STICKS
AND STONES

STICKS AND STONES

and

Other

Student

Essays

EIGHTH EDITION

EDITED BY

RISE B. AXELROD
UNIVERSITY OF CALIFORNIA,
RIVERSIDE

CHARLES R. COOPER
UNIVERSITY OF CALIFORNIA,
SAN DIEGO

BEDFORD/ST. MARTIN'S
Boston • New York

For Bedford/St. Martin's

Developmental Editor: Amy Saxon
Senior Production Editor: Peter Jacoby
Senior Production Supervisor: Jennifer Peterson
Executive Marketing Manager: Molly Parke
Copy Editor: Sarah Zobel
Permissions Manager: Kalina K. Ingham
Art Director: Lucy Krikorian
Cover Design: Marine Bouvier Miller
Composition: Ewing Systems
Printing and Binding: RR Donnelley and Sons

President, Bedford/St. Martin's: Denise B. Wydra
Presidents, Macmillan Higher Education: Joan E. Feinberg and Tom Scotty
Editor in Chief: Karen S. Henry
Director of Development: Erica T. Appel
Director of Marketing: Karen R. Soeltz
Production Director: Susan W. Brown
Associate Production Director: Elise S. Kaiser
Managing Editor: Shuli Traub

Manufactured in the United States of America.

8 7 6 5 4 3
f e d c b a

For information, write: Bedford/St. Martin's, 75 Arlington Street, Boston, MA 02116   (617-399-4000)

ISBN 978-1-4576-1262-6

Preface for Instructors

Sticks and Stones and Other Student Essays is a reader designed to accompany *The St. Martin's Guide to Writing*. Now in its eighth edition, *Sticks and Stones* continues the tradition of its predecessors: to celebrate student writing.

Enduring features of *Sticks and Stones* include the following:

- *Thirty-seven student essays* written in each of the *Guide*'s nine genres, from "Remembering an Event" to "Analyzing Stories."

- *Chapter introductions* that motivate students to write in each genre. In each chapter introduction, we aim to increase students' interest and investment by explaining in simple terms the distinctive features and purpose of each genre, how the genre relates to and builds on the others, and what they will gain academically and personally by working in it.

- *Headnotes for each essay* that invite students to become attentive readers of each genre. Headnotes help students approach the essays as models for their own writing by spotlighting how the writers' essays were effective and inviting further reflection on the genre and their own writing.

- *Two final sections, "A Note on the Copyediting" and "Sample Copyediting,"* that explain the role of editing in published writing and let students see the editing process in black and white.

- *An essay submission form* designed to encourage students to submit their own essays. As an instructor, you should feel free to provide extra encouragement to a student who writes an outstanding essay. Few students have ever thought their assigned essays could be published for a national audience to read. You might work with a student on further revision and assist with filling out the submission form. You may submit essays online at **bedfordstmartins.com /theguide** or by emailing **SubmitAnEssay@bedfordstmartins .com.**

NEW TO THE EIGHTH EDITION

Important new features enhance this edition:

- **New student essays.** Joining the most popular essays from the seventh edition, eight new essays offer students helpful and reliable examples of effective writing. These essays focus on topics that are current and relevant, such as laissez-faire economic policies and embryonic research.

- **New Critical Reading Guides** follow each chapter introduction. Each guide provides a framework within which students learn to evaluate peer writing. These guides include additional clarification of the genre's key features and may serve to direct class discussion.

- **A list of the basic features in each genre** helps students spot the conventions writers employ to achieve specific rhetorical goals.

SUGGESTIONS FOR USING *STICKS AND STONES*

Sticks and Stones is an ancillary that can be used alongside *The St. Martin's Guide to Writing.* You could ask students to read a chapter in *Sticks and Stones,* select a favorite essay, and analyze how it exemplifies the genre as outlined in the relevant *Guide* chapter's Basic Features section. Because the essays in every chapter of *Sticks and Stones* vary so much in subject and approach, you and your students could explore essays that model the many different ways writers organize ideas, structure sentences, use vocabulary and tone, address an audience, and center themselves in a genre.

You might want to walk students through a few paragraphs of the copyedited essay at the end of the book. The editing displaces, replaces, adds, and subtracts in order to focus and speed the reading and make the relationships among ideas clearer. Students could learn from speculating about reasons for some of the edits, not all of which are so local as they seem (as you will readily recognize).

To inspire thoughtful revision and editing, you could have your students submit essays that were based on assignments in the *Guide*—or even inspired by essays in *Sticks and Stones* itself—to be considered for publication in the campus newspaper or the next editions of the *Guide* and *Sticks and Stones*. You will find a submission form at the end of this book.

These suggestions address but a few of the numerous possible uses of *Sticks and Stones*. We would be delighted to learn how you use this book, as well as what you would like to see in the next edition. Please feel free to send comments and suggestions to us by way of the editorial staff at Bedford/St. Martin's:

The St. Martin's Guide Editor
Bedford/St. Martin's, 10th Floor
33 Irving Place
New York, NY 10003

ACKNOWLEDGMENTS

We are grateful to many people who made this edition of *Sticks and Stones* a reality. Most of all, we would like to thank the hundreds of students who have conceived, drafted, written, revised, and polished the essays we have received over the years. Although we cannot include every essay submitted to us, we have read each one with interest and care.

We also thank the instructors who encouraged their students to submit their work for this collection or who submitted their students' work themselves. *Sticks and Stones* would not exist without the generous efforts of these instructors.

Many thanks go to the instructors whose students' work is published in this edition: Sandra Baringer, University of California, Riverside; Sebastian Beauclair, Grand Rapids Community College; Kristin Brunnemer, Pierce College; Sean Connelly, Chaffey College; Rob d'Annibale, University of California, Riverside; Michelle Dowd, Chaffey College; Shelley Garcia, University of California, Riverside; Sean Henry, Mt. San Jacinto College; Lesa Hildebrand, Triton College; Chandra Howard, University of California, Riverside; Eva Mutschler, Oakland Community College, Orchard Ridge; Gray Scott, Texas Woman's University; Megan Stein, University of California, Riverside;

Shannon Tarango, University of California, Riverside; Hannah Tenpas, University of California, Riverside; Ruthe Thompson, Southwest Minnesota State University; and Janice Zerfas, Lake Michigan College.

We would also like to extend our sincere appreciation to Amy Saxon of Bedford/St. Martin's for her thoughtful guidance, invaluable editorial suggestions, and careful organization of this project. And of course, we thank Ruthe Thompson, Elizabeth Rankin, Paul Sladky, and Lawrence Barkley, whose fine work on previous editions of this book set the standard for everything that followed.

Rise B. Axelrod
Charles R. Cooper

Contents

To the Student 1

The essays in *Sticks and Stones* weren't selected based on subject matter (though many diverse and fascinating topics are covered), nor because they were flawlessly written, but rather because each of these essays offers you a great example of organized, carefully researched, and diligently edited student writing. These essays were written by students just like you in writing classes like yours across the country. If you think you're not like the students whose essays appear in this book, that you could never write this well—let alone get your work published—take heart! The truth is, the essays in this book didn't always look like they do now. They began as just a few sentences: notes taken from a research source, an idea written on the back of an old receipt, a tentative paragraph in a first draft.

And as you may have found with your own writing, even when the essays began to take shape, it was a rough shape. Some essays shifted from one rough shape to the next for a long time. But the writers persisted. They tested the advice of their peers and instructors. They gathered more material to support their arguments, whether that meant interrogating their memories, returning to a profile place, consulting more books and electronic databases, or watching a film a second time. They pushed themselves to think of new ways to say what they wanted to say. And they took the time to edit and revise and rewrite so their arguments would be clear and persuasive to their intended audiences.

There's no question that writing something good enough for publication is hard work. But there's also no question that doing so is possible for every student reading this book. As you read through these essays, the Critical Reading Guides that follow each chapter introduction will help you spot some of the techniques each student used to craft his or her essay.

1

Here's an easy way for you to increase your chances of getting published: As you write, ask yourself, "What can I do to help the readers of *Sticks and Stones*—other students like me—understand what I am trying to say in this essay?" A metamorphosis will begin. You will no longer think of yourself as someone who is merely completing an assignment for your writing class; you will begin to think of yourself as a writer in conversation with your readers.

You will notice that the writers whose work is collected here are determined to seize their readers and provoke a response. The tone of their writing is not "Hey, would you mind reading my work?" nor is it that of a class assignment written for an audience of one—the instructor. Instead, these essays clearly belong to writers who have something to say, who are writing for an audience they know exists beyond themselves and those grading their work.

What are you passionate about? What are you curious about? We can't wait to hear what *you* have to say.

Remembering an Event 2

Narratives like the ones you'll find in this chapter are some of the most common essays we read. They connect us to other people and teach us about ourselves. In fact, your sense of who you are—your personal identity—depends on narratives: the stories told and retold in your family and among your longtime friends, the stories you tell and retell yourself in moments of reflection. These stories may calm and center you, or they may alarm and agitate you, but together they define who you are and provide the foundation for your future.

Listening to gossip, watching a film, or reading a short story can be enjoyable. But to be on the shaping end of a story—to tell or write a story about your own life—is even more rewarding. Telling about an event might allow you to discover its particular significance in your life. For example, by writing about her first construction job, Julia Barojas discovered new respect for her hardworking brother. Or it might help you see more clearly how the past shapes the future: Aaron Forshier's story about a tragic accident can be seen as a case study in how an event can alter personalities and relationships.

Essays that relate a remembered event take on a variety of topics but always include several basic features. Most important, a remembered event essay is a well-told story; it features vivid descriptions of people and places; and it holds autobiographical significance for the writer. To tell a story is to re-form an event in your mind and examine it from your current perspective, through the greater knowledge you have gained from more education and a larger life experience. As you write and revise your remembered-event essay, take advantage of this perspective: take time to see your story anew, to read each draft as if you didn't already know its details. That way you can look for contradictions and inconsistencies in your thinking, and examine and reconsider any rapid conclusions you may initially have drawn about the experience. Sharing drafts with classmates and your instructor will give you even more perspective on the event and your response to it, and will refine and deepen your insight into the event's meaning.

Whatever you do, as you cull your memory for details of a remembered event, keep an open mind. Re-seeing events can lead to self-judgment and judgment of others: "I wish I had done this," or "if only she hadn't said that!" But these seemingly useless reflections can be important, allowing you to notice unresolved tensions below the surface of your memory and teaching you to reserve judgment as you struggle to understand the event.

Although language is slippery and imperfect, writing about your past is a powerful tool, allowing you to revisit remembered events, bring together your scattered thinking about them, and achieve significant insights. Your revised essay will document this voyage toward understanding.

Use the guidelines in the Critical Reading Guide (below) to practice peer review using the essays in this chapter.

A CRITICAL READING GUIDE

A WELL-TOLD STORY

How effectively does the writer tell the story?

Summarize: Circle or highlight the inciting incident and the climax of the story.

Praise: Give an example in the story where the storytelling is especially effective—for example, a place where the story seems to flow smoothly and maintain the reader's interest, or where narrative action is compelling or exciting.

Critique: Tell the writer where the storytelling could be improved— for example, where the suspense slackens, the story lacks tension or conflict, or the chronology is confusing.

VIVID DESCRIPTION OF PEOPLE AND PLACES

Do the decriptions help you imagine what happened?

Summarize: Choose a passage or description and analyze how and how well it uses the describing strategies of naming, detailing, and comparing.

Praise: Identify a description that is particularly vivid—for example, a graphic sensory description or an apt comparison that makes a person or place come alive.

Critique: Tell where the description could be improved—for example, where objects in the scene are not named or described with enough specific detail (colors, sounds, smells, textures), or where the description is sparse. Note any description that contradicts the dominant impression; it may suggest how the significance can be made more complex and interesting.

AUTOBIOGRAPHICAL SIGNIFICANCE

Is it clear why the event was important to the author?

Summarize: Briefly describe the story's dominant impression, and tell the writer why you think the event was significant.

Praise: Give an example where the significance comes across effectively—for example, where feelings are expressed poignantly, where the present perspective seems insightful, or where the description creates a strong dominant impression that clarifies the significance.

Critique: Tell the writer where the significance could be strengthened—for example, if the conflict is too easily resolved, if a moral seems tacked on at the end, or if more interesting meanings could be drawn out of the experience.

Sticks and Stones

Nicole Ball

Niagara University
Niagara, New York

Nicole Ball retells a remembered moment from her childhood that many may relate to. The title alludes to a familiar childhood saying: "Sticks and stones may break my bones, but words will never hurt me." Ball's purpose, however, appears to be much deeper than a tale of classic school yard bullying. Her essay confronts both the power of words to hurt, as well as the failure of words in response. The narrator's attempts to ignore the bully's harsh taunts are futile, school authorities refuse to help, and parental words of advice prove useless. As you read, notice how Ball offers small details to suggest familial solidarity. She denies her readers a happy ending, but in so doing she paints a memorably realistic coming-of-age story.

James Nichols was short and scrawny, the smallest kid in the entire eighth grade class. But he had a foul mouth and a belligerent attitude to make up for it. And he was a bully.

James sat in the front seat of the school bus, relegated there by the bus driver after some infraction or other. The driver, a balding, heavyset man who paid little or no attention to the charges he shuttled back and forth, rarely spoke and, except for that act of discipline, seemed disinclined to do anything else. The punishment, however, didn't seem to faze James; in fact, he reveled in it. Sitting in the front put him at the head of all the action and surrounded him with easy victims: those too timid or meek to trespass into the "tough" zone at the back of the bus.

I was a year older than James and, though not very tall myself, was at least a foot taller than he was. But by my last year in junior high school, I had a terrible complexion, a mouthful of braces, and a crippling shyness. I sat in the second seat on the school bus, only because I couldn't get any closer to the front.

My brother, Greg, who was a year younger, generally sat with   4
me because while he was a bit shorter, and much more confident,
he had no more desire to mix with the cigarette-toting crowd in
the back of the bus than I did. And although we didn't always get
along well at home, we both felt that it was nice to have someone
to sit with on the bus, even if we didn't talk much.

In our junior high, as in all junior highs, skill at socializing   5
outranked skill in classes. And since Greg and I were both social
outcasts, we endured our share of teasing and taunts. But James
Nichols set out to top them all.

At first, of course, his words were easy to ignore, mostly be-   6
cause they were nothing new. But as his taunts grew louder and
nastier, he developed the habit of kneeling on his seat and leaning
over the back to shout his unrelenting epithets down upon us. The
kids in the back of the bus relished every moment of our humiliation, often cheering him on. James puffed up with pride over his
cruelty. The bus driver never said a word, though he could not have
helped but hear the barrage of insults. Inside, I seethed.

"Ignore him," my parents insisted. "He'll eventually stop when   7
he realizes that you're not going to react." Their words were well
meant, but didn't help. The taunts continued and even intensified
when we got to school. Upon arrival, the buses lined up in front of
the school building, waiting until exactly 8:10 to release their passengers. Those long moments sitting in the parking lot, staring at
the red plastic seat in front of me, praying for the bell to ring so I
could escape James, were pure torture.

Each morning, Greg and I would flee from the bus. "I can't   8
take this much more," I would rage under my breath. Oh how I
longed to tear James to pieces. And although I knew I would never
physically attack James, I felt better imagining myself doing so.
Greg, though, would never respond to my frustrated exclamations,
which only added to my wrath. After all, didn't he hate James too?
But more often than not, I was just too furious to care what Greg
might have been thinking.

The showdown, I suppose, was inevitable.   9

One morning as we sat in the school parking lot, James took   10
his taunting too far. I don't remember what he said, but I remember what he did. He pulled a long, slender, wooden drumstick from
his pocket. He started to tap Greg on the top of the head, each hit
emphasizing every syllable of his hateful words. My brother stared

straight ahead. James laughed. The kids in the back of the bus laughed. The bus driver ignored everything.

My anger boiled over. "Don't you touch him!" I shrieked, striking out and knocking the drumstick from James's hand. At that moment, I didn't care that my parents had advised us to ignore James. I didn't care that everyone turned to gape at me. I didn't care that even the bus driver glanced up from his stony reverie. I only wanted James to leave my brother alone. As the stick clattered to the floor, audible in the sudden silence, I bit my lip, uncertain of what I had done and afraid of what might result. 11

My mistake, of course, was thinking my screams would end the taunts. The crowd at the back of the bus waited to see James's reaction. With his authority threatened, James turned on me like a viper. "Shut up, bitch!" he hissed. Coming from a home where "shut up" was considered strong language, James's swear word seemed the worst of all evils. 12

My eyes wide, I shuddered but didn't respond. Words were words, and if I had done nothing else, at least I had caused the bully to revert to words instead of actions. I turned my face to the window, determined to ignore his insults for the few remaining minutes before school. But a movement from Greg caught my eye, and I looked back. 13

In one swift movement, Greg reached into the front seat, grabbed James by the coat, yanked him out into the aisle, pulled him down, and delivered two quick, fierce jabs to James's face. Then he released him without a word and settled back into his seat. James, for once in his life, was speechless. His cheek flaming red from where the blows had struck, he stared at my brother without moving until the bus driver clicked open the doors a moment later, indicating we could go into school. 14

My parents heard about the incident, of course, and called the assistant principal about the entire matter. When the vice principal questioned my brother, Greg's explanation was simple: "He called Nicole a swear word, and no one calls my sister that." Greg had never said anything more touching. 15

I have heard it said that violence never solves anything, and it didn't. The bus driver was advised to keep an eye on James, but no admonition would have spurred the driver to interfere in anything. The teasing went on, cruel as ever, until James threatened to slit our throats with a knife he swore he had hidden in his locker 16 at school. After that, even though a locker search turned up nothing, my parents drove us to school every morning, and my mother talked to us about what to do if James ever pulled a knife on us at school.

But for me an imagined weapon paled when compared with the vivid memory of the complete silence on the bus, the blazing red mark on James's face, the calm little smile that tugged at the edges of my brother's mouth, and the click of the bus doors as they opened to free us. 17

In a Ditch

Stephanie Legge

University of California, Riverside
Riverside, California

In this essay Stephanie Legge relates a moment that holds particular significance in her life: the freedom of a new driver's license soon followed by a terrifying car crash. Legge engages readers by using dialogue throughout, allowing them to feel as though the event is happening at this very moment. Note the way she begins her story with a measured pace and then slowly builds urgency. Was she successful in creating suspense? You might not have a near-death experience to write about, but Legge's essay can still teach you a lot about how to use vivid descriptions and dramatization to enhance a remembered event.

"You're going to get us lost again," Nathan muttered from the passenger seat. "I told you we should have waited for Dad." 1

"Shut up!" I growled back. "It was your fault we got lost last time anyway!" 2

"Yeah sure, Stephanie," said Nathan. "You're the one driving. Can't you even figure out where you're going?" He leaned forward so he could peer through the window at the houses flowing by. "Where are we?" 3

The truth was I had no idea. We (or rather I) must have turned too early from the main street into a different neighborhood. We had been driving for an hour on our way to our dad's friend Marty's house, where Marty was holding a barbecue, and along the way, we lost sight of our father on his motorcycle between the mass of cars moving steadily along the freeway. I trusted my instincts to find the way to our destination, but it seems my instincts were slightly askew. My brother's and my heads turned left and right as we scanned our surroundings for any familiar sign. I didn't tell Nathan, but a nervous- 4 ness was creeping its way through my stomach; I'd had my license for only two weeks and if I made a mistake while looking for the right path out of that neighborhood, I'd be in trouble with the DMV for driving my younger brother before I was eighteen. That nervousness on top of being lost was beginning to show as I gripped the steering wheel harder.

"There!" I pointed through the windshield. "Jurupa Road! We 5 can follow that to Van Buren and just follow it to Marty's house." The nervousness drained out of me like cool water. I turned to Nathan with a cocky smile. "See? I can find my way around."

"Yeah, right!" said Nathan, picking the calluses of his fingernails. 6 "After following every road in Riverside, you'll eventually find your way to the right place."

"One slight detour and you think I can't find my way anywhere!" 7 I sighed. I scrubbed a fingerprint off my dashboard with my sleeve; I hated it when my car got dirty. "Anyways, at least we know where we are. Daddy's probably already at Marty's house by now. I'll tell him it was your fault."

"My fault!" Nathan slapped his hands down onto his thighs and 8 glared at me. "My fault! Who's driving here? You can't even find your way to a place we've seen Dad drive us to a hundred times and you think I should be the one watching where you're going?"

"Why not?" I replied, looking over my left shoulder to change 9 lanes. "You obviously seem to know a lot more than I do about everything. Maybe if you'd been paying attention more, we'd be there by now."

"Maybe if you weren't such a loser, we wouldn't get lost so mu— 10 Steph!"

I didn't have time to look at Nathan. I didn't even have time to 11 complete my lane change. I snapped my head to the front and saw a flash of white in front of me so close—too close. A white truck was slamming its brakes and I was still driving at sixty miles per hour. We were flying right at it. Nathan braced himself in his seat and I frantically swung to the left knowing it was useless; I waited for the crash to sound. Yet amazingly enough, I missed the truck by centimeters and felt a rush of relief so great it made my body prickly with goose bumps.

Then the screeching started. Not from me or Nathan, but from 12 beneath us. The world started rotating and suddenly we were sliding sideways at the same frightening speed. Trees flashed by so fast it was sickening. I raced the steering wheel the other way and then we were facing the opposite direction, watching a rock wall become a blur. Left and right—left and right—fishtailing round and round—Nathan next to me shrieking "Steph! Steph!"—things were bouncing around inside the car and hitting us painfully—now we were spinning uncontrollably and everything became obscured in one big twirl of color—BAM—CRUNCH.

The radio was still playing and the engine was still running, but after the screech of the tires and the pounding of whatever damage was being done, it seemed utterly silent. I was frozen in my seat, not entirely sure of what I was seeing; the sky was blue through the windshield, partially blocked by the twisted branches of a thrashed tree that was on its side. My car had spun around to face the opposite direction we had been traveling so that I could see the path of the ditch my car was in winding away into the distance, and I could see the white truck parked on the side of the road. After picking up the mangled table that had fallen out of the back of his truck, the driver climbed back in and started down the road toward us. He slowed as he came close, and I looked back at him, not sure of what to do or even if what had happened really happened. He looked at me curiously, then without another glance, picked up speed and drove away. 13

Nathan and I were alone. My father had no idea of where we were, and we had no way of reaching him. Suddenly, the weight of the situation fell on me like a sack of bricks and I felt the sickness of grief well up in my throat. Nathan was the first to react. He pushed at the door but found it wouldn't open. I didn't watch him as he climbed over the seat and got out through the back, but I saw his face clearly as he went around to the front and looked at my car with wide eyes and a dropped jaw. 14

"Oh my God, Steph," he whispered. I knew then I couldn't look at my car. 15

"Nathan," I gasped. "Oh my God . . ." I stared ahead and, feeling the engine start to shudder, a flicker of panic jump-started my heart. "Nathan, I've got to move my car!" 16

We were stranded with no communication, no help, so moving my car seemed like the logical thing to do. I clumsily put my hands on the steering wheel and revved up the motor, but beneath me I could hear the wheels spinning in place. The engine shuddered so violently that in another spurt of panic, I imagined the car catching fire. I let off the accelerator, shut off the engine, and the silence set in so dramatically it was frightening. Images flashed before me again of sliding 17 down the road, and the white truck driving away, and the blue sky with the broken tree. It was so hard to believe that we weren't still driving to Marty's house for a fun day at the pool. It felt so much like a dream.

After a few minutes of sitting there frozen in my seat, I heard the 18 clapping of someone hurrying toward us. A man and a woman appeared from behind the tree and their faces were filled with fear.

"Are you okay?" stammered the woman. "We saw everything 19 from the street!"

I found it hard to speak and could only stare. 20

"We're okay," said Nathan. "Someone stopped ahead of us and 21 we barely missed him." He paced back and forth in front of my car, surveying every inch of damage. At that same moment, someone called to us.

"Hey! Are you guys alright?" A man was stepping from a white 22 convertible. "It looks like you need some help."

I could hear the man talking to the couple and my brother, but I 23 wasn't quite sure what they were saying. Then the man approached me in my car. He was fairly young with black hair and eyes hidden behind a pair of shades. "Do you have a cell phone?"

"No," I croaked. 24

"Have the police come by yet?" 25

"No," I answered and swallowed hard. It was becoming easier to 26 talk. "We need to find my dad."

"Here," said the man and he handed me a black cell phone. "Call 27 who you need to call so they know what's happened."

I didn't know Marty's phone number and I knew no one would 28 be at my house, so I called my friend Jim who'd helped me get my car a year before. When I heard his voice on the other end, I could feel mine grow hoarse.

"Hi. Jim?" I murmured. 29

"Yello there, Stephanie!" Jim chuckled. He was eighty-two years 30 old and always cheerful. "What's goin' on?"

"Jim . . . I'm, um, in a ditch on the side of the road," I replied, 31 glancing again at the mutilated tree.

"You're what?" 32

At that moment, a shiny, black-and-white police car pulled up. The 33 officer, a tall man, stepped out and walked over to us as if this was a normal part of his day. The man in shades spoke to him first. I was grateful for this because I wanted to let my friend know where I was.

"Jim, I'm in the center-divider on Van Buren, just past Jurupa 34
Road. Can you find us?" I said hurriedly.

"Well, sure I can find ya, but—are you okay?" he replied with a 35
note of worry in his voice.

"We're fine," I said. "We're just really shook up." 36

I could see Nathan talking to the policeman, and the policeman 37
was expressionless. Then with a sickening jolt, I remembered I was in
more trouble than I anticipated; I had been driving Nathan and that
was illegal since I wasn't eighteen yet. I made sure Jim knew exactly
where we were and after I handed the cell phone back to the man in
shades, the policeman marched through the debris from the tree and
stood at the open car door to peer inside at me.

"Hello," he said calmly as if I was parked outside a grocery store. 38
"Everyone okay here? No one hurt?"

"No, nobody's hurt," I said. I found it hard to look into his eyes 39
and instead stared at my shoes.

"Well, I need you and your younger brother to stay inside the 40
vehicle so we can stop the traffic and get you out of here," said the
police officer, "and I'm going to need your license and registration." Nathan was already climbing into the backseat as I rummaged
through my purse and handed the policeman my license, then I realized as I opened my glove compartment that I had taken my registration out of my car when I signed up for insurance. It was unhelpfully
at home.

Well, everything else that day had been going horribly. One more 41
screwup wouldn't be too inconvenient. I told the policeman I didn't
have the registration, and the look he gave me was enough to make
the lump in my throat even sorer. He marked something on his clip-
board and then asked me for a detailed account of the accident.

Ten minutes later, the man in the sunglasses had left and Jim had 42
pulled up alongside us over the ditch. He greeted us with the sentence that we would hear a thousand times that day. "Thank goodness
you aren't hurt!" he said as he shuffled over to us. He waited with us
for twenty minutes until the tow truck chugged its way up the street.
Finally, I was forced to leave my car and look at the scene from the
outside. I could hardly keep my emotions under control.

The passenger's side looked like a piece of crumpled paper. All 43
along the door and the fender, the impact of the tree had caused the
whole side to dent inward. Three tires were flat, and the wheel that
had hit the curb was bent the wrong way. Even the side of the car that

hadn't hit the tree was dented in places; the hood was bent and the headlight hung miserably from its socket by a wire. The tree was in the street, cut clean off at the roots. A track of winding skid marks led to the wreck. To top it off, everything was covered in a thick layer of dirt.

I watched as the truck driver hitched up my car and dragged it 44 up onto the bed. I couldn't believe how wrong everything had gone. Jim and Nathan stood next to me talking about how fortunate we had been, but I couldn't see any of it. Sure, nobody had been hurt, but I had broken the law, been unable to present registration, and been left at the scene when the white truck had left us there. Also, insurance rates were going to rise, and worst of all, my car was most likely totaled. The best thing I had been looking forward to for two years was dashed in a matter of seconds; I wouldn't be able to drive again for a very long time.

We prepared to move out, taking the crumpled car with us, and 45 I told the driver that I wanted the car to be taken to my house. He dumped the car on my driveway as pitifully as it had been dragged up, and finally we knew we had to find our dad. Jim offered us the ride to Marty's house and along the way, I couldn't imagine how I would ever be able to tell my dad what had happened. We parked in front of Marty's house and noticed that Dad's motorcycle was missing.

"He must be looking for us," said Nathan as he climbed out of 46 Jim's car.

"Now listen," said Jim. "Make sure Marty's there and if he knows 47 where yer dad is. If he's not there, yer welcome to stay at my house 'til someone shows up, 'kay?"

"Thanks a bunch, Jim," I said and followed Nathan up the steps 48 to the front door. As expected, the living room was empty except for the movies, chips, and sodas still stacked up for the party that had never started because the company had never shown up. We walked to Marty's room where he was sleeping lightly. He woke when he heard Nathan say his name and blinked in surprise.

"Your dad's looking for you," he said, chastising. Nathan and I 49 looked at each other. I didn't feel right telling Marty the story before telling Dad.

"When did he leave?" I asked instead. 50

"He called from his house about ten minutes ago and he's on his 51 way back here," said Marty. He sat up and rubbed his eyes. "He's been looking all over Riverside and San Bernardino for you. Where've you been?"

I knew then I couldn't keep it from him before Dad got back.   52
"Marty . . . we crashed."

He froze. I could see he hadn't been expecting that kind of expla-   53
nation. Marty put his hands down and raised his eyebrows. "Really?"
I nodded and he chuckled with a sad note. "Your dad's going to be
really upset. How'd you crash?"

I gave Marty a brief description of the crash, but I wanted my dad   54
to know the whole story first. When I had finished, I heard the deep
rumble of a motorcycle approach. Nathan looked up at me with a look
of anticipation. We knew it had to be Dad.

My brother and I left the room at the same time and headed to   55
the front door almost dreamlike. How was I going to start? Would he
be angry? What would he say when he found out what had really happened? Nathan stopped in the doorway as I walked ahead of him onto
the porch. I didn't want to have to confront him alone, but then everything had been my fault. I could hear the thud of boots and my dad
rounded the corner, and we froze, staring. There was silence deeper
than when all the thrashing had stopped at the accident. Then my dad
removed his sunglasses and looked at me with an expression I had
never seen him give me. It was unreadable.

"I saw the car," he said.   56

The lump in my throat rose again. Not having to tell him the   57
reason for us being gone was worse than having to. My dad moved
toward me quickly and I shrank, not knowing what he would do.
Then his arms fell around me and he hugged me so tightly it shocked
me. I could feel him shaking all over and I realized I was shaking too.
For the first time since the crash, tears poured down my cheeks and I
buried my face into my dad's shoulder. Everyone kept saying we were
lucky not to have been hurt, but I didn't believe how fortunate we
were until my dad proved the gravity to us. Nothing else had mattered
until that point, when all emotions were let loose.

We later learned that steering mechanisms had broken when the   58
car hit the curb at sixty miles per hour. It would be three months and
a thousand dollars later before I could drive it again. Our insurance
placed me at fault for "driving down a highway, losing control of the
vehicle, and hitting a tree." Visiting the site again, we learned how vital
the tree had actually been in the accident; at that speed, had the tree
not have been there, the car would have flipped over and rolled onto
the railroad tracks. Far from being an object of destruction, the tree
ironically brought relief. I drive by that scene often, observing how the

skid marks flow left and right, swirl, then end at a blank spot between the line of trees.

Today, the car remains dirty and dented, and the door can only be   59
closed if the passenger slams all his weight into it. Of course I'm restoring it piece by piece, but I understand now that it's not as important as it was before. Suddenly everything seems so different, as if the world changed. My car is no longer my flashy pet, but my clumsy, mechanical legs. Likewise, roadsides, deep rivers, and the tops of mountains are tangible in a way that's not defined simply by peering through a window at them. I'd seen that ditch in the roadside hundreds of times, but being in it gave me a whole new perspective of the landscape around me. I felt vulnerable and small, like how a baby bird must feel when it falls from its nest. I don't know if this was a good or a bad experience for me, but the experience changed me from a bouncy teenager to a conscious adult.

Jet Fuel and Good Fairies

Elizabeth Schaap

Grand Rapids Community College
Grand Rapids, Michigan

Often, events that occurred when we were quite young leave lingering impressions throughout our lives. In this essay, Elizabeth Schaap recalls a moment when she was just a girl; though she was only four years old at the time, Schaap successfully interweaves narrative with remembered feelings and sensations. The security, excitement, and "weightless" freedom surrounding the event offer the reader a glimpse into what childhood meant for the narrator. As you read, notice how Schaap describes the tiny details that stand out in her memory—details that help make the story resonate with readers.

I spent an inordinate amount of time in airports as a child. I spent more time in airplanes in my first five years than some people do their entire lives. And I had never even flown commercially at that point. But it's been awhile since my family stopped flying private planes. The last time I visited an aircraft hangar with the intention of boarding, I was four years old. My father was a furniture store owner attempting to break into the charter business. Actually, that's not entirely correct. He was an air force veteran turned furniture store owner turned private pilot trying to break into the charter business. By the time I was born, my father had been flying planes of various shapes, sizes, and capacities for over twenty years. He had even begun passing on the torch to my oldest sister, Rachel, who was fourteen at the time and served (illegally) as copilot for many of our transcontinental journeys. 1

On this particular junket our destination was Florida—Marco Island to be exact—to stay at a friend's condo for the two weeks my sisters had off for spring break. We'd all stayed up late packing the night before; and in the morning (a bright and sunny 7 a.m.), my 2 mother had hurried all six of us into the Suburban and we'd driven to the airport.

I was a small child, and entering the hangar never failed to thrill me. I could hardly distinguish all the sensations. The first thing I noticed (and the thing I remember most vividly) was the smell. It was something like rubber and jet fuel and one other unnamed scent I could never identify; a mystery ingredient that I still associate with airplanes. It seemed to come from the exteriors of the planes themselves. It seemed to radiate off the wheels and the engines and the waves of heat steadily rising from the runway and waft through the brightly lit steel beams that held the ceiling thirty feet above my head.

The air was always clean in that particular hangar; never hot, never cold. Its architecture was simple and calm and very practical. Pieces of machinery were spaced at prudent intervals along the walls, ready and waiting to be put to use at any moment. There were always a handful of young men in matching work shirts moving around the room, always busy, always ready, making whatever preparations were necessary to get this particular client into the air with speed and efficiency. I remember watching them with a child's curiosity, feeling that they were benevolent forces working toward our good. Perhaps in another child's world they would be imagined as good fairies, though I'm not sure they would be particularly fond of such a description.

As I watched, my father inspected the plane with a confident, critical eye, looking for any lapses in security. He called Rachel over to him and had her go through what she remembered of the safety checklist with him. They started on the back left side and dipped in unison under the broad, gleaming wings to inspect the engines, jiggling, rattling, making sure everything stayed in place. They observed the front and right side of the plane, each stopping to test the wing flaps. My father walked toward the back end of the plane, his hand resting on the unyielding metal of the aircraft's trunk, and finally reached up to test the tail flaps, which were stable.

My two other sisters and I waited with our mother by the door that led to the hangar from the airport lobby. The anticipation began like static electricity in my belly. I bounced from one foot to the other, knowing the inspection was complete and the next move would be for my father to turn around and give us a wave, signaling that it was time to board. Soon we would be in the air, I said to myself. My stomach dropped another inch and I held my breath as my father turned his head and raised an arm.

"Alright, ladies."   7

This was our sign. Forgetting my mother, I let go of her hand and   8
walked proudly forward, duffel bag in hand, as if it were my airplane
we were about to fly out of there. Part of me felt that it was. I looked
around at the men navigating the hangar as if they were my comrades.
One of them, who was pushing a cart of something toward the lobby,
caught my conspirator's glance and gave me a wink in return. I smiled
and hid my face, the blush adding color to cheeks that were already
pink with excitement. As I climbed the escalator-like stairs, the smell of
leather nearly overwhelmed me. I tossed my bag on my seat and stood
looking out over the cockpit toward the runway. My enthusiasm could
no longer be contained. I was shimmying and trembling like an ecstatic
puppy, so ready for takeoff that I couldn't even bring myself to sit.

I turned around and watched my family pile in. My sister Stephanie   9
sat opposite me, across a little table with a map of the fifty American
states printed on it. Jessica, the second oldest, and my mother occu-
pied the seats next to us. The front two, closest to the cockpit, were
unoccupied. After a moment of situating ourselves and our travel bags,
my mother made us sit and buckle ourselves in. She checked our seat
belts and then sat down to attend to her own. After a few more minutes I heard a shout and a wave from my father to the airport crew and
I knew it was time. Rachel, with a smile at my mother, came aboard
and walked past to sit in the left seat of the cockpit. I heard my father
climb the ladder of stairs and the plane shook as he heaved the door
shut and locked it. I could barely catch my breath.

I watched his back as he calmly and happily made for the front of   10
the plane, taking his seat next to my sister and mirroring her by putting a pair of giant green headphones over his ears.

The engines started. The faint whining sounds only increased my   11
ardor as they spun to life and slowly sped up. Our small cabin gave a
lurch as my father released the brakes and began to carefully maneuver
the aircraft out of the hangar.

Fuel was our last stop. If you've ever smelled jet fuel while it's being   12
pumped, you know it's a smell not easily forgotten. It mercilessly pen-
etrates your nose with ten times the power of gasoline and to this day,
even though it's been over fifteen years since I've been in that plane, I
can still tell the difference between the two.

The man fueling the plane finished and communicated with my   13
father in a series of hand gestures. My father spoke in his headpiece

to the people operating what I referred to as only "The Tower." They gave us permission to move onto the airstrip.

Taxiing down the first half of the runway was the most agonizing experience of my four years. And the slowest. I gripped the armrests of my seat with fierce agitation as we taxied, taxied, taxied . . . and slowly made the turn at the end of the pavement. We waited, facing the opposite direction from which we came. Then suddenly the plane vibrated almost violently as its engines were thrust to full power. I listened as the pitch of the spinning fans rose higher and higher. We catapulted down the runway, faster and faster and faster until . . . I stopped hearing the wheels against the asphalt. I smiled to myself as the plane jostled me in my seat. My ears popped. I looked out my window to watch the ground shrink. I looked through the cabin and out the windshield as we gained altitude; the endless blue sky was like a welcoming sea of air and freedom and we sliced through it at 400 knots. Nothing on Earth could claim us. This is what I had wanted, what I had been waiting for. We were weightless.

14

The Accident

Aaron Forshier

Des Moines Area Community College
Ankeny, Iowa

Remembered-event essays often present people, and Aaron Forshier's paper about a tragic car accident introduces us to a very real, very complex character—Forshier's grandfather, who was profoundly affected by the crash. Forshier writes about his grandfather with the same tenderness that seems to have characterized their relationship. He refers to him not as "my grandfather" or even "my grandpa" but simply and affectionately as "Grandpa," and sketches the contours of their relationship with both general examples (a list of their favorite activities) and specific ones (the events of the morning of the accident). Forshier's attitude toward his grandfather is not only tender but also nonjudgmental, especially in the aftermath of the accident. When he shows, rather than tells, what his grandfather must be feeling, Forshier accomplishes a difficult feat for the autobiographer: He steps outside the personal experience of the event and examines it from a perspective unaffected by his own sorrow.

I began spending summers with my grandparents on their farm   1
when I was three years old. What began as three- or four-day visits gradually turned into most of the summer by the time I was seven years old. Time spent with Grandpa was always fun and exciting. Riding side by side in the tractor cab as Grandpa cultivated fields of beans and corn, harvested oats, or put up hay; hauling water and ground corn to the cattle in a distant pasture; repairing fences and farm equipment; helping in the garden; constructing and running his model train; fishing in the neighbor's pond; and relaxing on the porch swing at the end of the day, laughing over the stories he told

about my mom when she was growing up: These were just a few of the wonderful things that we did together. This all changed in the months and years following the accident; the time that I spent at the farm wasn't the same—Grandpa wasn't the same. As a result, visits to my favorite childhood place became fewer and fewer as the years passed.

I was eleven years old on that hot July day in 1999. It began as many days did on the farm, with Grandpa sticking his head into my bedroom and calling, "What? There's work to be done and my best farmhand is still in bed? Rise and shine, sleepyhead." I jumped out of bed, excited for the day to begin. It was the first summer that Grandpa had let me drive a tractor by myself, and we had started putting up hay the day before. I had spent most of the afternoon proudly hauling loads of hay from the field to the farmyard and unloading them onto two growing haystacks, and I was eager to get back on the tractor and continue my first grown-up job on the farm.

Grandpa and I finished the hay by lunchtime. After devouring my favorite lunch—Grandma's crispy fried chicken; creamy mashed potatoes covered with thick, savory gravy; and a big slice of juicy, sweet watermelon—Grandpa and I headed to town to deliver eight loads of bulk feed to the local Kent Feed and Supply business. Since he owned a big grain truck, Grandpa earned extra income by delivering feed to area farmers once or twice a month. We had made seven deliveries and were going back to town for the final load when Grandpa said, "It sure is hot—must be ninety-eight degrees in the shade. What do you say to stopping at the Dairy Den for an ice-cream cone before making our last delivery?"

"Great idea! You always know what I'm thinking," I eagerly replied. "There's nothing I'd like more right now."

With visions of the cool, delicious treat filling my head, I was almost unaware of the passing countryside until Grandpa began slowing down. I then noticed the four hayracks parked in a single row on the right shoulder of the highway a few hundred feet in front of us. A farmhouse and outbuildings flanked the right side of the highway, and three farmers were baling hay in a field on the left side. When our truck was almost even with the first hayrack, a little girl suddenly darted onto the highway from between the third and fourth hayracks. Grandpa screamed, "Oh, God, no! Hang on, Aaron." I remember screaming, and then everything happened so fast. Slamming on the brakes and turning sharply to the left, Grandpa tried desperately to

2

3

4

5

avoid hitting the child. Sounds of squealing brakes and screeching tires filled my ears as Grandpa managed to whip his powerful truck to the left side of the highway, but not quickly enough; the right rear wheel hit something with a heart-stopping thud that sent a chill through my body on one of the hottest days of the year. Barely missing a car approaching from the opposite direction, Grandpa tried to regain control of the truck, which left the highway, stumbled across a shallow ditch, tore through the wire fence surrounding the hay field, and was finally stopped by a huge, round hay bale.

Stunned, Grandpa and I both sat still, momentarily paralyzed. After a few seconds, Grandpa asked in a shaky voice, "Are you hurt?"   6

Still trying to catch my breath and waiting for my heart to stop pounding, I replied, "No, I think I'm okay, but I'm really scared. Did the truck hit that little girl?"   7

Grandpa didn't answer my question; once he knew that I wasn't hurt, he became silent and stared straight ahead, as though he were dreading what he had to face next. Without saying a word, Grandpa slowly opened the driver's door and stepped out of the truck, and I did the same. I watched him walk to the highway on trembling, jelly-like legs. He collapsed beside the girl; picked her small, limp body up in his arms; and held her close. As I came a little closer, I saw tears streaming down Grandpa's face. He was sobbing softly and moaning, "No, dear God, no! What have I done?"   8

I stood frozen in my tracks, suddenly unable to move closer. This was a side of Grandpa that I was seeing for the first time; I'd never seen him cry before. He had always been so strong—an unsinkable ship. I didn't see him cry at Great Grandpa's funeral, or when Grandma was very sick and in the hospital for weeks, or when he heard the news that his neighbor's son had died in a hunting accident. Seeing Grandpa break down surprised and upset me. I didn't know what to do.   9

As I continued to stand there, immobilized by what I was witnessing, the girl's mother ran onto the highway crying, "My baby, I want my baby! Please, dear God, help my baby!"   10

As the mother grabbed her daughter from his arms, Grandpa somehow choked out the faint words, "I . . . I . . . am . . . so . . . so . . . sorry."   11

Suddenly, there seemed to be people everywhere. The farmers who had been baling hay, including the girl's father, rushed to the scene. Witnesses to the accident were trying to help in any way   12 they could. A highway patrol car had just pulled up and another was close behind. Traffic was at a standstill, but police officers from town had arrived and were starting to detour vehicles onto nearby gravel roads. When I began walking toward Grandpa, a man took me by the arm and led me to his car, even though I kept telling him, "I want to be with my grandpa. Let me go."

The stranger was very persistent and insisted that I wait in his car. He kindly explained, "You can help your grandpa the most right now by staying here. The highway patrol officers are here, and they need time to talk to your grandpa and everyone who witnessed the accident. The ambulance will be arriving soon. The medics need to work quickly, and they can't do that if lots of people get in their way. I promise that I will come and get you as soon as you can be with your grandpa." Finally convinced that he was probably right, I agreed to wait in the car. 13

As I sat and waited, I noticed that my shirt was wet; I had been crying along with Grandpa and hadn't even realized it. Tired and concerned about Grandpa, I closed my eyes and tried to push both the picture of him crying and the accident out of my mind. I heard people talking and crying, the muffled voices of officers questioning witnesses, a siren blaring to announce the arrival of the ambulance, tractors idling impatiently in the hay field, and the distant, lonely howl of a dog. Mixed with these sounds were the pungent aroma of freshly cut hay, the overpowering odor of a nearby hog farm in ninety-degree temperatures, and the smell of hot rubber from smoldering tires that had left their outer layer of skin on the highway in a desperate attempt to stop the truck in time. The combination of the sounds and smells, along with the intense heat, had almost lulled me to sleep when a loud wail of despair suddenly brought me back to reality. 14

When the stranger finally came back to his car, he said, "The ambulance is almost ready to leave, and the police officers are finished with their reports, so you can go to your grandpa now." 15

I immediately ran over to Grandpa, who was still sitting beside the highway, and gave him a big hug. At the same time, I asked, "Grandpa, are you all right? Can we go home now?" When he didn't answer, I looked at him more closely and saw that he seemed to be in some sort of trance. I sat down beside him and held his hand, waiting for him to return to me from wherever he had gone. Watching the ambulance slowly leave, I remember wondering why it wasn't speeding away from the scene with its siren blaring or its 16

lights flashing. Even though I knew in my heart that the girl probably would not survive, I wondered why the medics weren't rushing
her to the hospital. Wasn't that their job? I learned later that the
girl had died in her mother's arms shortly before the ambulance
arrived. It had been the mother's wail of despair that I heard while
sitting in the stranger's car.

Grandpa and I walked to his truck and sat beside it, but he   17
still didn't give me any indication that he knew I was there. I said,
"Grandpa, I'm here. Can you hear me?" Although he didn't answer me, he did squeeze my hand to let me know that he heard
me and knew that I was there. I was worried about Grandpa. Even
with a summer tan, he seemed too pale, as though the life had been
drained out of him. His eyes looked hollow and distant, giving
me the eerie feeling that he was in a place shut off from the rest
of the world—a place where I could not be with him. Pain and
guilt glazed his eyes; tears continued to ooze and trickle down his
cheeks, etching mournful trails through layers of dust and sweat.
Not knowing what else to do to help Grandpa, I sat silently beside
him, holding his hand and resting my head against his arm while he
dealt with the pain in his own silent way. I had my own pain to deal
with—what had happened to the Grandpa I'd always known? Why
wasn't he talking to me?

After we had been sitting beside the truck for a while, my mom,   18
grandma, and uncle arrived. Grandpa rode home with Grandma,
and my uncle drove the truck home. Before leaving, Grandma took
me aside and said, "I'm sorry that you were with Grandpa this afternoon. Are you okay?"

With trembling lips, I replied, "I guess I'm okay, but Grandpa   19
won't talk to me. Did I do something wrong?"

Grandma returned my question with a hug and said, "Why   20
would you think that? You did nothing wrong. Grandpa is hurting
very deeply right now, but he still loves you very much. Go home
with your mom, and I'll call you in a few days and let you know
how Grandpa is doing. Don't worry; he'll be okay."

I gave Grandpa a good-bye hug and said, "I love you,   21
Grandpa." He managed to give me a weak hug but still didn't say a
word. He seemed to be drained of every ounce of strength he had.
It had been a long, horrible afternoon for both of us.

I cried myself to sleep that night, not only for the little girl and   22
her family, but also for Grandpa and me. Grandpa had always been

so strong and full of life, but today he reminded me of a deflated balloon. Even so, I truly believed that everything would be better in a few weeks—but it wasn't. The grandpa that I'd bonded so closely with for more than eight years never really came back to me; a special part of who he'd always been died with that little girl. He lost interest in most of the activities that we had always loved doing together—fishing, farming, and model railroading. His truck collected dust in the machine shed for two years before he finally sold it. He changed from a man who had enjoyed every moment of life to a man unjustly imprisoned by guilt.

Nearly six years have passed since the accident occurred, and 23 I've come to realize that Grandpa will probably never be able to forgive himself for what happened that day. Unable to forgive himself, he has become unable to reach out to others like he once did. I still have a grandpa, and I know that he still loves me; that will never change. But a part of him is missing—the part that made the two of us such a special team. I continue to spend time with Grandpa now and then, but we never recaptured the close bond that we once shared. Today, I cherish many unforgettable memories of the summers I spent with him, and I am grateful for the powerful bond we shared. Yet at the same time I feel cheated out of what could have been. Fate—that invisible something that brought Grandpa's truck and a little girl to the same place at the same moment in time—cheated me out of many more special years with my grandfather and cut short a wonderful chapter in my life.

Almost Quitting

Julia Barojas

University of California, Riverside
Riverside, California

Julia Barojas's essay is about perseverance. Barojas vividly describes the physical experience of suffering through a difficult first day as a construction worker—the hot sun, the blisters on her hands, the overpowering smells, and the pain in her back. Just as she is about to quit because the work is too hard, a comment by her supervisor makes her change her mind. You won't be surprised at this turn of events—the essay is called "*Almost* Quitting," after all. Barojas is not trying to create suspense about whether she will quit, though; she is writing about an event that ultimately filled her with confidence in her own abilities.

I awoke to the loud drone of my alarm as it rang directly next to my head. My eyes opened instantly, but it took me quite some time to understand what was going on. Then it finally clicked: It was 4 a.m. and I needed to get ready for my first day of work as an apprentice carpenter for a concrete company called Shaw & Sons. Somehow I found the strength in my feeble arm to turn off the alarm. The ringing echoed in my ears for a few seconds. 1

I sat up in bed and was surrounded by a piercing silence. The room was pitch-black and I staggered out of bed, waving my hands in front of me as I frantically searched for the light switch. After what seemed like hours, I found the switch and flipped it; my eyes slammed shut instantaneously. It took me some time to grow accustomed to the brightness, but little by little I regained my sight. 2

I began to get ready for work. As I laced up my black work boots and put on a bright green shirt with the company name "Shaw & Sons" written on the front in bold black letters, I heard 3 the loud rumble of my brother's truck and realized it was nearly time to go. I made my way through the dark hallway, out the front door, and into the truck.

My brother and I talked the entire way to work.   4

"Are you excited?" he asked.   5

"Of course I am! I'm going to be making my own money," I   6
responded.

"Well, you know it's not going to be easy, right?"   7

"What are you talking about? Of course it's going to be easy!   8
Anything you can do, I can do better. If you can manage, then so can I."

I felt very confident in myself and expected work to be a piece   9
of cake. In my mind, I would simply show up, do some simple work, go home, and then get a paycheck at the end of the week.

The drive went quickly and before I knew it we had arrived at   10
the work site, located on the Pacific Coast Highway in the city of Huntington Beach. We parked and as I opened the truck door an aroma of salt and fish filled my nostrils.

My brother and I walked for a few minutes and passed dozens   11
of boutiques and restaurants. Soon the massive foundations of hollow, unfinished buildings came into sight. I followed my brother as we made our way to our work location. There, he introduced me to the other workers and my new boss, Gilbert Gomez. Gilbert gave me a quick tour and went over some basic rules and expectations. Then he led me to the orientation room, located in what would soon become an underground parking structure. There I was given my hard hat and safety glasses, and strict instructions to wear them at all times.

After the orientation I made my way back to the work site but   12
got lost in the maze of pilasters that sustained the heavy foundation above. I eventually found an exit and it led me straight to our location.

I was put to work right away. It was almost 9:00 a.m. and the   13
heat of the sun was warm and comforting. My first task was to glue half-inch-thick strips of foam all along the base of the buildings. At first the task seemed simple, but after a while the strong smell of the glue spray started to get to me. My legs began to quiver from squatting and standing repeatedly. My back began to ache tremendously. My knees felt as though they would break soon from all the pressure I was placing on them. A small red blister formed on the

tip of my index finger from spraying adhesive onto the foam and the building. I checked the time on my cell phone and the clock read 9:47 a.m — I had been working for less than an hour.

After I finished gluing the foam, my next task was to nail plastic 14 devices called Speed Dowels onto the wooden framework. One by one I nailed the Speed Dowels. After I nailed about twenty of them the hammer began to feel heavier and heavier. I picked up the third-to-the-last dowel and placed it against the wood. I put the nail in its proper position and swung the hammer with a mighty force. As I hit the nail, my finger slipped and the hammer smashed down on my middle finger. The hammer dropped to the ground as I shook my hand in a desperate attempt to alleviate the pain.

As the day dragged on, the heat coming from the sun grew 15 more intense. The initial comfort I had felt that morning was long gone. My forehead was soaked with sweat and my head was throbbing viciously.

I stood up from my workplace and decided it was time for a 16 break. Without realizing it, I took a step back and stumbled over a broomstick that had been left on the floor. I landed heavily on my right hip and elbow.

That was the last straw! This job was more than I could handle. 17 I was sweaty and tired. Both my hip and elbow ached. Despite the fall, the hammer remained in my hand. I threw it and it hit the ground with a loud "thud." I stood up and marched over to Gilbert, preparing a long speech about why I would not be returning to work the next day.

As I neared my destination, I looked to my right and caught a 18 glimpse of my brother. I stopped dead in my tracks and just stared at him. He was on his knees, his face smeared with black streaks of concrete and blotches of white powder all along his shirt and pants. He had been working at this job for nearly two years and I could not remember ever hearing him complain about how difficult work was.

As I stood there, transfixed in admiration, I was startled by a 19 loud voice that came from behind me.

"He's a hard worker, isn't he?" 20

I nodded my head in agreement. I turned around and saw that 21 it was Gilbert.

"Hey Gilbert, you're just the person I was looking for," I said. 22 "So . . . um I . . . I . . ."

I wanted to tell him that I quit, that I was hot and hungry and   23
frustrated, but somehow the words just wouldn't come out.

After an awkward moment of silence I suddenly blurted out "I   24
want to thank you for hiring me . . . and I want you to know that I
truly appreciate it."

"It's my pleasure," he responded.   25

We exchanged smiles and I made my way back to my workplace.   26
The hammer I had thrown to the ground was still there, waiting for
my return. I picked it up and resumed my duties. My index finger
still had a painful blister on the tip, I was still hot. My middle finger
continued to throb. I was sweating profusely. However, things didn't
look as bad as they had just a few minutes ago. This wasn't the
most exciting job in the world, or the easiest, but it could be worse.

I began to work intensely and before I knew it, my phone read   27
3 p.m.; the day had finally ended. As my brother and I made our
way back to the truck I removed my safety glasses and hard hat. With
the back of my dirty hand I wiped away the ring of sweat that had
formed on my forehead. I looked at my brother's dirty clothes and
then looked down at my own. The layers of dirt that had accumu-
lated throughout the day would have repulsed me a few days ago,
but today I felt a sense of accomplishment; I hadn't given up. I simply
smiled and climbed into the truck, and away we went.

3 *Writing Profiles*

The essay you write for this chapter will almost certainly be the one you least expected to write in this class. It will not draw you back into memory, as the remembered-event essay did (Chapter 2), nor will it lead you to the library, as the other kinds of essays in this book are likely to. Instead, it will take you off-campus to see someone else's environment and—stranger still—require you to ask that person about it and capture what he or she says as a primary source for your essay.

It may seem daring or even reckless to walk into an unfamiliar place and ask strangers about their activities. Countless students given this assignment have nevertheless done so, gaining self-confidence and satisfying their curiosity about some unfamiliar corner of the everyday world—such as the soup kitchen, supermarket, printing press workshop, drive-in movie theater, and dragon boat festival visited by the student essayists in this chapter. The biggest surprise for many profilers is how willing strangers are to talk about their work and other interests.

As you read through the profiles that follow, note some of their basic features: detailed information about the subject, a clear and logical organization, the writer's role as either a participant or a detached observer, and the writer's unique perspective on the subject.

You may find your expectations about the people or place confirmed, but more likely you will be surprised or even astounded by what you learn—so surprised you may need to make a second visit to gather more information and to figure out how it all fits together. What you need in this special situation of observing and writing is an open mind—or better, a curious mind. Cultivating a curious mind will help you to think productively in any writing situation you encounter in college and, later, in your career. Anticipate that you will be surprised at what you see and hear in your visit and interviews. Embrace that surprise, use it in your essay, and continue to cultivate the curiosity that inspired it.

Use the guidelines in the Critical Reading Guide (below) to practice peer review using the essays in this chapter.

A Critical Reading Guide

DETAILED INFORMATION ABOUT THE SUBJECT

Does the writer portray the subject in enough well-chosen detail to show us why it's interesting?

Summarize: Tell the writer one thing you learned about the subject from reading the essay.

Praise: Point out one passage where the description seems especially vivid, a quotation stands out, or another writing strategy works particularly well to present information.

Critique: Point out one passage where description could be added or where the description could be made more vivid, where a quotation that falls flat should be paraphrased or summarized, or where another writing strategy could be used.

A CLEAR LOGICAL ORGANIZATION

Is the profile easy to follow?

Summarize: Identify the kind of organization — narrative, topical, or a blend of the two — that the writer uses.

Praise: Comment on the cues the writer gives that make the profile easy to follow. For example, point to a place where one topic leads logically to the next or where transitions help you follow the tour or narrative. Also, indicate what in the opening paragraphs grabs your attention or why you think the ending works well.

Critique: Point to information that seems out of place or instances where the chronology is confusing. If you think the opening or ending could be improved, suggest an alternative passage in the essay that could work as an opening or an ending.

THE WRITER'S ROLE

Is the author's role, whether spectator, participant-observer, or both, clear?

Summarize: Identify the role the writer adopts.

Praise: Point to a passage where the spectator or participant-observer role enables you to identify with the writer, enhancing the essay's immediacy or interest.

Critique: Point out any problems with the role—for example, if the participant-observer role becomes distracting, or if the spectator role seems too distant.

A PERSPECTIVE ON THE SUBJECT

Does the author have a clear point of view on the subject?

Summarize: State briefly what you believe to be the writer's perspective on the subject and the dominant impression you get from the essay.

Praise: Give an example where you have a strong sense of the writer's perspective through a comment, description, quotation, or bit of information.

Critique: Tell the writer if the essay does not have a clear perspective or convey a dominant impression. To help him or her find one, explain what interests you about the subject and what you think is important. If you see contradictions in the draft that could be developed to make the profile more complex and illuminating, briefly explain.

Our Daily Bread

Linda Kampel

Pennsylvania State University, York
York, Pennsylvania

When confronted with abject poverty, we are so often overwhelmed by it—the enormity of the problem can make us feel powerless and we simply turn away. But when a writer is able to put a name and a face on an issue, it becomes personal again. We can't help everyone, but maybe we could help someone like Andy or Carol, two people Kampel introduces us to. She describes Our Daily Bread soup kitchen with a journalistic look at the bleak surroundings; yet she manages to shine a light not on the desperation there, but on the tireless workers who bring hot food and hope to the nearly three hundred souls who depend on them.

To anyone who has the luxury of regular meals and a safe place to call home, walking through the entrance of Our Daily Bread soup kitchen is like stepping into a different world. Our Daily Bread operates out of a two-room cinder-block building in York, Pennsylvania, that has been transformed into a kitchen and dining area, where nearly three hundred poverty-stricken people come every day to eat. The front doors open at 10 a.m. on a large room with rows of six-foot metal tables, dim lights that cast gray shadows, and walls that are painted in 1970s "harvest gold," which has dulled with time. 1

In the back of the room there is a stainless-steel cafeteria-style serving counter, where people line up to be served hot coffee and do-nuts. As gloomy as the surroundings may sound, the majority of the people in the place seem to be comfortably familiar with the daily routine of standing in line, waiting for a meal. Occasionally, someone tells a joke or a funny story and one or more people laugh, making the atmosphere seem almost cheery. 2

35

A tall, heavyset black man wearing a dark cap suddenly starts yell-   3
ing at an invisible companion who has obviously upset him. "F—you!
I'll do what I want!" he yells. Everyone else in the room goes on with
their business. "I said I'm going to do what I want. Just leave me
alone!"

At first, it seems like this man could be a real threat, but when I   4
ask him what his name is, he very calmly says, "My name's Andy."

There is something sad about the look in Andy's eyes, and within   5
a few minutes, he's arguing again with whomever it is that has made
him so unhappy.

At 11 a.m., the crowd grows to about 80 people, and volunteers   6
are preparing to serve lunch. By 11:30, the number increases to 120,
and by 12:15, there are close to 250 men and women, and a handful of
children, making their way into the line that moves like a well-rehearsed
act in a play. Today's meal consists of vegetable soup, broccoli, bread,
and tuna-noodle casserole, with a choice of either lemonade or coffee
to drink. People of every age, gender, and race move through the line.
No one is turned away.

Carol, a thirty-five-year-old black woman dressed in clean but   7
worn-out clothes, says that she has been coming here for about two
years. "Most people who come here aren't homeless," she says. "We all
have a place to live and all. It's just that sometimes meals are a problem. Some people come here because it's a social thing, you know. You
take a break from whatever you're doing. You come in here and have
some food and talk to people you know."

A tall white man, about sixty-five years of age and dressed in dirty,   8
old clothes, walks past us. He has donut powder all over his mouth
and chin. "That's so sad," Carol says. "He doesn't even know it's
there. That poor man. Now he needs help. At least he's here in a place
where he'll be taken care of."

At first it's easy to think that Carol's problems aren't all that bad,   9
perhaps because she has become so good at convincing herself that this
way of life is normal. I fall right into her train of thought. But later,
thinking back, I can't help realizing that the majority of the people
who come to Our Daily Bread do need help of some kind or they
wouldn't be there. They're either so lost that they can't find themselves anymore or have accepted this daily routine as the reality of a
bad hand they've been dealt in life.

Around 12:30 p.m., a volunteer worker walks over to a microphone   10
at the end of the serving counter and asks, "Has everyone gotten the

food they need to eat?" No one says a word. "If anyone needs more to eat, please come up and get as much as you want."

A few people return to the counter for second helpings, but most people are beginning to leave. They've been well fed and maybe somehow given the boost they need to make it through the day.   11

At the helm of this well-run operation are two people, Joe Mc-Cormick and Marie Rohleder, both of whom seem to have a genuine and unconditional interest in making sure that for at least two and a half hours a day anyone who needs a hot meal or emotional support in a warm, dry place can find it within these walls.   12

Joe McCormick, the business manager, is a tall, white-haired, sixty-year-old man whose smile lets you know right away that he is a very special human being, the "real thing." Joe cares about every inch of this place and about the people who come here for help. Joe is semi-retired now, but he still takes care of all the expenses of Our Daily Bread, keeps track of the donations, and sends out thank-you notes to all those who contribute food or services. Every Monday, Joe is in charge of food preparation and serving.   13

"We've been here for seven years now," he says. "We're open Monday through Friday from 10 a.m. to 12:30 p.m. You should have seen the place we were in before we moved here. It was hell on earth, in the basement of Cristo Salvador, a local Spanish church. The kitchen was about a third of the size of this one here. There was barely enough room for a dishwasher and a stove. That place used to get about 150 degrees in the summertime when we were making food, and there were times when the water on the floor from rainstorms was six inches deep. We were afraid to use anything electric." Joe lights a cigarette. "Back then we were serving about 107 people a day. Now we're serving around 300. It used to be 400 before September House started its senior citizen outreach program, but I'll let Marie tell you about that later."   14

Cartons of pastries arrive through the back door, so Joe goes over to help bring them in. When he returns, he leans against a stack of crates.   15

"Last Thanksgiving we were really sweating it out because we supply Helping Hands with their turkeys, and we hardly had any turkeys at all. Then right after the holidays, we got a call to come and pick up fifty of them. It's feast or famine around here. When Chuck E. Cheese closed down last year, I got two truckloads of pizzas and birthday cakes. Boy, were they good. People still come in here and ask, 'Do   16 you have any more of those birthday cakes?' We're never at a loss for resources for food, it seems. It's not always the greatest, but it's out there. York County is a very giving place."

"Just a second," Joe tells me, and when he returns, he is with a 17 dark-haired woman about thirty-five years of age who is wearing a blue nylon jacket. She has the same welcoming smile that Joe has, and I can't help thinking how lucky everyone here is to have these two people on their side. Joe introduces the woman as Marie, who is, by her own definition, the inventory-control specialist.

"In other words, I make sure that all the food gets put in the 18 freezer, which explains the jacket. I also rotate the food on the shelves so that nothing stays around too long."

Marie also takes on the responsibilities of food preparation and 19 serving on Thursdays and Fridays.

"There's a guy named Charlie who takes care of Tuesdays and 20 Wednesdays, but he's not here right now. Anyway, an organization called September House started an outreach program a couple of years ago. They go and pick up our senior citizens and take them for meals at their senior citizen center. They're much better off over there because they get the attention they really need. That's why the number of people we serve here has dropped off slightly. It's a wonderful organization. It's hard not to get involved sometimes. There are some people you can't help but get involved with. They need that. And there are some people who come and go. We just found out today that one fellow we get involved with a lot just got sent to jail last night. Busted for drugs. It's heartbreaking sometimes because you know how hard they've been trying. There was one guy who used to do dishes for us. Lester. He tried so hard to stay sober, and he just couldn't do it. Eventually he died from alcohol poisoning."

"That's the hardest kind," Joe says. "You see these people and 21 you know that no matter what the hell they do, they're in a hole. And they're never gonna get out."

One of the volunteers comes over and asks where to put a tray 22 filled with pumpkin bread.

"That's Pat," Marie says after she points her toward a storage 23 shelf. "She's one of our regular volunteers. She comes in almost every day, along with the volunteers from at least one church group. "We get about fifty volunteers a week. The only problem is that no one wants to clean up—everyone wants to serve or cook, but as soon as 12:30 hits, boom, they're out the door. York College is sending over a group of students this Saturday to paint these walls. And the group Up with People is coming in tomorrow, I think, to help out. I'm glad they're coming because Fridays are the worst. For some reason, that's the day when the people who really are in desperate need come in, so that they can load up for the weekend. We always have extra bread, so we can give out a couple of loaves to everyone."

When 12:45 arrives, the volunteers are finished serving lunch. 24 There is clean-up work to be done, and Joe and Marie take their place among the volunteers so that they will soon be able to call it a day.

True Worker

Erik Epple

Bowling Green State University
Bowling Green, Ohio

Erik Epple offers readers a look behind the scenes of a large chain supermarket store when he introduces us to Larry Harshman. A detached observer, Epple evaluates Harshman's reputation as Kroger's hardest-working employee. As you read, notice the various writing strategies Epple employs. For example, he *contrasts* Harshman with his coworkers; he *narrates* the sequence of tasks Harshman performs; he explains the *causes* of Larry's preference for the night shift and reveals the *effects* of his years of hard work—his failed marriage and bad back. These strategies assist in showing a complete and nuanced picture of Larry Harshman.

I've been working at Kroger supermarket in Springville, Ohio, for 1 two weeks now, and my coworkers keep mentioning Larry Harshman, head of the store's grocery department. Depending on whom I talk to, Larry is either the most solitary, antisocial person on staff, or some kind of mythic hero, like Paul Bunyan or Pecos Bill.

I decide I want to meet Larry for myself. The mystique around 2 him only grows when I learn he works the graveyard shift. I head back to the supermarket at 11:00 one Thursday night and introduce myself to Larry. As we talk, I begin to realize that Larry Harshman is a far more complicated person than my coworkers would have me believe.

The chattering of mechanical devices, the smashing of falling 3 crates, and the ripping of cardboard would cause most people to cover their ears. Larry welcomes the noise, though. It proves to him that he is working hard and also eases his loneliness.

Sitting across from Larry in the dimly lit break room, I am inspired 4 by his work ethic. Over twenty-seven years, Larry has worked his way up from a bagger to head of the grocery department. Clark Carr, the store manager, has nothing but praise for Larry: "He is a very reliable worker, one that I go to every time I need something done."

Larry, however, is beginning to feel his age: "It's my back; I just   5
can't move as quick anymore."

Other Kroger employees, however, believe that no one there can   6
outwork Larry, despite his aging body. Whether he is cutting open boxes or unloading a truck, he seems to defy his limitations and works in a flurry of activity, in an environment of ordered chaos. Efficient, practiced, and precise are words that best describe Larry.

Larry's days are exact: arise, go to work, return home, sleep. The   7
routine is periodically interrupted when he goes out to eat with a friend, but such interruptions are rare. And while Larry works nine to five, he does not go to work in the morning, like most other Americans, because his workday begins at 9 p.m.

"I've never been much of a social person," Larry states with   8
downcast eyes. "That's why I work third shift." Larry prefers to work alone and would rather have just one good friend than many. He likes those nights when only he and Carol—a night cashier and close friend of his—work the shelves. His obsession with work and desire for solitude have destroyed his home life. His wife of twenty-five years filed for divorce, leaving Larry totally dispirited.

"I like being alone," he comments, "but alone doesn't mean with-   9
out anyone to care about you. She was always that one special person in my life and was always there when I needed someone to listen to me. Now she is gone, and all that I have left are my friends at Kroger."

After a moment's quiet, I ask Larry to explain his job. He sips his   10
Pepsi and responds: "After my break, I'll show you."

Fifteen minutes later, he hauls himself out of the metal chair and   11
nods toward the door. Following him into the back room, I am surprised by his change of mood. His eyes narrow, and cursing under his breath, he falls into step with another employee as they survey the work left undone by the day crew.

"Looks like another long night for us, Oscar," Larry proclaims to   12
his companion, cursing again.

"Just once," Oscar growls, "I'd like to see those lazy bastards   13
work a night shift."

Grabbing the handle of a pallet jack—a large machine that re-   14
sembles a miniature forklift—and rolling the jack toward him, Larry begins speaking to me over his shoulder.

"First, we unload the truck, which usually isn't too bad but can be   15
a pain in the ass at times," he declares, as the twin prongs on the jack
slide under the first pallet of groceries.

I watch Larry repeatedly maneuver the forklift in and out of the   16
semi's trailer, each time appearing with another pallet stacked with
boxes; within a half hour the sixty-foot trailer is empty. When all of the
pallets are lined along the back wall, Larry pulls a box cutter out of his
rear pocket.

I watch as Larry mechanically slits the tops, one by one, off of   17
each box. Although working at a frenetic pace, he never cuts into the
groceries inside. After removing each top, he places the open boxes on
cart like devices called wheelers. Four workers appear from the front of
the store to take the now-filled wheelers inside. As the night continues,
I discover Larry always has a wheeler filled before someone comes back
for a new one.

Everyone agrees Larry is the key to a successful night.   18

"It worries me sometimes, watching him gimp around the break   19
room, but his age never shows through his work," comments Rita, an
employee who works the wheelers.

"He gets six weeks out of every year for vacation. During those   20
weeks, Oscar loads up the wheelers and Spencer unloads the truck, and
everything just goes to hell," complains Mark, another worker.

Returning the box cutter to his pocket, Larry calls break over the   21
loudspeaker. As everyone else begins shuffling toward the break room
for a few smokes or a snack, Larry heads for the front of the store, buys
himself a can of soda, then sits down on one of the register belts.

"It's just not like it used to be around here," Larry mumbles.   22
"Clark takes away all of our help, and the ones who are working don't
take it seriously. It's all a big joke these days. Some of the workers
spend most of their time on the clock talking on the telephone to God
only knows who. Others just joke around and never go beyond what is
expected of them. The spirit of working and earning your pay is gone.
That gets to me sometimes."

Glancing around me, I see exactly what Larry means. Empty boxes   23
are scattered up and down the aisles, left on the floor for the morning crew to pick up. The six workers unloading the wheelers inside
the store cannot keep up with Larry, the only person working in the
back on the dock. Not only are wheelers spread around the store, still
loaded, but many more are choking the back; I weave my way through
a narrow canyon of wheelers to reach the break room.

"He just takes his job too seriously. He needs to lighten up, enjoy 24
himself," remarks a cocky, tall worker, whom I later find out is Greg.
"If you want my opinion," he continues, "he needs a woman."

As if to add gloom to the picture of Larry's personal life, Rita 25
chimes in: "Oh, you know old Larry will never get himself another
woman; he doesn't even know how to act around one anymore."

The crew falls into its own private thoughts. Through the canyon 26
of wheelers, I can see Larry still sitting by himself in the front. Half an
hour later, everyone is back at work.

"No reason to keep stacking up the wheelers," Larry growls, as 27
he stares at the many wheelers waiting to be taken into the store and
unloaded. "They'll just get so backed up that no one can get into the
back."

Larry turns and begins stacking the now empty pallets and clean- 28
ing up the docking area. When he is satisfied that everything is in
order, he takes the remaining wheelers out to the front. Instead of
leaving the work to the other employees, Larry begins to help them
stock the shelves. With Larry helping, the others finish in less than an
hour.

"Now is when I slack because all the work is done," Larry states. 29
"There is nothing left to do, even if anyone wanted to. It makes no
sense to slack before the work is over."

Driving away that night, I realize that Larry Harshman is neither 30
mythic hero nor recluse but someone who represents a time when how
well a person performed his job was a measure of that person's worth.
It is an attitude that his coworkers, both those who see him as Super-
man and those who don't, do not seem to perceive or understand. But
in just one night, I learned not only to appreciate him as a hard worker
but also to respect him as someone who refuses to let unenthusiastic
coworkers or his own physical decline stand in the way of getting the
job done.

Bringing Ingenuity Back

Linda Fine

University of California, Riverside
Riverside, California

When you interview someone who is passionate about something, you may discover—as Linda Fine did—that a commonplace process can turn into a memorable story. Using a straightforward interview style, with quotations and paraphrases, Fine allows the librarian in this essay to detail the arduous steps involved in old-fashioned hand presses. As you read, notice how Fine's perspective changes throughout the course of her essay and how her concluding analogy leads the reader to join her in a new appreciation for the dedication and personal touch involved in this unique craft.

As I made my way to a set of elevators in the rear of our sleek new campus library, I passed students and librarians working at monitors wired into the university's online system. I also passed students sitting at tables with their laptops open and books piled nearby. A few students were using the photocopiers to scan pages onto their jump drives, and two printers on a corner table spewed paper as students stood nearby chatting. I was on my way into the past to see hand-printing presses dating from the Civil War. The antique presses were donated to the university by Dr. Edward Petko because he favored the hand-press method over modern laser printing, and he hoped that the university would help keep the traditional process alive.

Entering an unmarked room in the basement, I saw numerous weathered wooden cases stacked twice my height and, beyond them, old iron machines in various shapes and sizes. I stepped into the room clueless but eager to learn about this nearly forgotten printing process.

Sara Stilley, a thin, dark-haired woman in her late twenties, works in this room five days a week. After welcoming me, she showed me some samples of artwork she has printed. One of her most recent works was a greeting card she had made for another staff member. The finished product looked very professional, but then Sara proceeded to explain to me the frustration behind this masterpiece.

The preparation work takes hours, and in some cases, days. Sara's   3
difficult task is to carefully align each individual letter by hand. The letters are made up of very thin rectangular prisms, which make them difficult to handle. Not only does Sara need manual dexterity, she also needs skilled eyes to be able to tell the letters apart. If a wrong letter, font, or size has been used, she has to go back to tediously correct the frame and setup by hand. Familiarity with what the letters will look like is essential for the setup of hand printing because the letters can be confusing. The leaded letters in the printing process work like a stamp. Instead of arranging them the way they are read, the operator must position the letters upside down and backward, like a mirror image. It takes time and effort to train the eye to recognize letters this way. Letters such as *n* and *u* are easily mixed up, as are *p* and *q*, and *b* and *d*. Formatting the letters correctly is a critical step in the printing process because any careless error in the setup leaves a noticeable flaw in the printed document.

In addition to the letter conflict, Sara said, "Many times after cen-   4
tering the text, I would find out that I made a mistake in the forma-tion. Instead of making it perfectly centered, I was supposed to align it to the left." I could imagine that going back and correcting the spac-ing would be a wearisome task.

This old-fashioned printing process has other problems and dif-   5
ficulties too. For example, humid weather causes the ink to spread out, leaving the text appearing smudgy and smeared. There also may be too much or too little ink used in a working press. Sometimes Sara will run out of a specific letter for a page. The only solution to this problem is to break apart her work into two printing processes and print half the page at a time.

Sara explained that back in the 1800s, printers did not number   6
their pages when printing a book. In order to keep the pages orderly, they had to use the same word twice. For example, if a page ended with the word "boy," then the following page would have to begin with the word "boy." Not numbering the pages can easily cause them to fall out of order.

At this point in the interview, I had to ask her, "If using hand- 7
printing presses can cause so many problems, why would anyone still
prefer using them over laser-printing presses?"

Sara answered, "I feel better with what I produce. For example, 8
personally baking a cake for someone is better and much more appre-
ciated than simply buying one."

After she said that, I got the point. If I were to send out Christmas 9
cards, each individual card would mean so much more if I had personally hand-printed it myself rather than buying a box of pre-printed
cards at Wal-Mart. Craftsmanship adds value and meaning that you
can't find in industrialized commodities that you just buy.

I walked around the room and explored the shapes and sizes of the 10
various printing presses. I saw that each machine had its own unique
maneuvers. Some levers had to be pulled clockwise and pushed down.
Others simply needed to be rolled across the printing bed and back.
The cases and crates stacked around the presses contained lead-filled
letters and hundreds of neatly stored rectangular pieces. There were
keys, metal washers, wooden blocks called "furniture" to keep the letters in place, ink, and galleys—all of which, I learned, were required
for the printing process.

At the very end of my interview, Sara demonstrated one of the 11
many printing presses to me, the "Asbern." First she carefully arranged
the lead-filled text blocks on the printing bed and used a key to tighten
the furniture securing the letters. As she switched the power button
on, the ink rollers began to spin. A low, soft mumbling sound stirred
and filled the room. Sara slipped a piece of plain white paper into the
slot and steered the machine from left to right. Steering the wheel
seemed like a very tough job because she was jerking her entire body
to create enough torque to rotate the wheel. Soon she turned off the
machine and took the paper out. After a careful examination, she an-
nounced that it wasn't perfect. Sara handed the page to me expecting
me to see what she saw, but as I looked at it, I found nothing wrong
with the printing.

Squinting, she told me, "The text is not perfectly centered on 12
the paper. It's a bit crooked because I slipped in the paper at a slight
angle."

Who ever would have thought that small errors, like slipping in 13
the paper slanted, would make such a big difference? This is one of the
many things that make hand-printing more difficult than using a modern printing press.

Had Sara not pointed out to me the imperfection of her work, 14 however, I never would have caught it. It is amazing how she can spot a flaw in her work as quickly as a professional chess player can call a checkmate. Sara's keen expertise in the area of hand-printing presses impresses me. I never thought such an old-fashioned job would provide deep insight into the beauty and value of works made by hand.

As I left the room filled with irreplaceable treasures, I thought of 15 the time when my sister, Irene, knitted a scarf for her friend on duty in Iraq. Irene was very worried about making the scarf "perfect." She was so concerned about making a mistake—or not having enough time to finish the scarf—that I wondered why she didn't simply buy a scarf at Macy's. After interviewing Sara Stilley and learning more about the ingenuity of her work, I now understand why Irene chose to make the scarf by hand. The scarf she knitted for her friend had more meaning in it than a typical scarf purchased at a department store. She expressed her loving care and support through the gift she made because it took time and effort, and not just money. There are a few holes and gaps in that scarf, but I'm sure her friend, like me, didn't see the imperfections and thought the gift was simply perfect.

Modernizing a Remnant of the Mid-Century

Bonnie Lapwood

Mt. San Jacinto College, Menifee Valley
Menifee, California

Bonnie Lapwood profiles an institution in transition: a drive-in movie theater that is modernizing to meet the needs of the twenty-first century. Lapwood begins the essay by describing the theater from a moviegoer's point of view, but she also interviews the theater manager to find out more about the theater's history and upcoming renovations. Using both of these strategies provided Lapwood with enough detailed information to profile the theater effectively for her readers. As you read, ask yourself whether Lapwood takes a spectator role, a participant role, or both in her profile.

1　A giant, neon pink Stater Bros. sign looms out of the darkness as we approach Mission Blvd. The glowing letters spill out across the unseen background in a streamlined, atomic-age font. The same sign probably greeted those headed to the drive-in fifty years ago. After turning right on Mission, the sign for the Rubidoux Drive-In appears. The Rubidoux is the oldest operating drive-in theater in Southern California, and still attracts a large following. Roy C. Hunt opened the Rubidoux Theater in 1948. The miniature railroad and petting zoo that once surrounded it have now disappeared, but every night, the screen still leans gracefully over an increasing number of cars filled with expectant viewers.

2　At night, the large slab of screen one is visible only as a black monolith behind illuminated palm trees. Red-vested teenagers stand joking and laughing when the entrance is empty, but snap to attention when prospective moviegoers approach the stone ticket huts. Our attendant is a fresh-faced young man who jovially asks us which movie we are seeing, and tells us the radio frequency of the audio track for our screen. Radio-broadcast movie soundtracks are a relatively recent innovation, replacing communal speakers and individual speakers. Of course, this means that the quality of the movie audio is only as good as the quality of the car stereo, but the broadcast is clear and static-free. The parking lot is uneven, with raised rows allowing the viewers a form of tiered seating. Once parked, viewers can leave their cars to visit the brightly lit snack bar and restrooms, housed in a pink stucco building with teal trim that sits in the middle of all three screens.

Before the movie begins, people arrange themselves to enjoy it 3 comfortably. People with SUVs generally park with the back of their car facing the screen and sit on the ledge with the hatch open and the radio blasting, using blankets for warmth. Most people with sedans simply park facing the screen and sit in the car as they would if they were driving. Others eschew their car entirely, sitting on lawn chairs close to their sedans or pickups, so they can hear the sound. Some people occupying lawn chairs have neon glow sticks, which they either wear around their wrists or wave in the air. Children run around their parents' cars until chided to sit down and behave. The parking lot is almost full by the time the previews begin, and the constant stream of people moving between their cars and the snack bar has slowed to a halt. The massive screen and lack of distractions make it much easier to get absorbed in the movie than in a regular theater. Sitting in a car, it feels like the movie is being projected just for you.

Although drive-in theaters have become less popular since the 4 1960s, this drive-in theater has grown in popularity over the last six years.

"The drive-in appeals to families because it's a bargain, and there's 5 no worry over parking, or being late," says Frank Huttinger, a vice president at De Anza Land & Leisure,which owns the Rubidoux as well as five other drive-in theaters. Frank decides which movies are appropriate for drive-in audiences, negotiates their purchase with the studios, and groups them together by screen. Family-friendly movies are always included, as are large horror and action releases (Frank says that he personally prefers to see action movies at the drive-in, and light comedies and dramas at a traditional theater). De Anza Land & Leisure itself is a family-owned company, as are most drive-in companies, and has been operating drive-in theaters in California, Utah, and Georgia since the 1960s. With twenty- five screens spread over six theaters, it is the second largest drive-in corporation in America. Frank is a member of the family, having seen his first drive-in movie—H. G. Wells's *The Time Machine*—at ten years old. Yet he worked in new media—CDs and the Internet—for over twenty years before joining the company.

"I've been in movies for about six years. It's a fun market," he   6 says. Frank's experience in media has influenced the rebranding of the De Anza theaters, which has been taking place over the last five or six years. "We've completely moved away from newspapers, and now all our advertising is on the Internet," he states proudly. Money has also been put into revising snack-bar menus and improving technology at the theaters. Frank sees the drive-in business in a very practical, realistic light. He buys movies for their mass appeal, and despite the success of a recent series of old films shown through a partnership with Turner Classic Movies, he recognizes that audiences desire twenty-first-century entertainment. "You can't rely on nostalgia—you have to keep up and be current," he affirms. This seems to be somewhat of a personal mantra of his. The Rubidoux, with its retro coral-pink and sky-blue color scheme, is due for a "serious" remodelling in the next year or two.

Frank also acknowledges the non-movie side of the business. "We   7 wouldn't be able to keep up without the swap meets," he reveals. Swap meets take place at the Rubidoux from 6 a.m. to 2 p.m. on Wednesday, Friday, Saturday, and Sunday. They form the daylight side of the drive-in business, and make use of the giant parking lot when sunlight prohibits movies from being projected. They have been held since the 1960s, and are an integral part of the drive-in industry—which in part explains why so few drive-ins have been refurbished or newly built. Along with the difficulty involved in buying the large amounts of land and equipment required to run a drive-in, Frank noted that it takes about five years to build up swap meets to the point of being profitable.

The drive-in experience appeals to many, as it offers low admission   8 fees, the freedom to either bring your own food or buy concessions at lower prices than at traditional movie theaters, and an opportunity to relax in the privacy and comfort of your own car. The potential discomforts of a traditional theater—overzealous air-conditioning, babies crying, popcorn on the floor, taller people blocking the view, teenagers carrying out public displays of affection, having to sit apart from companions because of a lack of seats—are eliminated at the drive-in, where the air conditioner is adjustable, the seats are comfortable, and the other viewers cannot interrupt.

I was originally attracted to the drive-in theater out of sentimen-   9
tality for the design and technological innovations of the American
mid-century. However, as Frank told me, nostalgia is not enough to
sustain a business. I found the Rubidoux Drive-In to be a worthy rival
to the modern movie theater since it has the charm of an older drive-in
with the convenience and technologies of today. This drive-in theater's
resurgence in popularity may inspire more innovations in the way the
American public watches movies, which may lead to more alternatives
to traditional movie theaters.

"Paddlers Sit Ready!" The Enduring Sport of Dragon Boating

Katie Diehm

The Catholic University of America
Washington, D.C.

While other profile authors do occasionally insert themselves into their essays—reflecting on an interviewee's comment, for example, or briefly joining the scene they are describing—for the most part they are detached observers, reporters rather than participants. Katie Diehm, however, makes her subject come to life by describing dragon boat racing from an insider perspective. Diehm's participant-observer role allows her to offer readers not only the look and sound of the race, but also its feel. Readers are invited into the sensory experience—to feel the muscle strain, the adrenaline, the wind—which impresses on them the urgency of the moment.

As we bob up and down in the river, our arms begin to shake in antic- 1
ipation. Our hands grip our paddles tighter as we hold them down straight into the water, bracing the boat and willing it to stay still despite the rain blowing into us. From my seat on the left side of the fifth bench, I can see the call boat over the heads of my nervous teammates. The timer watches us intently until that exact moment when all four teams are lined up and he can give us the go.

Over the sound of water hitting the sides of the boats, we can hear 2
cheering from the excited spectators on the shore. From the other side of the river, the spectators appear as a long streak of moving color lined up in front of perhaps the most colorful of festivals. Tents with various Chinese wares, food, and music cover the lawn, all part of this joyous celebration of the dragon boat tradition.

Dragon boats first originated more than two thousand years
ago in China when, as legend has it, disgruntled Chinese poet and
scholar Qu Yuan committed suicide by jumping into a river after
his village was overrun with enemies. As *Washington Post* journalist
Paul Schwartzman tells us, "local fishermen searched for him in their
boats, pounding drums and beating the waters furiously to ward
off the water dragons they feared might eat him" (2). Dragon boat
racing soon developed in honor of this event, often as part of the
Chinese Festival of the Dragon Boat, meant to honor and appease
the dragon ruling over the river. Today's dragon boat races are often
accompanied by a festival, which generally begins with a flag-raising
ceremony the day before the races. This ceremony, in which the Chinese flag is raised over the river, symbolizes China's lasting importance in the event. A far cry from the fishing boats of Qu Yuan's era,
today's dragon boats are forty-five feet long and made of fiberglass,
complete with a dragon's head and tail at either end. Sixteen paddlers line both sides of the boat and paddle in synch in a way unique
to dragon boating.   3

"Boat Three draw left!" the timer yells over the wind, and the left-
side paddlers on the boat in the third lane begin to work hard, paddling sideways to move their boat farther away from the second lane.   4

"Boat Four hold! Paddle back!" the timer yells as the wind shifts
and their team begins to pull forward past the starting line. The paddlers strain to hold their paddles down in the water, keeping the boat
still, and then slowly and steadily begin to paddle backward.   5

The beginning of a dragon boat race is often the hardest due to
elements like wind and the river current. Getting lined up often takes
the better part of ten minutes—an ironic beginning for a race that lasts
approximately three—and is grueling for the paddlers as they sometimes must paddle constantly just to stay in one place. As the boats
finally pull into place, the timer wastes no time in barking out orders.   6

"Paddlers sit ready!" he calls, signaling the time for all paddles to
be removed from the water and proper grip on the paddle—the upper
hand gripping the top of the paddle as if in a fist, the lower hand gripping the lower section of the paddle, directly above the wide part—to
be assumed.   7

"Attention!" At this call the teams lean forward, arms extended
and paddles raised about five inches above the water, ready to plunge
with all intensity into the river. Mike Dojc, a dragon boat enthusiast,
explains that the paddlers stretch their backs out straight, ready to pull   8

at the paddle with the muscles from their arms, stomach, and back by twisting their bodies and keeping their arms straight (Dojc 1).

"Go!" Instantly the teams spring into action. Simultaneously, my teammates and I drop our paddles down and forward and pull back with all our strength. The start time in dragon boat racing is extremely important—it's a thirty-second chance to gain additional speed that will last even when the paddlers fall back into a slower and more constant pace. The tiller—the person in charge of steering the boat—stands at the back and grips the till, willing through long strokes or skillful dips of the till that the boat stay on course. The caller, standing on the front of the boat and struggling to keep her balance despite the surging of the boat, beats out a fast rhythm on a drum, shouting the counts over the beat. 9

"One! Two! Three! Four! Watch-your-lead! Two! Three! Four! Keep-it-up! Two! Three! Four!" 10

As the boats leave the beginning of the race, the quick-start pace subsides and the paddlers begin to pace themselves. At ninety strokes a second, however, the pace is hardly relaxing. As arms begin to go numb, the paddlers begin to focus all their energy on keeping up with the rest of the paddlers in the boat, as they know that even the slightest delay on their paddle's entrance into the river can mean a demerit of a couple of seconds. Suzanne Ma, a journalist from the *Hamilton Spectator*, tells us that the aim is for the "rhythm of the boat to be like one collective heartbeat" (1). Each team has a unique way of keeping everyone in time using some division of the paddlers. My team divided the sixteen paddlers into two groups. The first ten paddlers (two per bench) watch the two paddlers in the front (called the lead strokes); the left-side paddlers watch the lead on the right, and the right-side paddlers watch the left. The paddlers on the fourth bench, called the mid-strokes, serve as pacers for the back half of the boat as they watch the lead strokes and are then watched in the same way by the back paddlers. From my left-side fifth bench position, I sit directly behind the mid-strokes and am dubbed a part of the "engine room," the part of the boat that is relied on for constant, steady paddling. The front of the boat is made up of paddlers who have long, solid paddle strokes. These paddlers must also be very strong, as they are paddling dead water. The rear three benches are made up of powerful paddlers called rockets. These six paddlers are perhaps the most important on the boat, as it is their strength that propels the boat forward. Some describe the feeling of paddling in rhythm as entering a Zen state, and 11

Schwartzman tells us that "if the boat is in tune, you can feel it glid-
ing" (2). Paddling in unison with proper technique and a tailwind, our
boat can get up to 6 mph.

As the boat reaches the end of the five-hundred-meter race, adre-   12
naline kicks in to counteract our fatigue. At one minute to go, our
designated flag catcher, chosen for her light weight and gymnast-like
frame, gets up, climbs behind the tiller, ties her feet into a strap se-
cured from the neck of the dragon, and lies down prostrate over the
dragon's head until she is extended a good two feet off the dragon's
nose. Her outstretched arm directs the tiller toward the flag that she
must catch or the team will receive a hefty demerit on its time.

The last thirty seconds of the race are often the hardest. Clearly   13
fatigued and struggling to maintain the pace, the paddlers rely solely
on adrenaline to get to the finish line. The pace accelerates to the beat
of a drum, and the caller urges the paddlers to "Finish-it-now!"—a
signal to paddle faster and firmer than before. As soon as the boats
speed through the finish line and flags are caught, the callers waste no
time in yelling, "Hold the boat!" We thrust our paddles straight down
into the water and attempt—despite the speed of the boat—to hold
them still. Our boat comes to a stop about eight feet away from the
grassy shore, and the tiller rapidly begins to spin the boat around and
back to the docks. With now-shaking arms and pounding hearts we
slowly make our way back, where we unload and trade places with the
next team waiting to go out. The races continue all day and into the
next, tournament style, until only four teams are left. These last four
compete against one another in one final race—the last of the season.

As the teams narrow down, the festivities increase, and teams that   14
are out of the running return to the shoreline to cheer for the teams
that are still competing. The smell of Chinese cuisine fills the air, and
ethnic music explodes from all corners of the grounds, reminding the
participants just how unique an experience the Chinese Festival of the
Dragon Boat really is.

WORKS CITED

Bradley, Theresa. "Students Revel in Asian Tradition: Dragon Boat Race."
Miami Herald 29 Sept. 2005: 1–3. *LexisNexis.* Web. 13 Oct. 2005.
Dojc, Mike. "Blazing Paddles: Q&A with a Dragon Boat Enthusiast." *Toronto
Sun* 26 June 2004: 1–3. *LexisNexis.* Web. 13 Oct. 2005.

Ma, Suzanne. "Pulling Together: Dragon Boat Racing Soothes the Mind, Energizes the Body." *Hamilton Spectator* 7 July 2005: 1–4. *LexisNexis.* Web. 13 Oct. 2005.

Schwartzman, Paul. "In Dragon Races, Team Spirit Sinks In, and That's Not All: Ancient Chinese Tradition Grows with Fourth Year of Competing on Potomac." *Washington Post* 29 May 2005: 1–3. *LexisNexis.* Web. 13 Oct. 2005.

Explaining a Concept 4

Explaining a concept might seem like a broad or daunting task at first. After all, as the student writers in this chapter show us, a "concept" can refer to anything from body language to stop-motion animation. A concept is an issue, phenomenon, or process: participatory culture, academic failure among college athletes, the dowry system in India, jihad, secular humanism, postcolonialism, bankruptcy, and machismo are all concepts. Nevertheless, you explain concepts much more frequently than you might realize. When you describe the latest technological feature on your smartphone to someone who has never seen it before, or list the reasons one might vote for a particular political candidate (perhaps citing authoritative sources or offering evidence), you are explaining a concept.

The concept essays in this chapter share the same basic features: a focused explanation (the main thesis), clear and logical organization, appropriate explanatory strategies (such as definition, classification, and comparison/contrast), and smooth integration of sources.

Once you have identified an issue you are familiar with or would be interested in knowing more about, your next step is to gain a quick orientation to it. Let's say you've heard about participatory culture and would like to know more. A bit of Web browsing reveals that the term *participatory culture* refers to the universe of file-sharing networks, blogs, wikis, and other platforms that enable ideas and content to flow among peers; the shared value of these participants; and the participants themselves. Voilà: a concept you could learn more about and write about!

Writing that explains a concept is not so personal as narrating a remembered event (Chapter 2) or profiling a place or activity you have observed (Chapter 3). It need not be so accommodating to readers' expected resistance as arguing to support your position on an issue (chapter 6) or proposing to solve a problem (Chapter 7). But it does invite you to attune yourself to your readers, precisely measuring what they will already know about the concept: You don't want to bore them or burden them, but to enable them to learn about your concept without too strenuous an effort. No showing off is allowed: Of course you know more than your readers about this subject, but to win their ear, you must remain tactful throughout, authoritative yet never talking down.

Every academic discipline, profession, career, sport, kind of work, governmental or political organization, local community, and religion has its concepts. Through concepts, we define, understand, and manage our world. We can't live without them. These are not just big words—they are required words. As a college student, you'll add hugely to your concept hoard. In doing so, you'll gain a wider understanding of the myriad aspects of your life and times, and you'll have the precise words—the concept names—to help you organize and deploy your new knowledge.

Use the guidelines in the Critical Reading Guide (below) to practice peer review using the essays in this chapter.

A Critical Reading Guide

A FOCUSED EXPLANATION

Is the explanation focused?

Summarize: Tell the writer, in one sentence, what you understand the concept to mean and why it is important or useful.

Praise: Give an example of something in the draft that you think will especially interest the intended readers.

Critique: Tell the writer about any confusion or uncertainty you have about the concept's meaning, importance, or usefulness. Indicate if the focus could be clearer or more appropriate for the intended readers or if the explanation could have a more interesting focus.

A CLEAR, LOGICAL ORGANIZATION

Is the explanation easy to follow?

Summarize: Look at the way the essay is organized by making a scratch outline.

Praise: Give an example of where the essay succeeds in being readable—for instance, in its overall organization, forecast of topics, or use of transitions.

Critique: Identify places where readability could be improved—for example, the beginning made more appealing, a topic sentence made clearer, or transitions or headings added.

APPROPRIATE EXPLANATORY STRATEGIES

Is the concept explained effectively?

Summarize: Note which explanatory strategies the writer uses, such as definition, comparison, example, cause-effect, or process analysis.

Praise: Point to an explanatory strategy that is especially effective, and highlight research that is particularly helpful in explaining the concept.

Critique: Point to any places where a definition is needed, where more (or better) examples might help, or where another explanatory strategy could be improved or added. Note where a visual (such as a flowchart or graph) would make the explanation clearer.

SMOOTH INTEGRATION OF SOURCES

Are the sources incorporated into the essay effectively?

Summarize: Note each source mentioned in the text, and check to make sure it appears in the list of works cited, if there is one. Highlight signal phrases and in-text citations, and identify appositives used to provide experts' credentials.

Praise: Give an example of the effective use of sources—a particularly well-integrated quotation, paraphrase, or summary that supports and illustrates the point. Note any especially descriptive verbs used to introduce information.

Critique: Point out where experts' credentials are needed. Indicate quotations, paraphrases, or summaries that could be more smoothly integrated or more fully interpreted or explained. Suggest verbs in signal phrases that may be more appropriate.

The Forgotten Personality

Katie Angeles

University of California, Riverside
Riverside, California

In order to explain a specialized term, Katie Angeles began with a discussion of a more widely understood subject: personality types. Aware that her audience might not be familiar with the topic, she briefly explains the history and concept of personality types. From this starting point, Angeles is able to contrast characteristics her audience may be more familiar with to those traits unique to the "forgotten" personality type—the *phlegmatic*. Note how Angeles uses the illustration of the way different people behave at a party to offer readers an example they can identify with throughout the essay. Is Angeles successful at seamlessly integrating sources throughout her own sentences?

The next time you're at a party or any other type of social gathering, look around. Some people are telling stories and making everyone laugh, others are making sure everything is running smoothly and perfectly, and a few individuals are the bold ones who liven things up and "get the party started." These are the obvious personalities—the "life of the party," the "busy bee," and the "leader." Personality experts call these personalities sanguine (the popular one), the melancholic (the perfect one), and choleric (the powerful one). However, there's one personality that's not so easy to spot, and therefore is usually forgotten—the peaceful phlegmatic. 1

What makes people the way they are? Why do some people command the spotlight, while others are experts at fading into the background? Personality types were first identified around 400 BC, when the Greek physician Hippocrates noticed that people not only looked 2 different, but also acted differently. He believed that each person's personality type was related to a particular body fluid they had in excess: yellow bile, black bile, blood, or phlegm. These were classified as the "four humors" (Funder 203). Around AD 149, a Greek physiologist named Galen built on Hippocrates's theory, stating that sanguines had an excess amount of yellow bile, melancholics had extra black bile, cholerics had more blood than others, and phlegmatics had an extraordinary amount of phlegm (Littauer 16). In later years, more theories evolved—American scientist William Sheldon believed that personality was related to body type, while people in India said that metabolic body type contributed to the way people behave (Funder 373). Ultimately, these theories were proven incorrect; but we still recognize different personality types. Today, what do we think determines personality?

As *Time* magazine reported on January 15, 1996, D4DR, a gene that regulates dopamine, is usually found in people who are risk takers (Toufexis par. 2). However, researchers suspected that the gene itself wasn't the only cause of risk-taking and that other genes, as well as upbringing, contributed to this phenomenon (Toufexis par. 3). At the time the report appeared, people were worried that parents would use prenatal testing to weed out certain genes that invoked undesirable personality traits (Toufexis par. 6). Since all personalities have their good and bad sides, this would have been a controversial development. Thankfully, parents are not yet able to test for their child's future personality. 3

Moreover, we know that even though people may be born with a certain personality, the way they are brought up can also contribute to how they relate to others later in life. For example, birth order has been shown to affect personality type (Franco par. 1). Firstborn children tend to be choleric since they have the job of leading their siblings; middle children are usually phlegmatic since they're in a prime negotiating spot; and the youngest are generally sanguine because they're used to being spoiled (Franco par. 2–4). Parents can also influence the way a child's personality turns out. 4

Each personality type has its strength, but a strength taken to an extreme can become a weakness. While sanguines love to talk, sometimes they may talk too much. Although cholerics are born leaders, they may use their influence in negative ways. Melancholics are perfectionists, but they may prefer being right to being happy, and phlegmatics tend to be easygoing and agreeable, but they may be too passive and have a fear of conflict. Their laid-back attitude can be very 5 frustrating to the most fast-paced personalities, such as cholerics and melancholics.

Phlegmatic people can be hard to notice because they're usually   6
not doing anything to call attention to themselves. While the sanguines are talking and loving life, the cholerics are getting things done, and the melancholics are taking care of the little details, the phlegmatics distinguish themselves by simply being laid-back and easygoing. Even though phlegmatic people tend to fly under the radar, it's very noticeable when they're not around, because they are the peacemakers of the world and the glue that holds everyone together. They are low-maintenance, adaptable, even-keeled, calm, cool, and collected individuals. They are usually reserved, yet they love being around people, and they have a knack for saying the right thing at the right time. Phlegmatics also work well under pressure. However, they hate change, they avoid taking risks, they are extremely stubborn, and it's very hard to get them motivated or excited, which can translate into laziness (Littauer 21). Aside from these traits, the phlegmatic's characteristics are hard to define, because phlegmatics tend to adopt the traits of either the sanguine personality or the melancholy personality.

Most people are a combination of personalities — they have a   7
dominant and a secondary personality that combine the traits of the personalities. For example, some phlegmatics are phlegmatic-sanguine, making them more talkative, while others are phlegmatic-melancholy, causing them to be more introverted. It's not possible to be phlegmatic-choleric, since phlegmatics avoid conflict and cholerics are fueled by it (Littauer 24, 25). People who try to resist their natural personality type can wind up unhappy, since they are trying to be someone they are not.

All personalities have emotional needs. The sanguine needs at-   8
tention, affection, approval, and activity; the melancholic needs space, support, silence, and stability; the choleric needs action, appreciation, leadership, and control; and the phlegmatic needs peace, self-worth, and significance (Littauer 22). If people don't have their emotional needs met, their worst sides tend to emerge. For example, if a phlegmatic, easygoing, type B personality is in a family of all cholerics, or "go-getter," type A personalities, the phlegmatics may find themselves masking their true personality in order to survive. This can be very draining for phlegmatics, and sooner or later, their negative side will emerge.

Phlegmatics are very adaptable — they get along with everyone 9
because they are able to meet the emotional needs of all the individual
personalities. They listen to the sanguine, they follow the choleric, and
they support the melancholic. In return, the sanguine entertains them,
the choleric motivates them, and the melancholic listens to them.
However, if phlegmatics feel like they're being taken for granted, they
will become resentful. Since they have an innate need for peace, they
won't say anything, and people won't know that there's a problem
(Littauer 125).

Even though phlegmatics are often overlooked, they have a lot 10
to contribute with their ability to work under pressure, their diplo-
matic skill, and their contagious contentment. So the next time you're
checking out personalities at a party, try looking for the phlegmatic
first. The forgotten personality might just be the most interesting person in the room.

WORKS CITED

Franco, Virginia. "Siblings Birth Order and Personality Types." *Essortment.*
Pagewise, Inc., 2002. Web. 21 Nov. 2006.

Funder, D. C. *The Personality Puzzle.* 2nd ed. New York: W. W. Norton, 2001.
Print.

Littauer, Florence. *Personality Plus for Couples: Understanding Yourself and the
One You Love.* Berrien Springs: Baker Publishing Group, 2001. Print.

Toufexis, Anastasia. "What Makes Them Do It." *Time.* Time, 15 Jan. 1996.
Web. 16 Nov. 2006.

Proxemics: A Study of Space and Relationships

Sheila McClain

Western Wyoming Community College
Rock Springs, Wyoming

Essays that explain a concept are often recognizable as research papers. The writer will use (and cite) sources to validate his or her perspective on the subject. Sheila McClain was interested in researching body language, but when she found the subject too broad for a focused essay, McClain narrowed her topic to a little-known term she knew readers could relate to. As you read, notice how McClain moves between the two concepts, allowing the larger, more familiar subject (body language, or "nonverbal communication") to lead her into an explanation of the smaller, less familiar one (proxemics). McClain does a good job of using sources to frame her discussion (with clarification of technical terms and difficult concepts) while still allowing her own voice to direct the essay.

Every day we interact and communicate, sometimes without even saying a word. Body language, more formally known as nonverbal communication, speaks volumes about who we are and how we relate to others. As Lester Sielski, an associate professor at the University of West Florida, writes, "Words are beautiful, exciting, important, but we have overestimated them badly—since they are not all or even half the message." He also asserts that "beyond words lies the bedrock on which human relationships are built—nonverbal communication" (Sielski). A group of pscyhology students at the University of Texas recently demonstrated just how profound an effect nonverbal communication can have on people. The students conducted an experiment to test the unspoken rules of behavior on elevators. Boarding a crowded elevator, the students stood facing and grinning at the other people on board. Understandably, the people became uncomfortable; one person even suggested that someone call 911 (Axtell 5–6). Why all the fuss?

Unspoken elevator etiquette dictates that one should turn and face the door in a crowded elevator, being careful not to touch anyone else and honoring the sacred personal space of each individual by staring at the floor indicator instead of looking at anyone else. Although they are not written down, strict rules govern our behavior in public situations. This is especially true when space is limited, as on elevators, buses, or subway trains (Axtell 5–6).

Patricia Buhler, an expert in business management and associate professor at Goldey-Beacon College, confirms the large role nonverbal communication plays. She asserts that as little as 8 percent of the message we communicate is made up of words. We communicate the rest of our message, a disproportionately large 92 percent, with body language and other nonverbal forms of communication (Buhler). While researchers have long known that nonverbal cues play a large role in communication, for many years they made no effort to learn more about them (Sielski). Amid rising public interest, several scientists pioneered new research in the field of nonverbal communication in the 1950s. Among these experts was anthropologist Edward T. Hall. He focused on a specific type of nonverbal communication called *proxemics*. Proxemics is the study of how people use space to communicate nonverbally. Whether we are conscious of it or not, our use of space plays a major role in our everyday interactions with others.

A review of some of Hall's main terms will help us better understand proxemics and appreciate just how much our use of space affects our relationships. For example, according to Hall, in our everyday interactions, we choose to position ourselves to create either "sociopetal" or "sociofugal" space. Sociopetal space invites communication; sociofugal space is the opposite—it separates people and discourages interaction (Jordan). A student in a school lunchroom may sit alone at an empty table in a corner, away from the other students (creating sociofugal space), or directly across from a person he would like to befriend (creating sociopetal space).

Hall identifies three kinds of general spaces within which we can create either sociofugal or sociopetal space. These are "fixed-feature space," "semi-fixed feature space," and "informal space" (Jordan). Fixed-feature spaces are hard, if not impossible, for us to control or change. For example, because my college English class is too small for the number of students attending, we have a hard time positioning ourselves so that we can all see the overhead projections. We cannot make the walls of the classroom bigger or the ceiling higher, and the overhead screen is likewise "fixed" in place. We must work within the constraints of the space. A semi-fixed feature space is usually defined by mobile objects such as furniture. The couches and chairs in a living room, for example, may face only the television, thus discouraging conversation and relationship building. But we are able to reposition the furniture to create a more social environment. Informal space is by far the easiest to manipulate. We each control our personal "bubble," and we can set distances between ourselves and others that reflect our relationships with them. Take, for example, the way that people approach their bosses. A man who is afraid of or dislikes his boss may communicate with her from as far away as possible. He might stand in her doorway to relay a message. Conversely, a woman who has known her boss for many years and is good friends with him might come right in to his office and casually sit down in close proximity to him. Individually, we have a great deal of control over our informal space, and how we use this space can speak volumes about our relationships with others.

After observing many interactions, Hall broke down informal space further, identifying four distances commonly used by people in their interactions with others: "intimate distance," zero to one and a half feet; "personal distance," one and a half to four feet; "social distance," four to twelve feet; and "public distance," twelve feet and beyond (Beebe, Beebe, and Redmond 231). Intimate distance, as the name suggests, is generally reserved for those people closest to us. Lovemaking, hugging, and holding small children all occur in this zone. The exception to this rule comes when we extend our hand to perfect strangers in greeting, allowing them to briefly enter our intimate space with a handshake. Personal distance, while not as close as intimate, is still reserved for people we know well and with whom we feel comfortable. This zone usually occupies an area relatively close to us. It can at times be applied, however, to include objects we see as extensions of ourselves. For instance, while driving, we may feel our personal space being invaded by a car following behind us too closely. We see our own car as an extension of ourselves and extend our "personal bubble" to include it. Social distance is often considered a respectful distance and is used in many professional business settings as well as in group interactions. There is a public distance between a lecturer and a class, or someone speaking publicly from a podium and his or her audience.

In positioning ourselves in relation to others—especially in choos-   6
ing nearness or distance—we communicate respect or intimacy, fear
or familiarity. We can improve a friendly relationship simply by using a
warm, personable distance, or drive potential friends away by seeming
cold and distant, or getting quite literally too close for comfort. We
can put people at ease or make them uncomfortable just by our proximity to them. The study of nonverbal communication, and specifically
proxemics, demonstrates the truth of the old adage, "Actions speak
louder than words."

WORKS CITED

Axtell, Roger E. *Gestures: The Do's and Taboos of Body Language Around the
World*. New York: Wiley, 1998. Print.

Beebe, Steven A., Susan J. Beebe, and Mark V. Redmond. *Interpersonal Communication: Relating to Others*. 2nd ed. Boston: Allyn, 1999. Print.

Buhler, Patricia. "Managing in the 90s." *Supervision* 52.9 (1991): 18–21. *EB-
SCOhost*. Web. 29 Sept. 2004.

Jordan, Sherry. "Embodied Pedagogy: The Body and Teaching Theology."
Teaching Theology and Religion 4.2 (2001): 98–101. *EBSCOhost*. Web.
29 Sept. 2004.

Sielski, Lester M. "Understanding Body Language." *Personal and Guidance
Journal* 57.4 (1979): 238–42. *EBSCOhost*. Web. 29 Sept. 2004.

Therapeutic Cloning and Enbryonic Research

Etoria Spears

University of California, Riverside
Riverside, California

Is it possible to explain a controversial topic without allowing personal biases to show? When Etoria Spears explains the concept of embryonic research, she asks her readers to consider a newborn baby who has contracted an incurable disease. Is this introduction meant to establish some sensitivity toward the benefits of embryonic research, or is it intended to open dialogue? Spears also presents reasons one might oppose the concept. As you read, consider how you might have written about a multifaceted issue such as this. If you were writing about a controversial topic, what focus might you take and how might you establish your authority on the subject without appearing biased?

Imagine the joy of having your first child. Hundreds of emotions run through your mind as you hold the tiny newborn in your arms. You wonder many things: Will I be a good parent? Can I support my child properly? Will I be able to give her all the love and attention she needs and deserves in order to grow into a strong adult? Such questions are common when it comes to raising a child. However, few can bring themselves to consider how they would feel if they learned their infant had a life-threatening disease for which there was no known cure. 1

Unfortunately, this was the case for Roger and Helen Karlin, whose daughter Lindsay Faith was diagnosed with the unique and fatal *Canavan disease* at the young age of three months. Canavan is a neurological disease in which the brain deteriorates at such an alarming rate, its victims usually die before reaching their teen years (Donegan). Upon discovering there was no known cure for their daughter's condi- 2 tion, the Karlins turned to gene therapy treatment to save their daughter's life. The treatment was intended to replace damaged brain cells with replicated ones created from stem cells. However, this would prove difficult because "scientists have had unexpected difficulty getting healthy genetic material to transfer successfully and remain functional in the living cells of patients suffering from genetic diseases" (Donegan). The odds of success were very slim, but they decided to pursue the treatment in hopes of buying Lindsay some time (Donegan).

The story of the Karlin family's struggle with Lindsay's disease 3 is just one of many cases that consider *therapeutic cloning* as medical treatment. Therapeutic cloning is defined as the cloning of human embryos in order to acquire stem cells for medical research. Stem cells, also called "master cells," are essentially blank slates with the ability to take the form of any type of cell present in a tissue. For example, a stem cell that is introduced to the tissue of the liver would take the form of a liver cell. Scientists hope to use cloned cells to replace damaged or dying cells in the human body. The ability to do so has the potential to cure hundreds of diseases, including Alzheimer's, Parkinson's, and diabetes. This form of cloning is very different from reproductive cloning, which is intended for creating new beings. However, the process of harvesting the stem cells required is exactly the same. Stem cells are obtained via Somatic Cell Nuclear Transfer, also called SCNT. An egg is stripped of its genetic material by removing DNA from the nucleus. The desired DNA is then inserted into the egg, which is given an electric shock to promote cell division. After about four to five days, the egg reaches the blastocyst stage and stem cells can be harvested by destroying the embryo (Hansen). Although the research could contribute a great deal of knowledge to the scientific field, many find it controversial due to the destruction of the embryo to reach the stem cells within.

It is not uncommon for groundbreaking research such as thera- 4 peutic cloning to raise a few eyebrows. Despite the possible benefits that could be gained, many people are hesitant to support this technology, mainly because of the debate over the moral status of an embryo. In general, there are three different views on this matter: the no–moral-status view, the middle view, and the equal–moral-status view (Chan 107). The aim of presenting the three views is to explain each of them respectively, not to grant authority to one view over another (107).

The no–moral-status view holds that the embryos created for thera- 5 peutic cloning have absolutely no moral status whatsoever (Chan 108).

One argument supporting this view suggests that these specific embryos lack key traits of human embryos that would develop into actual people, namely the fact they are unfertilized (108). Therefore, not only is it exempt from the moral status of a human being, it has even less moral status than a fertilized embryo. Its purpose is for research, proponents of this theory say, not for producing life, so there is room to argue if it has any moral status at all (108).

The middle view offers an understanding between those of no 6 moral status and equal moral status. The middle view suggests that although an embryo does not share the same status as a human being, it still deserves respect as a form of human life (Chan 110). This view permits distinction from an embryo and a person because, unlike people, supporters of the middle view say, there is no evidence that embryos can think or feel (110). At the same time, it can be said that embryos are a form of life and should be regarded as such, not merely things to be used at our disposal (110). With that in mind, some may still not be convinced it is morally permissible to use unfertilized embryos for research.

The final view is that of equal moral status. In this case, regard- 7 less of the fact that an unfertilized embryo will never be a person, the embryo still has complete moral status as if it were a living, breathing, human being. For advocates of this view, there is no question as to the ethics of embryonic research: It is absolutely unacceptable. Under no circumstances would scientists have a right to destroy an embryo, fertilized or not, for the sake of research or advancements in medicine. Some even go so far as to call it murder.

How one regards the moral status of the human embryo varies 8 based on one's personal beliefs and choices. In the past decade, scientific discoveries have advanced our knowledge in leaps and bounds. The new information we have gained has brought us one step closer to curing some of the most devastating diseases known to man. However, as innovative as this technology may be, there is constant disagreement over if and how it should be used. Regarding the use of therapeutic cloning to treat illnesses, the main issue is the moral status of the human embryo. Some claim it has no moral status, others feel it deserves our respect as a form of human life, and still others believe it's the same as a person and should not be used for research. While the debate rages on, people around the world will continue to suffer until a verdict is reached or another solution is found.

WORKS CITED

Chan, Jonathan. *The Bioethics of Regenerative Medicine.* Vol. 102. Ed. King
    Tak Ip. Springer Nederlands, 2008. Print.
Donegan, Craig. "Gene Therapy's Future." *CQ Researcher Online.* 5.46. Dec.
    8, 1995. n. pag. Web. 8 Nov. 2009.
Hansen, Brian. "Cloning Debate." *CQ Researcher Online.* 14.37. Oct. 22,
    2004. n. pag. Web. 8 Nov. 2009.

The Disorder That Hides Within

Max Wu

University of California, Riverside
Riverside, California

Max Wu approaches his essay from the assumption that although his subject—mental illness—might be difficult for his audience to identify with, they will almost certainly understand the nerves associated with public speaking. Wu then compares this common fear with its more extreme version, social phobia. When readers are able to relate to this disorder, they become curious and want to understand more. Once Wu has engaged his readers' interest, he considers current scientific research in this field. How effective do you think Wu is in narrowing such a large concept? Consider how the title of this essay frames Wu's discussion.

———————

Are you afraid of speaking in front of an audience? Do you get jitters and "butterflies in your stomach" as you approach the stage with weak knees? "Yes," he says. "Of course, all the time," she replies. Do you feel your general social performance in the world is so inadequate that you escape any and every instance where you might face public scrutiny? Ask this question and the room goes quiet. The fact of the matter is, most people get nervous and loathe the idea of public speaking, but some people feel nervous in every social situation. This fear of social scrutiny is referred to by mental health professionals as "social phobia." What separates common stage fright from social phobia is that social phobia is a crippling disorder that can obstruct a healthy lifestyle. However, it is easily treated once the individual realizes he or she needs help.

Social phobia is difficult to diagnose because of the way patients seem to subconsciously mask their abnormal behavior and practices. In an article written for *The Irish Times*, Marie Murray describes in great detail the actions that many patients practice that make it hard for the outside world to spot a problem. A clinical psychologist at University College Dublin, Murray has observed many students with social phobia and has made some breakthrough discoveries that have helped doctors around the world deal with the mystery surrounding social phobia. An unfortunate facet of social phobia that Murray observes is that "people become trapped by their false belief of how they appear to other people and . . . are unable to see evidence of when they are being successful in social encounters" (11). People with social phobia have a distorted view of the world that develops over time to a point where they become clinically depressed and believe that the world is against them. This hazy view of the world grows day by day as normal conversation becomes interpreted as personal attacks time and time again.

Murray also observed that patients with social phobia engage in activities that they feel make them more confident but in reality distance them from others and end up hurting their own psychological well-being. Murray knows this disorder is incredibly difficult to cope with and feels that the most important step in curing these people is to allow them to identify their own fears and understand that these fears are common and possible to be overcome. 3

J. A. den Boer, a professor of psychiatry and author of an article on social phobia in the *British Medical Journal,* has dedicated a large part of her career to research about social phobia. Through her numerous studies, she concludes that "social phobia is a poorly investigated and misunderstood condition" (796). She finds that social phobia starts when a child is under five years old and "may abruptly follow a stressful or humiliating experience" (797). After years and years of these unfortunate experiences, "the course of the disease is lifelong and unremitting unless treated" (797). Many patients who suffer from the disorder do not realize that the pain they have to endure is that of social phobia and thus further delay their treatment, which den Boer claims leads to increased risks of suicide (798). 4

Social phobia has not been well documented in the past or well diagnosed, but proper diagnosis and treatment are possible. In order to properly diagnose a patient, doctors need to pay close attention to the patient's medical history for any sign of events that might have triggered symptoms of the condition. The Diagnostic and Statistical Manual of Mental Disorders, or DSM-III-R, published by the American Psychiatric Association, issues criteria that must be met to diagnose social phobia. Drawing from the DSM-III-R, a doctor would ask questions 5 about how the patient would deal with certain social situations and the responses would determine the severity of the disorder.

After a patient realizes that something must be done to free his or her life from social phobia, what treatments are available? What can be done to free a mind from deep-seated nervousness and fear of humiliation that it has grown to accept? One promising form of treatment is being developed in Australia by Professor Gavin Andrews, the head of the clinical research unit at St. Vincent's Hospital (Fallon 16). Andrews invented a character named John, a first-year college student with social phobia. John has trouble going to class and surviving at school because of the overwhelming case of social phobia that haunts his daily life. By using this generic character in an online treatment program, Andrews manages to help those who feel trapped in their lives but would never have surfaced to receive treatment for their crippling disorder. Using "online exposure therapy, computer-aided training programs, virtual reality technology and enhanced cognitive behavioral therapies," Andrews successfully treated the almost 550 patients he received in the first year of his online treatment program, curing half of them completely (Fallon 17). It can be difficult for sufferers to seek treatment. In a study Andrews conducted in 2004, he found that 24 percent of Australians with agoraphobia (the fear of public places) and 7 percent of Australians with social phobia surfaced to receive medical attention from professionals (Fallon 17). The disorder is not difficult to cure, but sufferers must first confront their fears before they can find lasting relief.

Although social phobia was not well documented or often diagnosed in the past, doctors are becoming increasingly aware of how to identify and treat the disorder. Today, numerous treatment strategies exist, and sufferers are finding relief. Hopefully soon, the excessive fear of social situations will plague only a scarce minority.

WORKS CITED

den Boer, J. A. "Social Phobia: Epidemiology, Recognition, and Treatment." *BMJ* 315.7111 (1997): 796–800. *JSTOR*. Web. 7 Nov. 2009.

Fallon, Mary. "When Fear Takes Over." *Sydney Morning Herald* 28 May 2009, first ed., Health and Science sec.: 17. *LexisNexis Academic*. Web. 7 Nov. 2009.

Murray, Marie. "Anxiety Disorder Leaves You in Fear of Social Situations." *The Irish Times* 1 Apr. 2008: 11. *LexisNexis Academic*. Web. 8 Nov. 2009.

The Art and Creativity of Stop-Motion

William Tucker

University of California, Riverside
Riverside, California

For this assignment, William Tucker knew that he wanted to write about film or animation, but he realized that both "film" and "animation" were far too broad to cover in one essay. Instead, Tucker narrowed his topic to stop-motion animation, a subcategory that caught his interest. Although stop-motion animation is one of the oldest techniques in film animation, it is still popular both on the big screen and on YouTube. Tucker explains the concept by defining it, explaining its history, narrating the process used to make stop-motion films, and providing examples of popular stop-motion films. The enthusiasm for stop-motion Tucker developed while writing this essay ultimately led him to make his own film. Consider whether Tucker's enthusiasm is contagious: Does his explanation of stop-motion animation inspire you to try your own hand at it?

Cinematography and filmmaking are present everywhere today. It is virtually impossible to go about your day without occasionally seeing a motion picture, whether it is a sitcom, an advertisement, or an instructional video. The process of producing films has changed in the past century and many techniques have been invented and perfected. One style of film in particular has proven to stand the test of time. The style can be seen in popular productions such as *Gumby, Chicken Run, Fantastic Mr. Fox,* and the original *Godzilla* and *King Kong* movies. It played a key role in the origin of film and continues to be a relevant art form in the filming community, used both by famous Hollywood directors and by independent film students alike. It inspires creativity. This style, stop-motion film, is a critical part of film and cinematography.

Stop-motion, also known as frame-by-frame film production, is   2
an animation technique in which a still camera photographs an object
which is moved very small distances at a time. When these still images are played back quickly, they create the illusion of movement. The
frame rate, or FPS (frames per second—the speed at which the individual photos are shown during the sequence), varies. The original
stop-motion films usually never reached over 20 FPS, because of the
limitations of older technology (Johnson). However, today most stop-
motion films vary from 25 FPS to as high as 30 FPS, depending on
how quickly the director wants the inanimate object to appear to move
(Johnson).

The technique of stop-motion is nearly as old as the motion pic-   3
ture itself. Albert E. Smith and J. Stuart Blackton are credited with
being the first to use the technique in their 1898 film, *Humpty
Dumpty Circus,* where toys and puppets appear to come alive on screen
(Delahoyde). Stop-motion grew in popularity as it allowed directors
to depict fantasy and imagination while still providing realistic-looking
scenes. For example, before computer-generated imagery (CGI), if a
director wanted to make a dinosaur movie, the director could dress
humans in dinosaur costumes, hire animators to create a hand-drawn
animated film, or use stop-motion with clay dinosaur figurines. Using
dinosaur costumes would be easier than using stop-motion, but it
would more often than not make the dinosaurs look tacky and unreal.
Hand-drawn animation is lovely, but two-dimensional. A stop-motion
film takes a long time and meticulous work to create, but it captivates
audiences with its more authentic and "real" look. During the beginning years of animated film, stop-motion was critically acclaimed, win-
ning many Oscars in the animated film categories.

Stop-motion animators soon began to use clay figurines as the   4
main focus in stop-motion films; this technique is now known as claymation. Clay figurines allow inanimate objects to take on human-like
characteristics and are easy to manipulate quickly between individual
photographs. Famous claymation stop-motion films include the hit
70s television show *Gumby* and the short film *Vincent,* which helped
a young Tim Burton attract the attention of Walt Disney Studios
(Delahoyde). Burton would go on to revolutionize the stop-motion
industry by crafting feature-length stop-motion films, such as *The Nightmare before Christmas, James and the Giant Peach,* and *The Corpse
Bride* ("Tim Burton").

Stop-motion requires not only creativity but also patience and pre-   5
cision. With stop-motion films now playing back at as high as 30 FPS,
nearly nine thousand individual photographs are needed for just five
minutes worth of footage. Because of this, most stop-motion films,
even those with a professional crew, are in production for as long as
three years (Delahoyde). Stop-motion directors begin each scene by
choosing an inanimate object to be the focus point of the scene. After
the object is chosen, it is photographed and moved less than an inch
between individual photographs. The camera is placed in a station-
ary position (a tripod is almost a necessity in order to keep the camera
focusing on the same exact location for each photo) (Delahoyde). A
major problem that stop-motion enthusiasts face is making sure that the
backgrounds of frames are similar to one another. If the background
is not exactly the same for each frame, noticeable errors like splotches
and blurs can occur. Also, if the background is inconsistent, the film
will look less convincing, and may even give the audience headaches
from the lack of visual consistency. For this reason, most creators shoot
inside and make their own backgrounds, either by drawing one or by
making a CGI-based background ("Stop Motion Filming Technique").

Those brave enough to shoot a stop-motion film outdoors must   6
take into account all the variables that can hurt the overall presentation
of their film. If the film is being shot in a crowded place, the creator
cannot allow pictures to be taken with people in the background. People in the background of the shot will cause inconsistency in the frames
which will appear as colored splotches in the film, especially if the frame
rate is extremely high ("Stop Motion Filming Technique"). Stop-
motion directors must also take into account the weather and brightness of the outdoors. Since the process of taking photos for a stop-
motion film takes an exorbitant amount of time, people making films
may have to plan on being outdoors shooting a scene for many hours.
Lighting changes as the sun moves throughout the day. If the outdoor
scene doesn't have consistent lighting because of the sun's movements,
the scenes may suffer from unwanted shadows and different lighting at
separate points in the scene. Consistency and attention to detail are the
foundations of stop-motion film. They are perhaps the most important
factors separating professional stop-motion films from amateur films.

Stop-motion still plays a key role in the filming world today. It has   7
inspired new film art forms that are heavily used. For example, time
lapse photography is a well-known technique used in film to quickly

show the passing of time. Stop-motion helped lead to the time-lapse technique by stringing together individual photographs in order to represent movement and time ("Stop Motion Photography"). The time-lapse process does take longer than typical stop-motion. In time-lapse photography, a camera focuses on an object for as long as a year, taking pictures periodically of the slow changes that occur. Then the many pictures are played in quick succession to show the changes. Popular subjects include the growth and blooming of a flower, a day and night's worth of city traffic, and the movement of the sun and moon. These scenes in nature take anywhere from a day to an entire year to take place, but with time-lapse/stop-motion the entire process can be viewed in as little as ten seconds, which creates an interesting illusion for the audience.

Although newer forms of cinematography are constantly being invented and revised, stop-motion will forever be important in the film community. Although CGI has become the industry standard for movie animation, stop-motion is still flourishing. Popular sites such as YouTube allow creators to post original stop-motion videos; they can then be viewed by a wide audience. Some of the most popular films on the Internet today are stop-motion films, receiving hundreds of thousands of views daily. This art form will forever captivate viewers and inspire ingenuity, whether it is used for a simple amateur video or a feature-length film of epic proportions.

8

WORKS CITED

Delahoyde, Michael. "Stop-Motion Animation." *Dino-Source*. Washington State U, 25 Apr. 2006. Web. 7 Nov. 2008.

Johnson, Dave. "Make a Time-Lapse Movie." *Washington Post*. Washington Post, 9 Nov. 2005. Web. 5 Nov. 2008.

"Stop Motion Filming Technique." *Thinkquest*. Thinkquest, 1999. Web. 6 Nov. 2008.

"Stop Motion Photography." *SciFi2K*. SciFi2K, 11 Jan. 2004. Web. 6 Nov. 2008.

"Tim Burton Talking about Animation." *Tim Burton Dream Site*. Minadream .com, n.d. Web. 6 Nov. 2008.

Finding Common Ground 5

Every day, high-stakes issues fill the airwaves and the Internet and crowd the pages of newspapers and magazines. Most issues we only glance at, while a few may engage us deeply—either because we are curious or because we recognize that the outcome of those issues is important to us personally: Should prayer be permitted in public schools? Should an underage girl be required to get her parents' permission to have an abortion? Should online search engines release individuals' search records to researchers or businesses? Should phone and cable providers be able to charge Web users differently for different levels of service?

By definition, a controversial issue is unsettled, unresolved. A debate swirls around it. As we read or listen to this debate, we may be inclined at first to take sides. Often, however, if we pay closer attention, we realize that the issues aren't as black and white as they sometimes seem. In order to truly understand what's at stake and take a responsible position on an issue, we need to take some preliminary steps: Specifically, we need to analyze and explain the debate and then seek common ground among various existing positions.

The analysis and explanation of debates can be informative to readers who want to understand issues of the day. They can also clarify and even help resolve immediate dangers or crises in a business or corporation; inform debate in an elected governing body, like a city council or the U.S. Senate; or introduce newcomers to an ongoing debate among experts over an important academic discipline, like those from which you choose your college courses.

However, simply explaining the debate is not always enough. If we can identify points on which the stakeholders might be able to agree, we can move beyond analysis and toward *synthesis*. Essays that attempt to find common ground do not simply explain both sides or make arguments in support of one side or another; instead, they analyze the concerns shared by those who argue on either side and discuss ways in which seemingly irreconcilable positions might in fact be amenable to compromise or consensus, at least in part.

In "Finding Common Ground," you're asked to think more deeply about conflicting opinions. Instead of asking you to merely understand and then write about both sides of the issue, we encourage you to take a closer look into what each side has in common. If they truly had nothing in common, there would be nothing to argue about. What motivating forces are at work? What is at stake? And what shared values are driving the parties to argue? Essays that seek common ground employ certain basic features of the genre: an informative introduction to the issue and opposing positions; a probing analysis; a fair and impartial presentation; and a clear, logical organization.

You will encounter many disciplinary debates in your college career. By attempting to find the common ground behind these debates, you will hone your analytical skills and broaden your perspective, allowing you to imagine new solutions and acquire greater understanding of your field. Practice in explaining, analyzing, and finding common ground among different positions will in turn allow you to join the debate, arguing vigorously and responsibly in support of a position of your own.

Use the guidelines in the Critical Reading Guide (below) to practice peer review using the essays in this chapter.

A CRITICAL READING GUIDE

AN INFORMATIVE INTRODUCTION TO THE ISSUE AND OPPOSING POSITIONS

Has the writer explained the issue and opposing positions clearly and in a way that will engage reader's interest?

Summarize: Briefly tell the writer what you understand the issue to be and what the opposing positions are.

Praise: Indicate where the writer does a good job explaining the issue, introducing the authors, or engaging readers' interest.

Critique: Describe any confusion or uncertainty you have about the issue, about why it is important, or about the positions the essays being analyzed take on it.

A PROBING ANALYSIS

Is the writer's analysis of the points of disagreement and potential agreement interesting and insightful?

Summarize: Tell the writer what you understand to be the points of disagreement and the areas of potential agreement.

Praise: Identify one or two passages where the analysis seems especially effective—for example, where the opposing arguments are shown to be based on similar motivating factors, such as a shared value or common concern.

Critique: Identify places where additional details, an example or illustration, or more explanation would make the analysis clearer. Let the writer know if you detect any other motivating factors that might be used to establish common ground.

A FAIR AND IMPARTIAL PRESENTATION

Has the writer represented the opposing arguments in a balanced, unbiased way?

Summarize: Circle the words used to describe the proponents, and underline the words used to describe their views.

Praise: Note any passages where the writer comes across as being especially fair and impartial.

Critique: Tell the writer if the authors and their positions are presented unfairly or if one side seems to be favored over the other. Identify passages that seem critical of the proponents or their views, and suggest ways the writer could make the point less negatively, such as by using quotations to state criticisms or replacing negative words with neutral ones.

A CLEAR, LOGICAL ORGANIZATION

Is the essay clear and readable?

Summarize: Underline the thesis, and circle key terms that forecast the topics the essay will focus on. Then circle those key terms when they appear elsewhere in the essay.

Praise: Pick one or two places where the essay is especially clear and easy to follow—for example, where the writer has repeated key terms or synonyms for them effectively, or where the writer has used comparative transitions, such as *both* or *as well as* to signal similarity and *whereas* or *although* to signal differences.

Critique: Let the writer know where the readability could be improved—for example, where a topic sentence could be clearer or where a transition is needed. Suggest a better beginning or a more effective ending.

Gambling and Government Restriction
Luke Serrano
University of California, Riverside
Riverside, California

Discussions of governmental regulation versus personal autonomy can often become heated. In the case of gambling, is it the government's role to prevent gambling addiction, or should personal responsibility step in? In this essay, Luke Serrano successfully presents both sides of the argument as offered by a pair of psychologists and a financial analyst, but also finds a common thread: a belief that compulsive gambling is real, and serious. As you read, think about how harmful something has to be before you believe the government should ban or regulate it.

People often look for sources of entertainment to temporarily take their minds off responsibilities and problems. While some people are satisfied with a simple game or television show, others have the desire to make their entertainment even more interesting by investing money in it. Having something at stake in a game provides people with a rush that does not come from simply playing the game. Archaeological evidence suggests that gambling dates as far back as 2300 BC to ancient China, India, Egypt, and Rome ("The History of Gambling" 1). However, almost as long as there has been gambling, there have been people trying to put an end to it. Authority figures have noticed that gambling can serve as a distraction that keeps people away from what they are supposed to be doing. In medieval England, gambling was outlawed when King Henry VIII discovered that his soldiers were spending more time gambling than working on drills and marksman-ship (1). In the United States, gambling was outlawed in Nevada until 1931 when casino gaming was legalized and Las Vegas began its rise as one of the largest gambling hot spots in the world (1). It now brings in over 30 billion dollars in revenue each year (Dunstan 2). Two main views have arisen concerning the influence gambling has had on people. Both sides believe government regulation has a great effect on gamblers, and that gambling addiction is a real problem that requires treatment. Their viewpoints diverge because one side believes that gambling causes serious problems and should be illegal; the other believes that gambling is not a problem and that restrictions do more harm than good.

Those who argue that gambling is a problem point to the per-sonal and social issues created by those who gamble too much. Arnie and Sheila Wexler are both certified compulsive gambling counselors in New Jersey. Sheila developed the compulsive gambling treatment program at the New Hope Foundation in Marlboro, New Jersey (Wexler and Wexler 1). The Wexlers firmly believe that compulsive gambling is a disease similar to drug and alcohol addiction. They argue that "the disease can be much more insidious [than drug or alcohol addiction] because it is more difficult to detect and can have a more devastating effect on friends and families" (2). The devastating effects compulsive gambling can have on people have led the Wexlers to call for the outlawing of gambling in the United States.

Some people, however, believe that compulsive gambling is not a pressing issue. Quantitative analyst Guy Calvert represents a Wall Street firm and is an adamant believer that the growing prevalence of compulsive gambling is just an exaggeration (Calvert 1). In his essay "The Government Should Respect Individuals' Freedom to Gamble," Calvert says, "Individuals should not be prohibited from gambling just because some people find it addictive," and he claims the "dangers of prohibiting gambling outweigh the benefits" (1).

The argument for the prohibition of gambling is centered on the detrimental effects that gambling can have on people. The Wexlers argue that compulsive gambling is "a progressive disease" that goes through phases (3). The first phase of gambling addiction is the phase in which the gambler reports a series of wins or streaks. This phase can reoccur throughout the gambling addiction, but the initial win streak is the hook that draws the gambler in (3). This hook gives the gambler a taste of wealth and the illusion that the wealth and luck will continue. The next phase of compulsive gambling is the losing phase. The losing phase is the phase in which gamblers lose the money that they might have won and begin to chase their losses (3). At this point, the gambler begins to borrow money to cover bets that he or she cannot pay. This is when the desperation phase begins; it is the last phase, at which point the gambler will do anything to put down the next bet (3). Family, friends, and work no longer matter. The desire to get the same rush as from the first big win is the only thing that matters. Families are destroyed, friendships are ruined, and careers are lost because the gambler cannot go without betting long enough to take care of responsibilities. Studies estimate that "the number of compulsive gamblers in this country is between 10 million and 12 million, approximately 5 percent of the general population" (5). The sheer number of compulsive gamblers and the devastation that comes with them are the reasons that the Wexlers believe the only viable action is the prohibition of gambling.

In contrast to the prohibition argument, the no-restrictions argument says the prohibition of gambling would be detrimental to the United States. Calvert argues that measures to suppress gambling would "usher in a new era of public corruption, compromising the integrity of government officials, judges, and the police" (2). He gives the prohibition of alcohol as an example of what would happen if gambling became illegal (1). Crime would rise because of the underground lifestyle that is brought with illegal gambling. In addition to being harmful, Calvert says, the prohibition would be unnecessary because most people do gamble responsibly. Most people who go to casinos "are not crazed, welfare-dependent casino desperadoes; they are in many respects better off than the average American." Studies show that the average household income of casino players is 28 percent higher than that of the U.S. population (4). Gambling is used the majority of the time as a source of entertainment, not as a fix for the compulsive gambler. Furthermore, banning gambling would not deter the truly compulsive gambler (2). It is the nature of an addict to find the next fix no matter what the cost. Illegality would do nothing to stop the compulsive gambler, just as heroin's being illegal does nothing to stop the junkie. Like an alcoholic or a drug addict, a compulsive gambler has to want to get help to get better.

Although the two parties disagree on whether the government should regulate gambling, they do agree that compulsive gambling is a problem and an addiction. In one instance described by the Wexlers, a man came to a treatment center and seemed to be having withdrawal symptoms after a gambling binge. He had dilated pupils, he was sweating and shaking, and he suffered severe mood swings (2). The similarities between compulsive gambling and drug and alcohol addiction are undeniable. Calvert agrees, saying, "pathological gambling can and sometimes does result in genuine human misery" (5). Both parties agree that this is a problem that needs to be solved. People who have gambling problems need treatment because without it there is no stopping the addiction.

In 1996, members of an estimated 32 percent of all U.S. households gambled at a casino, amounting to about 176 million visits to casinos (Calvert 2). These staggering numbers show that gambling has a great effect on Americans, whether it is positive or negative. The arguments both for and against gambling bring forth valid points. On the one hand, the prohibition argument claims compulsive gambling is a serious problem and the only way to stop it is by prohibiting gambling completely. On the other hand, the progambling supporters argue that gambling is a legitimate institution that provides entertainment and economic growth for the United States; moreover, this party argues that the prohibition of gambling would cause more harm than good for the American people. Despite the different opinions that exist about gambling, it is a large part of American recreation and is an issue that should not be taken lightly.

WORKS CITED

Calvert, Guy. "The Government Should Respect Individuals' Freedom to Gamble." *Gambling.* Ed. James D. Torr. San Diego: Greenhaven P, 2002. N. pag. Excerpt from "Gambling America: Balancing the Risks of Gambling and Its Regulation." Cato Policy Analysis 18 June 1999. *Opposing Viewpoints Resource Center.* Web. 1 Dec. 2009.

Dunstan, Roger. "Pivotal Dates in Gambling History." *American Gaming Association.* American Gaming Association, 2003. Web. 2 Dec. 2009.

"The History of Gambling." *Gambling PhD.* Gambling PhD.com, 2003. Web. 2 Dec. 2009.

Wexler, Arnie, and Sheila Wexler. "The Hidden Addiction: Compulsive Gambling." *Legalized Gambling.* Ed. Mary E. Williams. San Diego: Greenhaven P, 1999. N. pag. Contemporary Issues Companion Ser. Rept. of "The Hidden Addiction." Professional Counselor June 1997: n. pag. Opposing Viewpoints Resource Center. Web. 1 Dec. 2009.

Are Laissez-Faire Policies to Blame?

Matthew Chrisler

University of California, Riverside
Riverside, California

The following essay does a great job of both clarifying an often confusing topic—laissez-faire economics—and investigating two differing perspectives on a frequently debated issue. Matthew Chrisler wrote this piece shortly after the financial crisis of 2008. Notice how, despite widespread frustration at the time, Chrisler was able to consider two opposing viewpoints without injecting his personal opinion—his tone remains balanced and thoughtful throughout. Because Chrisler remained impartial, his readers trust that he is presenting both sides accurately. After reading his essay, consider whether you think Chrisler was successful at maintaining a logical approach and refraining from taking a position on this issue.

Due to the recent collapse of credit and other economic troubles, many scholars have devoted themselves to analyzing the roots of the current market problems. Two papers illuminate polar points of view on the issue of whether "laissez-faire" economics is responsible for the current credit crisis. George Reisman's blog entry, "The Myth that Laissez-faire Is Responsible for Our Financial Crisis," argues that laissez-faire systems are not responsible because they do not exist; "The Conservative Origins of the Sub-Prime Mortgage Crisis," an article by John Atlas and Peter Dreier, argues that laissez-faire is indeed the reason we face the current global crisis. The two papers touch on what constitutes laissez-faire economics, government regulation and deregulation, subprime mortgages, the Federal Reserve, and congressional acts, as well as historical trends in the economy.

1

"Laissez-faire," or *hands-free* in French, is the economic school   2
of thought that promotes little to no government interference in an
economy. Taking the definition literally, George Reisman asserts that
laissez-faire market conditions do not exist in the modern economy.
In contrast, Atlas and Dreier argue that any movement toward less
regulation, or the act of deregulating and industry, is laissez-faire in
principle, and the ideal laissez-faire economy does not have to exist for
an action to be considered as such. In support of his claim, Reisman's
main argument is that after the Great Depression and the creation of
governmental banking regulations, increased taxes, farm subsidies,
apartment rent controls, and a veritable alphabet soup of regulatory
agencies, America ceased to be a laissez-faire nation in any sense of the
word. Conversely, Atlas and Dreier, building off their argument that a
move toward deregulation is laissez-faire economics, assert that America has had a long tradition of regulation tied with economic prosperity until the 1980s, during which deregulation of industries caused a
period of economic distress. Reisman conflicts with Atlas and Drier
on many levels because of differing opinions on what it means to be
"laissez-faire."

The two articles present opposing perceptions of the magnitude   3
and benefits of government interference in markets. Reisman places
blame for the recent financial crisis on the increased meddling of
government in the market, while Atlas and Dreier argue that it was
the deregulating of certain markets that led to today's crisis. According to Reisman, much of the crisis was caused by a combination of
the Community Reinvestment Act and the government guarantee on
loans. The Community Reinvestment Act mandated that banks make
loans to low- and moderate-income borrowers who would normally
not qualify for a loan. In addition, the government would guarantee
the mortgages of these low-income borrowers, creating a perfect niche
for the subprime lenders. Because these bad loans were guaranteed by
the government, subprime lenders sought profits by making loans at
exceedingly high interest rates, using bait-and-switch tactics and devi-
ous contracts to entice low-income borrowers to take out loans. On
the other hand, Atlas and Dreier give evidence that deregulation is responsible for the rise of the housing crisis, which spawned the financial crisis. In the 1980s, banks lobbying Washington were able to push
back the regulations that prevented banks from investing in private
markets and making loans. After this deregulation occurred, a massive
increase in loans was recorded, leading to a bust. Because no regula-

tions were enforced, banks were able to make high-risk, high-interest loans to those who would normally be excluded, leading to the take-off of the subprime market. According to Atlas and Dreier, a plethora of banks—including Countrywide, Washington Mutual, and Lehman Brothers—were responsible for almost two-thirds of subprime loans. Atlas and Dreier show that large banks, as the backers of these loans, are not blameless.

Using different information, the two articles present different arguments regarding the government's role in the crisis. Reisman asserts that through overregulation of the housing market, the government inadvertently caused the current crisis. However, Atlas and Dreier argue that because the government deregulated the banking industry in the 1980s, the subprime lenders were left free to practice predatory lending. 4

Separate from government, which controls monetary policy, are the actions of the Federal Reserve, which controls fiscal policy. Criticism coming from both sides focuses on the actions of the Federal Reserve and its chair, Ben Bernanke. They differ mainly in their opinion of whether it was laissez-faire or regulatory policy that was responsible for the Reserve's recklessness. Reisman bases his argument on the Federal Reserve's control of the nation's banking interest rates, which is essentially the interest rate at which banks lend one another money. Reisman asserts that the actions of the Federal Reserve were extremely irresponsible, because their use of the federal interest rate is responsible for much of the credit crisis. In the recent years before the crisis, the Federal Reserve continually lowered the federal interest rates in order to encourage people to take out money. The Fed also lowered the Federal Reserve ratio, or the percentage amount banks had to guarantee on a given deposit. The Federal Reserve hoped to increase the overall amount of capital in the market by means of the money multiplier. When there are low interest rates, and the Federal Reserve ratio is low, more capital, or credit, is available at lower cost, which led to a marked increase in loans. As Reisman explains, "In recent years, the Federal Reserve has so encouraged this process that checking deposits have been created equal to fifty times the actual cash reserves of the banks, a situation more than ripe for implosion." 5

However, when the federal interest rate decreased to the point where the overall increase in prices, or inflation, was greater than the interest rate, banks started losing money on loans, because they would be paid back in money that was worth less. Combined with the rapid 6 bust of the real estate market, banks became fearful of lending money to large businesses and private investors because the loans would usually end in foreclosure or a net loss for the bank. According to Reisman, this led to the large freeze in loans, which in turn contributed to the current chaos in today's markets. Much in the same vein as their other arguments, Atlas and Dreier argue that the lowering of the interest rate is not government regulation, but the absence of enforcement of the spirit of regulation. Again they stress that a move toward deregulation is a move toward laissez-faire economics, therefore reflecting the blame onto proponents of hands-off economics. On this subject the two articles do not contest information, but instead provide different perspectives on the same data.

The question of whether or not laissez-faire economics is responsible for the current economic crisis is one that cannot be decided in two articles, or even through a detailed study of the current economy. Reisman and Atlas and Dreier present convincing arguments on both sides of the question, but leave a lot of questions unanswered. Most important to many millions of people in the United States is "where do we go from here?" Both articles agree that while the causes are muddled, an answer needs to be forthcoming, and soon. Because their views are informed by different values and different information, they understandably differ on what that solution should be. However, as with the aftermath of the recent election, there is no time for division, recrimination, or revenge; the authors of these papers all agree that a unified solution based on sound economic principles rather than ideological positions should be implemented to relieve the economic pressures on the United States.

WORKS CITED

Atlas, John, and Peter Dreier. "The Conservative Origins of the Sub-Prime Mortgage Crisis." *The American Prospect*. The American Prospect, 17 Dec. 2007. Web. 15 Nov. 2008.

Reisman, George. "The Myth that Laissez Faire Is Responsible for Our Financial Crisis." *George Reisman's Blog on Economics, Politics, Society, and Culture*. Blogspot, 21 Oct. 2008. Web. 15 Nov. 2008.

Criminal DNA Databases: Enhancing Police Investigations or Violating Civil Rights?

Brittany Koehler

Oakland Community College, Orchard Ridge
Farmington Hills, Michigan

To capture reader interest and establish the timeliness of her topic, Brittany Koehler frames her essay with a reference to popular TV crime shows, then attempts to show her audience the relevance of this subject by detailing how these fictional scenarios may be more true-to-life than readers realize. When writing an essay that analyzes two opposing viewpoints, it is important to use quality research that equally represents both sides of the debate. Does Koehler succeed in finding common ground? How might additional information about the authoritative sources you cite make your essay more effective?

On television today, crime shows have captivated viewers' attention. The ratings of shows like *CSI: Las Vegas, New York,* and *Miami,* and all of the *Law & Order* spin-offs that circulate on television have sky-rocketed in recent years. On these shows, criminals are easily apprehended when police investigators enter fingerprints and DNA samples collected at a crime scene into a computer that matches them to a suspect's DNA or fingerprints in the computer's database. However, many people don't realize that having a DNA database is a very controversial issue.

DNA "fingerprinting" is a technique that police often use in their investigations. A DNA sample is extracted from someone suspected of being involved in a crime; this is generally done by the removal of

cells from the cheek with a cheek swab. Police compare the DNA of a
suspect with any genetic material removed from the scene of a crime.
From here, police create profiles of the evidence collected from a crime
scene or from the DNA samples removed from a suspect (Weekes 1).

In the United States, the profiles compiled by police investigators   3
are added to the Combined DNA Index System (CODIS), a central
database containing over a million DNA profiles. Created in 1994
with the DNA Identification Act, CODIS allows forensic profiles to be
inserted by every state in the United States of America. Not only are
profiles added to CODIS, police investigators are also able to search
the database for possible matches to DNA collected from crime scenes
("Genetic" 7).

In the years since the creation of the DNA database, those people   4
who support the existence of CODIS have been pushing for its ex-
pansion. In 2003, President George W. Bush called for profiles to be
created from all arrestees, including juveniles and illegal immigrants
(Driscoll 2). However, there are many who feel that a DNA database is
a violation of citizens' civil rights. The Electronic Privacy Information
Center (EPIC) and the American Civil Liberties Union (ACLU) are
two of the most vocal groups who strongly disapprove of CODIS.

John Pearson offers support in favor of DNA databases through-   5
out his essay "Counterpoint: The New Fingerprint: The Effectiveness
of DNA Profiling." Sally Driscoll's essay "Point: DNA Profiling Is a
Threat to Civil Rights" provides support for an opposing outlook on
the debate. Both essays agree on the benefits that a DNA database
would provide; however, they stand on opposing sides regarding the
reliability of DNA in criminal cases and the efforts needed to protect
the privacy of citizens.

The benefits of a DNA database are recognized on both sides of   6
the debate. Pearson claims that having a database of DNA profiles
improves the "ability [of] investigators to track criminals" (3). He cites
many benefits that have come from the creation of CODIS; for example, with the profiles from the database "about 7,000 previously
unsolved criminal cases nationwide" have had suspects identified, and
the Innocence Project "claims to have exonerated 131 people using
DNA evidence as of August 2003" (4). Similarly, Driscoll agrees that
there are benefits to having a criminal database of DNA. She admits
that CODIS is "a proven crime-fighting tool" and has "helped bring
closure to crime victims, their families, and the wrongly accused" (2).
Both sides agree that acquitting the "wrongly accused" and solving

previously unsolved cases are benefits of having a DNA database. However, while the benefits of a DNA database are great in number, the reliability of DNA in criminal cases comes into question.

The essays strongly disagree on how reliable DNA is in criminal cases. Pearson deduces that DNA fingerprinting is more reliable than classic fingerprinting. He argues that DNA "degrades very slowly" and DNA evidence can be found in the form of any bodily fluid, skin, or hair—even teeth or bone (Pearson 2). After declaring that DNA evidence can be extracted from "nearly any organic source," he points out that fingerprints "have to be isolated on a smooth surface to allow for a good impression" (2). Pearson also contends that criminals can easily avoid leaving fingerprints by wearing gloves whereas an "offender would have to wear something akin to hazmat . . . to prevent any contact that would shed hair or skin cells or draw blood" (2). Pearson argues that police investigators are more likely to collect DNA samples at a crime scene than a useable fingerprint.

In contrast, Driscoll asserts that DNA evidence is not as reliable as many people seem to believe it is. With DNA there is always the possibility for "corruption" and "misuse" (Driscoll 4). For support, Driscoll cites a research study performed by Stanford University that established that "as much as 3 percent of DNA samples have been mishandled" (4). She also states that not only can DNA be mishandled, but it can "easily be planted at a crime scene," whereas it is much more difficult to plant a fingerprint (4). These are not the only ways that Driscoll shows that DNA is not very reliable. She cites a case where an innocent citizen was implicated with DNA: "In one 'cold hit' DNA taken from a rape victim matched DNA in a database, except that it belonged not to the rapist, but to a man with whom the woman had consensual sex prior to the crime" (4). The collections of planted DNA, corrupted DNA, or DNA of innocent bystanders are all possible scenarios that would force one to question the reliability of DNA. How one feels about the reliability of DNA in criminal cases can factor into how one feels about the possible invasion of privacy that a DNA database could create.

Both sides have different ideas of how to protect the privacy of citizens who could possibly be invaded through the establishment of a DNA database. Pearson mentions that "strict guidelines" were instituted to protect the "privacy of individuals" with the DNA Identification Act of 1994. According to Pearson, the privacy is already extremely protected with "stiff criminal penalties facing those who would use such materials in violation of established laws" (3). He also argues that the DNA profiles are developed only "to the extent required for identification" (Pearson 3). Those who would abuse the privacy of U.S. citizens with what little information is included in the DNA profiles entered into the DNA databases would be severely punished by the judicial system. However, Pearson admits that "at some point in the future . . . additional regulation in regard to individuals and corporations will be needed" (3).

On the other hand, Driscoll argues that the DNA database "infringes on [U.S. citizens'] constitutional . . . right to privacy" (2). Driscoll cites a court case that supports her claim: "In 2006, a Minnesota Court of Appeals determined that the routine collection of DNA from citizens who had been charged with crimes, but were either not convicted or proved to be innocent, is in violation of the Fourth Amendment to the U.S. Constitution" (2). The Fourth Amendment protects citizens against unreasonable searches and seizures, which are an invasion of a person's privacy; the Minnesota Court of Appeals felt that the DNA of those who had been arrested but not convicted fell under the protection of the Fourth Amendment. 10

Nevertheless, while there is a difference of opinions on the reliability of DNA in criminal cases and the invasion of privacy that database would cause, both sides agree that having a DNA database would be beneficial. And as the debate of whether or not to have a DNA database continues, the techniques depicted on the crime shows of *CSI* and *Law & Order* are currently becoming realities. 11

WORKS CITED

Driscoll, Sally. "Point: DNA Profiling Is a Threat to Civil Rights." *Points of View: DNA Profiling* 2007. *Points of View Reference Center.* Web. 27 Mar. 2008.

"Genetic Privacy." Epic.org. 8 Apr. 2008. *Electronic Privacy Information Center.* Web. 31 Mar. 2008.

Pearson, John. "Counterpoint: The New Fingerprint: The Effectiveness of DNA Profiling." *Points of View: DNA Profiling* 2007. *Points of View Reference Center.* Web. 27 Mar. 2008.

Weekes, Rob. "DNA Database for Criminals." IDebate.org. 4 Oct. 2001. Web. 27 Mar. 2008.

Chris McCandless: His Supporters and Critics

Eve Lee

University of California, Riverside
Riverside, California

Eve Lee chose a more unusual approach to her essay. Rather than addressing a controversial issue, she takes on a polarizing public figure: Chris McCandless. In 1992, McCandless struck out alone in the Alaskan wilderness, determined to survive by hunting and foraging. Author Jon Krakauer based *Into the Wild* on McCandless's story, and in 2007 the book was adapted for film, making McCandless a nationally known figure. Some have admired McCandless's fearlessly adventurous spirit, while others criticize his attempt as foolish. As you read, notice how Lee smoothly integrates quotations into her sentences and paragraphs to support her own ideas with her sources.

Chris McCandless's journey to Alaska has been a controversial topic ever since writer Jon Krakauer first reported on it in *Outside* magazine in 1993. People have differing opinions about Chris McCandless and his adventure. While Krakauer, a defender of McCandless, believes that he was just a determined adventurer, critics such as Terry Tomalin, a journalist, believe that McCandless was an overeager and foolish man. Krakauer seems to respect McCandless's actions, comparing him to a monk and stating, "one is moved by [his] courage, [his] reckless innocence, and the urgency of [his] desire" (97). McCandless's critics argue that McCandless was a "kook" and that "[he] had already gone over the edge and just happened to hit bottom in Alaska" (Krakauer 71). Although both sides disagree on many points, they acknowledge that Chris McCandless was an intelligent man, that his solitary journey to Alaska intentionally lacked thorough plans, and that he did not go to Alaska to commit suicide.

Critics and supporters alike agree that McCandless was deliber-   2
ately journeying with minimal supplies, although they do not agree
with that decision. McCandless's critics do not understand or support
his decision to journey without proper equipment and backup plans.
Terry Tomalin, for example, the outdoors and fitness editor of the *St.
Petersburg Times*, wonders why McCandless didn't use the $24,000
his parents had given him for college to get "the best outdoors gear
money could buy." In addition, he argues "[had McCandless] brought
a map, he would have seen there was an avenue of escape within a
day's walk. Had he told a friend or relative where he was going and
when he planned to return, he might have been rescued." Critics deem
McCandless's actions to be arrogant, and they believe he was "lucky"
to have survived for as long as he did (Krakauer 71–72). This is evident when Krakauer states that "[b]y design McCandless came into
the country with insufficient provisions, and he lacked certain pieces of
equipment deemed essential" (180). Krakauer even cites a critic who
thinks McCandless was "purposely ill-prepared" (Krakauer 71).

Krakauer, on the other hand, seems able to relate to and under-   3
stand McCandless's need to forsake everyone and everything during
his great experiment in the wild. He suggests that his ability to empathize with McCandless may be because he had problems with his
father, as McCandless did. Krakauer seems to see himself mirrored
in McCandless: "We had a similar intensity, a similar heedlessness, a
similar agitation of the soul" (155). He understands that McCandless
thought if he got down to basics, like Thoreau, he could "fix all that
was wrong with [his] life."

While critics assume that McCandless's lack of planning was ig-   4
norance, arrogance, or carelessness, Krakauer argues that McCandless
"knew precisely what was at stake" (181). According to him, "Mc-
Candless, in his fashion, merely took risk-taking to its logical extreme."
Because he thinks McCandless just wanted to see how far he could
push himself, while trying his best to come out unscathed, Krakauer is
convinced McCandless did not intend to kill himself (156). He claims
"McCandless's death was unplanned, that it was a terrible accident"
(134). Tomalin agrees. He interprets McCandless's "forag[ing] for
wild plants" as evidence that he was fighting for his life.

Nevertheless, the two sides disagree on the cause of McCandless's   5
death. Tomalin believes that the desperation and "panic" of starving,
coupled with eating the "wrong" seeds, led to McCandless's death.
He explains: "It is that critical moment that panic rears its ugly head.

Give in to it, you die. Resist, you live." Krakauer believes that Mc-
Candless did not eat naturally poisonous seeds. Instead he argues that
McCandless made an error, and put nontoxic wild potato seeds in a
damp plastic bag, causing them to rot, and making them poisonous
and fatal (194).

Chris McCandless's death garnered much attention because of the   6
strange circumstances in which it occurred. It is not unexpected that
an unprepared person would die in the wilderness, but it is strange
that someone would go into the wilderness unprepared. Like in every
mystery, there are many factors to consider. At first, critics and supporters of McCandless appear to view his story in drastically opposing ways—critics think he was foolish, but supporters see something
in him to admire. However, both proponents and opponents of Mc-
Candless agree that he was an intelligent young man seeking adventure. A critic named Nick Jans states that McCandless "overestimated
[himself]" and "underestimated the country" (Krakauer 71). Krakauer
asserts that "[McCandless] wasn't incompetent—he wouldn't have
lasted 113 days if he were" (85). They also believe that Chris Mc-
Candless made some regrettable decisions that could have saved his
life. Krakauer states that there were "avoidable blunders" (185). Unfortunately, since it is impossible for McCandless to change his actions,
the most people can do is "learn from his mistakes," according to Tomalin, and hope that he died peacefully.

WORKS CITED

Krakauer, Jon. *Into the Wild*. 1996. New York: Random House/Anchor Books,
     1997. Print.
Tomalin, Terry. "Mistakes Can Be Deadly in the Wild." *St. Petersburg Times*
     16 Nov. 2007, South Pinellas ed., sports: 2C. *Academic via LexisNexis*.
     Web. 3 Dec. 2009.

6 *Arguing a Position*

If you're like most people, when you think of an "argument" you probably think of a disagreement. A constructive and reasoned argument, however, is something else altogether. A constructive argument is more thoughtful and less dramatic than the heated exchanges people have when they are upset; building such an argument can be both challenging and enjoyable.

The purpose of an argument essay is not to "win," but rather to present a thoughtful case that clearly supports your logic. In writing a reasoned argument, you must first examine all sides of the issue you're discussing: As you gain knowledge of your issue, you will move beyond what you've perhaps always thought about it, expanding your perspective in order to understand its advantages, drawbacks, and ambiguities. When you fully understand all aspects of your subject (including opposing viewpoints), you are better equipped to present a logical argument. By anticipating other positions, accommodating those you find plausible, and refuting those you find flawed or weak, you construct an effective argument.

When you have strong feelings about an issue, it can be easy to overlook or dismiss positions that differ from your own. A good argument, however, demonstrates that it is possible to respect those who hold different views, even if you hope to convert them to your way of thinking. By using well-supported reasons to justify your position, and in thoughtfully addressing readers' potential objections, you present yourself as informed and reasonable. Your careful consideration of both sides of an issue and your use of authoritative sources to support your claim helps readers trust your argument. And when readers see the validity of your position, you can make a difference. In fact, inserting your views into the debates that swirl around contested issues is one of the most valuable and satisfying contributions to American life and culture that an educated person can make.

Reasoned argument is always more effective when it is addressed to particular readers. Your goal in addressing this specific audience is to challenge their thinking without ridiculing their values or beliefs. You should assume that whomever you are addressing is informed and intelligent and can understand and empathize with a reasonable argument.

The student writers in this chapter use certain basic features of the genre to build their positions: a focused, well-presented issue; a well-supported position; an effective response to opposing views; and clear, logical organization. They offer facts, statistics, and expert testimony, in addition to writing strategies such as narration, description, exemplification, and comparison and contrast to present their arguments. Mary Hake, for example, calls attention to the unseen hardships of migrant farmworkers by citing facts and statistics, but she puts this data in context by narrating the history of migrants' presence in the United States and by comparing their population to the population of several states. Tan-Li Hsu uses facts, statistics, and abundant examples to show how marketers are selling potentially dangerous energy drinks directly to teenagers. Courtney Anttila cites numerous research studies, as well as credible firsthand observations, in her argument that texting is part of the natural evolution of language.

Writing an argument like those presented here may cause you to question your own beliefs and assumptions, but this uncomfortable confrontation will expand both the boundaries of your thinking and your ability to effectively communicate what you truly believe. So take a position. Study the issue. Consider likely differences between your viewpoint and your readers'. Speak out reasonably. The world is waiting to hear from you.

Use the guidelines in the Critical Reading Guide (below) to practice peer review using the essays in this chapter.

A CRITICAL READING GUIDE

A FOCUSED, WELL-PRESENTED ISSUE

How well does the writer present the issue?

Summarize: Tell the writer what you understand the issue to be. If you were already familiar with it and understand it differently, briefly explain.

Praise: Give an example from the essay where the issue and its significance come across effectively.

Critique: Tell the writer where more information about the issue is needed, where more might be done to establish its seriousness, or how the issue could be framed or reframed in a way that would better prepare readers for the argument.

A WELL-SUPPORTED POSITION

How well does the writer argue in support of the position?

Summarize: Underline the thesis statement and the main reasons.

Praise: Give an example in the essay where the argument is especially effective; for example, indicate which reason is especially convincing or which supporting evidence is particularly compelling.

Critique: Tell the writer where the argument could be strengthened; for example, indicate how the thesis statement could be made clearer or more appropriately qualified, how the argument could be developed, or where additional support is needed.

AN EFFECTIVE RESPONSE TO OPPOSING VIEWS

How effectively has the writer responded to others' reasons and likely objections?

Summarize: Identify where the writer responds to a reason others use to support their argument or an objection they have to the writer's argument.

Praise: Give an example in the essay where a concession seems particularly well done or a refutation is convincing.

Critique: Tell the writer how a concession or refutation could be made more effective, a reason or objection the writer should respond to, or where common ground could be found.

A CLEAR, LOGICAL ORGANIZATION

How clearly and logically has the writer organized the argument?

Summarize: Find the sentence(s) in which the writer states the thesis and forecasts supporting reasons, as well as transitions or repeated key words and phrases.

Praise: Give an example of how or where the essay succeeds in being especially easy to read, perhaps in its overall organization, clear presentation of the thesis, clear transitions, or effective opening or closing.

Critique: Tell the writer where the readability could be improved. Can you, for example, suggest better forecasting or clearer transitions? If the overall organization of the essay needs work, make suggestions for rearranging parts or strengthening connections.

TXTing: *h8 it or luv it*

Courtney Anttila

Southwest Minnesota State University
Marshall, Minnesota

English instructors often complain that texting and the casual style used in text messages have negatively affected the quality of student writing. Some argue that the proliferation of this style confuses students who are still learning how to write correctly. However, Courtney Anttila suggests that texting is simply another phase in the evolution of the constantly changing English language. Using research in linguistics, she argues that the use of texting slang in formal writing is less common than alarmists might think. Anttila further argues that most students can "code-switch" between the language they use when sending a casual text message and the language they use in academic papers or professional e-mails. As you read, consider how one might contradict this argument.

In 2005, about 7.3 billion text messages were sent within the United States every month, up from 2.9 billion a month the previous year (Noguchi). In August 2007, there were 92.5 million (or 43 percent) of mobile users actively using short-message-service (SMS), also known as text messages, and 41 million subscribers sent texts nearly every day ("M:Metrics Study"). Just imagine how many thumbs are typing messages at this moment. Human beings have been communicating in shorthand languages for years using different techniques such as Morse code, smoke signals, and other encrypted codes (Barker). Texting has created a "code" that people can decipher because most abbreviations are spelled phonetically, the slang is used in everyday life, and it is an extremely convenient way to communicate (Barker). Some see texting slang as butchering the English language. However, texting demonstrates the constant developmental change and manipulation of

1

language that happens over time and creates a new literacy for people to communicate with (O'Connor).

During the 1990s, instant messaging on a computer was the craze. A type of slang developed to communicate quickly while typing — "LOL" instead of "laughing out loud," "gr8" instead of "great," and other abbreviations and letter replacements. But using this shorthand form of communication just on the computer was not enough. Now texting has become more popular than ever, and people can send 160-character messages from their phone to anyone who can receive them — allowing them to communicate with practically anyone at any time. Most texters don't even need to blink when deciphering the texting and instant messaging (IM) language used today.

Students and other text-message users have made the new language increasingly detailed over the years, letting people send more information in a smaller amount of space. This "texting language" can become so encoded into the minds of the users that they don't even have to change how they read or think to understand the message. But it is not appropriate all the time. Imagine a fifteen-year-old boy applying for a summer job and writing this: "I want 2 b a counselor because I love 2 work with kids" (O'Connor). It is clear what he is saying, but most people would be appalled at this language on an application because it isn't Standard English. Fortunately, people change their type of language depending on their situation daily; children rarely talk to their parents the same way they talk to their friends, and parents do not speak to their children the way they speak to their coworkers. Students' academic writing is not as negatively impacted by texting as some people think. In the article "Txts r gr8 but not in exams," Ian McNeilly, a twelve-year secondary English teacher and director of the National Association for the Teaching of English, states, "I don't think text message and MSN messenger styles are a sign of declining standards, but changing literacies. Children are usually capable of differentiating between the two" (Barker). Texting slang is not a threat to students' writing for school or for work.

People may assume that texting replaces or damages Standard English because adolescents who text are not writing grammatically correct messages. Although there have been some instances where the "texting slang" has been used in inappropriate places, there is no direct correlation between people who text and poor scores on standardized English texts. In fact, the use of text-message abbreviations is connected positively with literacy achievements (Smith). There has been research suggesting that using text abbreviations might have a correlation to children's reading and writing skills. Researchers at Coventry University studied thirty-five eleven-year-olds and related their use of cell phones to their English reading, writing, and spelling skills. The researchers found that the children who were better at spelling and writing were the ones who texted the most (Smith). They found no evidence linking children who texted and a poor ability to use Standard English. Researcher Beverly Plester is "interested in discovering whether texting could be used positively to increase phonetic awareness in less able children, and perhaps increase their language skills, in a fun yet educational way" (Smith).

Texting slang is also considered to be much more common than it actually is. A researcher in language and communication at the University of Washington, Crispin Thurlow, studied 135 nineteen-year-old students at Cardiff University and analyzed 544 of their text messages (Barker). Thurlow found only 20 percent who used abbreviations, and 35 percent who used apostrophes correctly in their messages (Barker). Tim Shortis, who is carrying out a PhD in text messaging as a vernacular language at London University's Institute of Education, said "You get initialisms such as LOL for laugh out loud and letter and number homophones such as r and 2, but they are not as widespread as you think. There are also remarkably few casual misspellings" (Barker). 5

Not only do people make the wrong assumption that using texts is automatically a burden to the English language, but they also worry that texting has brought more cheating into classrooms. Now instead of passing notes, there is the option of sending electronic messages with cellular phones. It is true that phones allow their users to send and receive messages relatively quickly and secretly; however, students who cheat will find a way regardless of texting. And although some students text during class, teachers are getting better at detecting when students are using their cell phones. Cheating is not a new phenomenon; it has always been an issue in school, and it will continue to be. But it is not a problem solely because of texting. 6

Texting technology has not only made communication easier, it has also allowed young people to become more comfortable with writing daily. Although students have always had to write in school, they previously mostly talked to their friends on the telephone. E-mail and instant messaging have made writing to people less intimidating—and hassle-free. Now with texting, this generation has shown improvement in writing ability. Today's students write more and are better able 7 to explain their thoughts and feelings with words (O'Connor). Even though they might not use the best grammar, kids are getting practice with their writing, and it shows. Adolescents have now surrounded themselves with less formal writing, and they are familiarizing themselves with the strategies that are important for written communication.

Until the next communication innovation comes along, texting 8 and its language are not going to go away. Texting is a part of the continual development of English and has a large impact on today's world. Though texting is a distraction when abused, it has helped put the written word back into our lives, making people more comfortable with the skill of writing. Texting has shown students a way to practice their writing skills outside of class. It is a convenient way for many people to get in touch . . . & it's a fast, EZ way 2 communic8.

WORKS CITED

Barker, Irena. "Txts R Gr8 But Not in Exams." *The TES*. TES Connect, 9 Feb. 2007. Web. 7 Feb. 2008.

"M:Metrics Study: 92.5 Million Active SMS Users Make Short Code-Based Mobile Marketing the Most Effective Platform for Mobile Advertisers." Blog posting. *Club Texting*. Club Texting Wireless Promotions, 25 Oct. 2007. Web. 2 Nov. 2007.

Noguchi, Yuki. "Life and Romance in 160 Characters or Less." Washington Post. *Washington Post,* 29 Dec. 2005. Web. 22 Oct. 2007.

O'Connor, Amanda. "Instant Messaging: Friend or Foe of Student Writing?" *New Horizons for Learning Online Journal* 11.2 (2005): n. pag. Web. 22 Oct. 2007.

Smith, Alexandra. "Texting Slang Aiding Children's Language Skills." *The Guardian*. The Guardian, 11 Sept. 2006. Web. 7 Feb. 2007.

Banning Cell Phone Use While Driving

Thomas Beckfield

Mt. San Jacinto College, Menifee Valley
Menifee, California

In this essay, Thomas Beckfield takes on both the cellular industry—which claims public safety training will resolve the problem of cell phone–related accidents—and drivers who may not realize the extent to which cell phones compromise concentration. People tend to think that using a cell phone in the car might be dangerous for irresponsible drivers but does not inhibit their own ability to drive safely. Beckfield seeks to influence public opinion and ultimately inspire legislative change by presenting statistics based on authoritative research. Do you think Beckfield's purpose is clear throughout the essay?

On February 4, 2002, a driver of a Ford Explorer lost control of his 1
vehicle while commuting on a Washington highway and hurtled over a guardrail into oncoming traffic. The driver of the SUV and four unsuspecting passengers in the minivan with which it collided were killed ("Car Accident"). Until this accident, federal investigators with the National Transportation Safety Board (NTSB) had never "identified use of a cell phone as a possible factor" in a fatal automobile crash ("Car Accident").

Most of us, as either a driver or a passenger, have been behind 2
someone who is driving erratically as he or she tries to use a cell phone. Living in Los Angeles, I have seen countless drivers dangerously weave and zigzag in and out of traffic, fight to stay in their lane, and almost lose control of their vehicles as they talk on their cell phones. Such recklessness can be terribly scary, made all the more sobering by the sight

of a young child or infant seated in the back of the wayward vehicle. With many lives put at risk each day by drivers who disregard their own safety and the safety of others, cell phone use while driving a vehicle should be banned.

Exactly how dangerous is it to use a cell phone while driving? 3 Opinions differ. On the one hand, safety advocates insist that cell phone use in cars should be banned completely. A California Highway Patrol report found that "[s]ome 4,700 accidents in 2001 could be traced to cell phone use while driving. . . . Of those accidents, 31 people died and nearly 2,800 people were hurt" (Bell). Federal investigator Dave Rayburn, the NTSB agent in charge of the February 4, 2002, case, reported, "Some of the issues we are looking at are the fact that the (Explorer) crossed the median and overrode the barrier. The other is cell phone use. Witnesses said the victim was on a phone conversation two or three minutes at the time of the crash" ("Car Accident").

Ever since cell phones became a part of our national culture in the 4 1990s, scientists and researchers have debated their impact on driving. The most notable research to date was a 1997 study published in the *New England Journal of Medicine*. The study found, in part, that cell phone users were four times more likely to have an accident than those same drivers when they were not using their phones. To clearly convey the findings' seriousness, Redelmeier and Tibshirani, the study's authors, equated the increase to "driving with a blood alcohol level at the legal limit" (456).[1] Redelmeier and Tibshirani also noted that personal characteristics, such as age and driving experience, did not have a significant "protective effect" against the dangers of cell phone use while driving (455). In short, the study provided significant evidence that the driving skills of different groups of people are seriously affected when using a cell phone while behind the wheel of a car.

Other studies have also linked cell phone use to poor driving 5 or increased accident rates. Researchers at the University of Rhode Island (URI)—Manbir Sodhi, professor of industrial engineering, and Jerry Cohen, professor of psychology—demonstrated a correlation between cell phone use while driving and reduced field of view. Funded in part by the URI Transportation Center, the researchers chose to concentrate on a specific attribute to measure one's driving skill: the breadth of the visual field to which the driver is paying attention. The subjects in Sodhi and Cohen's experiment wore a head-mounted tracking device that recorded—approximately fifty times per second—where the drivers' eyes were focused (McLeish).

Sodhi and Cohen concluded that a considerable decrease in driver   6
alertness occurred when the participants conducted cognitive tasks,
such as remembering a list of items, calculating math in one's head,
or using a cell phone, while driving (McLeish). The URI researchers
discovered another interesting finding: tunnel vision caused by cell
phone use continues well after the conversation ends. This dangerous
occurrence while driving probably occurs because drivers are still
thinking about the conversation they just completed on their cell
phone (McLeish). Their minds are simply not focused on their driving
environment.

While the cellular industry recognizes and acknowledges the re-   7
lationship between cell phone use and accidents, they believe banning
cell phone use while driving to be overzealous, that problems associated with driving and cell phone use may be easily corrected with
education and training. In 1997, the Cellular Telecommunications
Industry Association committed nearly $15 million to educate their
customers on using cell phones safely while driving (Koffler). With
public service announcements, television commercials, and radio spots,
the campaign advocated the use of hands-free devices, such as headphones, earpieces, and voice-activated dialers, as well as common sense
when using a cell phone while driving (Koffler). Yet study after study
concludes similarly: It is the talking, the cognitive distraction of conversation, that leads to accidents, not the dialing.

If we do not change the laws regarding the use of cell phones   8
while driving, countless lives will be put at risk. In an interview with
the *Washington Post*, NTSB spokesman Ted Lopatkiewicz commented,
"We expect down the road to investigate more crashes involving cell
phones as they come up" (qtd. in "Car Accident"). And while the cellular industry lobby is still advocating the freedom to use a cell phone
as an American right, when one's cell phone call made while driving
causes another's injury, some restrictions on freedom are warranted.

NOTE

1. In a survey conducted by InsightExpress, 23 percent of respondents
believed that using a cell phone while driving was as dangerous as driving
drunk. While 70 percent believed that using a cell phone while driving was
dangerous, 61 percent disagreed with proposed legislation to ban cell phone
use while driving, and 54 percent disagreed with the idea that cell phone use
while driving should be regulated by the government ("Don't Ban").

WORKS CITED

Bell, Rick. "Time for Drivers with Cell Phones to Hang Up." *San Diego Business Journal* 18 Nov. 2002: 38. Print.

"Car Accident May Be Blamed on Phone." *CBS News*. CBS, 4 Feb. 2002. Web. 24 Mar. 2003.

"Don't Ban Dialing Drivers." *Fairfield County Business Journal* 16 Oct. 2000: 11. *EBSCOhost*. Web. 24 Mar. 2003.

Koffler, Keith. "Outside Influences: Speed Bumps for Cell Phones." *Congress-Daily* 21 June 2000: 12. *EBSCOhost*. Web. 24 Mar. 2003.

McLeish, Todd. "URI Study on Cell Phone Use Attracts National Attention." *The University Pacer.* U Rhode Island, Sept. 2002. Web. 24 Mar. 2003.

Redelmeier, Donald A., and Robert J. Tibshirani. "Association between Cellular-Telephone Calls and Motor Vehicle Collisions." *New England Journal of Medicine* 336.7 (1997): 453–58. Print.

Energy Drinks

Tan-Li Hsu

University of California, Riverside
Riverside, California

In this essay, Tan-Li Hsu considers such weighty concerns as ethical marketing and consumer deception. However, rather than getting lost in such a large issue, Hsu investigates something much smaller: He offers a focused look at energy drinks, including how they are marketed and their potential effects on health. Hsu cites news articles reporting studies about caffeine abuse in teenagers; he also cites the American Beverage Association, which defends its labeling practices. By bringing his opposition into the debate and refuting their claims, Hsu strengthens his own position. Like many of Hsu's other readers, you may never have thought before about caffeine levels in energy drinks or the dangers of caffeine. As you read, think about how Hsu presents the issue to his readers, and consider his strategies for convincing them of his argument.

Ever since Red Bull energy drink was introduced in the United States in 1997, the market for energy drinks has been continually expanding. Roland Griffiths, a professor of psychiatry and neuroscience at Johns Hopkins University School of Medicine and author of a study published in the journal *Drug and Alcohol Dependence,* estimates that the market for energy drinks now totals at least $5.4 billion a year (Doheny). These popular drinks are packed with caffeine, a stimulant that is able to freely diffuse into the brain and temporarily increase alertness. Although the Food and Drug Administration places a limit on how much caffeine food products can contain—71 milligrams for each 12-ounce can—energy drinks are considered to be dietary sup-

1

plements and not food products, allowing the caffeine content of these drinks to remain unregulated (Roan). As a result, hundreds of brands of energy drinks with ridiculous amounts of caffeine not specified on labels flourish in the market.

Furthermore, marketers intentionally target teenagers who are   2
more susceptible to drinking multiple cans because they tend to live active lifestyles that leave them sleep deprived. It's no wonder that "[t]hirty-one percent of U.S. teenagers say they drink energy drinks, according to Simmons Research. That represents 7.6 million teens" ("Teens"). With the increased usage of energy drinks combined with the lack of caffeine content warning labels on cans, emergency room doctors and poison control centers are reporting more cases of caffeine intoxication (Seltzer). Energy drink manufacturers are putting teenagers in danger by not clearly indicating the amount of caffeine on labels and by marketing highly caffeinated energy drinks to teenagers.

All energy drinks list caffeine as an ingredient on labels, but many   3
don't specify how many milligrams of caffeine are in the drink. Some brands, like "Wired" and "Fixx," have 500 mg of caffeine per 20-ounce serving, about ten times the caffeine found in cans of soda (Doheny). Another ingredient, guarana, is a source of caffeine that adds to the drinks' already high caffeine content. Unsuspecting teens who crave a buzz by drinking several cans of energy drinks are un-knowingly putting themselves at risk for the irregular heartbeat and nausea associated with caffeine intoxication. In rare cases, such as that of nineteen-year-old James Stone, who took "two dozen caffeine pills for putting in long hours on a job search," intoxication may even lead to death by cardiac arrest (Shute).

It is possible to promote responsible consumption of energy   4
drinks by including possible health hazards along with caffeine content on can labels that encourage drinking in moderation. The reason why such warning labels don't already exist is because marketers are more concerned with money than the health of consumers. "Vying for the dollars of teenagers with promises of weight loss, increased endurance and legal highs [. . .] top-sellers Red Bull, Monster and Rockstar [. . .] make up a $3.4 billion-a-year industry that grew by 80 percent last year" ("Teens"). By warning about the possible health hazards of drinking too much caffeine, manufacturers of energy drinks risk a decrease in purchases. Maureen Storey, a spokeswoman for the American Beverage Association, argues that "most mainstream energy drinks contain the same amount of caffeine, or even less, than you'd get in

a cup of brewed coffee. If labels listing caffeine content are required on energy drinks, they should also be required on coffeehouse coffee" (Doheny). This argument has some validity, but it fails to include ingredients in energy drinks that function as a hidden source of caffeine, such as guarana. Guarana is a berry that grows in Venezuela and contains a high amount of guaranine, a caffeine derived from the guarana plant. Assuming that energy drinks and coffee have the same amount of caffeine, the risk of caffeine intoxication from energy drinks is much higher because of the guaranine.

Marketers take advantage of teens by encouraging them to drink 5 more with attractive brand names such as Rockstar, Monster, and Cocaine Energy Drink that promise to enhance performance. There are many reasons why marketers target teenagers instead of a more mature age group. The first is that teens are more easily tricked by claims that energy drinks will increase endurance and mental awareness. Also, teens are more enticed by the thought of an all-night party than adults are. It's no surprise that marketers are targeting exhausted teenagers who are more likely to purchase these drinks than an adult who makes sure he is in bed by 10 p.m. However, marketers fail to realize the consequences of such marketing techniques. A study led by Danielle McCarthy of Northwestern University showed "a surprising number of caffeine overdose reports to a Chicago poison control center" ("Teens"). "Although adults of all ages are known to use caffeine, it is mainly abused by young adults who want to stay awake or even get high, McCarthy said" ("Study").

Another reason why marketers shouldn't incite teens to buy 6 energy drinks is that the half-life of caffeine in a young body is significantly longer than in an adult's body (Shute). Half-life is the time required to remove half the amount of a substance to prevent accumulation in the body. With a longer half-life in teens, caffeine can accumulate more easily and increase the risk of caffeine intoxication. Preteens are getting hooked on caffeine as well: "A 2003 study of Columbus, Ohio, middle schoolers found some taking in 800 milligrams of caffeine a day — more than twice the recommended maximum for adults of 300 milligrams" (Shute). The problem for preteens is especially dire because "their body weight is low," as Wahida Karmally, the director of nutrition for the Irving Center for Clinical Research at Columbia University Medical Center, explains (Shute). Moreover, researchers do not know how such high levels of caffeine consumption affect the child's developing body.

Manufacturers argue that marketing to teenagers and preteens   7
is acceptable because energy drinks can be part of a balanced lifestyle
when consumed sensibly. While convincing, this argument does not
demonstrate a clear understanding of the scope of the problem. If a
student drinks an energy drink while studying at night and can't sleep
because of it, he might drink another in the morning to help wake up.
According to Richard Levine, a professor of pediatrics and psychiatry
at Penn State University College of Medicine and chief of the division
of adolescent medicine and eating disorders at Penn State Milton S.
Hershey Medical Center, "too much caffeine can make it harder to
nod off, even when you're tired. Then you risk falling into a vicious
cycle of insomnia caused by energy drinks followed by more caffeine
to wake up" (Seltzer). Those who fall into this cycle become addicted
to energy drinks and this addiction threatens the very idea of sensible
consumption. For example, 15-year-old Eric Williams explained that
"he used to drink two to four energy drinks a day, and sometimes
used them to stay awake to finish a big homework project (Seltzer).
The headaches he got when he didn't drink them convinced him to
quit "although it took him two weeks" to break the habit (Seltzer).
Teens shouldn't rely on energy boosters to achieve a balanced lifestyle;
they should learn time management and get into the habit of a good
night's sleep every day.

Exciting brand names, appealing promises of enhanced perfor-   8
mance, and lack of clear warning labels have allowed energy drink
manufacturers to intentionally target a younger audience. With these
tactics, the energy drink market has grown into a billion-dollar industry. Although manufacturers are enjoying profits, consumers are
placing themselves at risk for serious health problems associated with
caffeine intoxication. The most susceptible to intoxication are teenagers who drink either to delay exhaustion or to get a buzz. Caffeine content and overdose warnings must be placed on energy drinks in order
to make teens aware of the potential dangers of drinking too much.

WORKS CITED

Doheny, Kathleen. "Energy Drinks: Hazardous to Your Health?" *WebMD Health* News. WebMD, 24 Sept. 2008. Web. 18 Jan. 2009.

Roan, Shari. "Energy Drinks Can Cause Caffeine Intoxication." *Booster Shots.* Los Angeles Times, 28 Sept. 2008. Web. 16 Jan. 2009.

Seltzer, Rick. "Heavy Use of Energy Drinks Can Threaten Teens' Health." *Atlanta Journal-Constitution*. Atlanta Journal-Constitution, 27 Aug. 2008. Web. 16 Jan. 2009.

Shute, Nancy. "Over the Limit?" *U.S. News*. U.S. News & World Report, 15 Apr. 2007. Web. 12 Jan. 2009.

"Study: More People Abusing, Getting 'High' on Caffeine." *Fox News*. Fox News, 24 Feb. 2009. Web. 24 Feb. 2009.

"Teens Abusing Energy Boosting Drinks, Doctors Fear." *Fox News*. Fox News, 31 Oct. 2006. Web. 24 Feb. 2009.

With Each Seed a Farmer Plants

Mary Hake

Pierce College
Lakewood, Washington

Farms are an important part of the United States' national self-image—we take for granted the "amber waves of grain" that provide food for us and for the world. Mary Hake writes about a grimmer side of this story: the plight of migrant farmworkers. By citing statistics and evoking reader sympathy for the migrant workers, she eloquently argues for rights for these workers. Hake claims that United States agriculture is a "broken system" that cannot survive without abusing the labor force it depends on. As you read, think about Hake's purpose in writing this essay, and what kinds of audiences she might have written it for. How effectively does Hake use her sources to support her claims?

When we sit to eat our meals and join in the family chatter Thanksgiving Day, many of us will have tables laden with food. Americans live in one of the richest nations on earth. We have fertile farmland, agricultural techniques that are modern and efficient, agreeable rainfall in many areas and irrigation provided by flowing rivers in others. Seeds are plentiful, orchards bloom and flourish, grains ripen each year. Yet within this framework are the harvesters of our bounty: the migrants who have fought for decades for a decent wage, livable housing, clean water, and enough food to feed their own children even as they pick our celebratory feast. As Edward R. Murrow referred to these people on Thanksgiving Day, 1960: "The under-educated, unprotected, under-fed and unclothed. The forgotten ones" ("Harvest of Shame"). How is it, then, that they can still be "forgotten" so many years later? 1

Living in a country that prides itself on its heritage of personal 2
freedom and individual rights, we have neglected an entire group of
people who are without the strength or the voice to demand otherwise
from us. The same science that tells us that unclean water and over-
crowded living conditions breed disease, that great fatigue can cause
dangerous accidents in the field, and that poverty is a reason why those
who are sick or injured do not seek the medical care they need to stop
its spread, also tells us how to grow even more food in less time, ne-
cessitating many more harvesters to do this dirty work each growing
season. With each seed a farmer plants, he grows two things. One is
a valuable crop; the other is poverty. Seen in this light, every migrant
farmworker who harvests food in the United States should have equal
access to the health care and basic human services we deem to be our
right as Americans, for to do anything less is to put the nation's food
supply in danger.

Our current use of a migrant workforce has its roots in the 3
1940s, when the United States government instituted a program
to provide cheap labor for the fruit and vegetable farmers (Reynolds). These farmers needed help picking their produce in the limited
amount of time they had before it began to rot in the fields. Many
of their previous helpers had been lost in World War II. The cheap-
est and fastest way to provide these replacement laborers was to
go into Mexico and hire more than three million Mexican nationals between 1942 and 1964 (Reynolds). This plan, named the Bracero Program, brought these workers across the border by bus for the length
of the harvest season. Then, without ceremony, these farmhands were
sent home again. For almost twenty years, American agriculture sent
for foreign help to harvest our food in this revolving-door fashion and
in relative secrecy.

By the 1960s, however, that began to change, largely through 4
the efforts of one man, Cesar Chavez. A farm laborer from the age
of ten, Chavez realized that American farmhands were being denied
a fair wage and safe working conditions (Wheeler 33). As business-
men, the field owners wanted to increase their profits, a goal they accomplished by paying the lowest possible wage to the braceros. Some
farmworkers, like Chavez, were born in America of Mexican heritage,
while others were Mexican citizens who were bused across the border directly to the fields each growing season. Through a philosophy
of nonviolence and the action of "organized sit-down strikes in the

fields," Chavez worked to protest this situation (Wheeler 33). When the braceros returned the next season, Chavez became convinced of the need to organize the farmworkers into a Union that would eventually become known as the N.F.W.A, or the National Farm Workers Association (Wheeler 36). In 1965, after much struggle, the N.F.W.A. reached its goal of a national boycott to call attention to the plight of the American migrant.

Migrant workers, as they will be defined for this essay, are farm laborers who travel more than one day to reach their places of employment. Men, women, and children have historically performed this role, often from a very young age and for very little money. Some have been born into it, some forced by financial need to take any work they could find. An anonymous farmer speaking of his workers more than forty years ago said: "We used to own our slaves, now we just rent them" ("Harvest"). It is within this context that the modern American must examine how we pay for the food that we eat.   5

Most migrants have an income far below the poverty line and are rarely in one place long enough to acquire the legal residence necessary to apply for aid. As writer Eric Schlosser states, "Migrants are among the poorest workers in the United States. The average migrant is a twenty-nine year old male, born in Mexico, who earns less than $7,500 a year for twenty-five weeks of farm work" (*Reefer Madness* 79). Many have no money at all and work only to feed themselves.   6

This transient life has a direct impact not only on the adult laborers but on the entire family as well. Some have argued that migrants are culturally unable to sustain permanent residence, and that they actually enjoy moving with the seasons and would feel limited otherwise. There is absolutely no evidence to support this point of view. Moving as they must, the children are often malnourished owing to a lack of money to feed them and a lack of time to prepare meals. They have little or no warm clothing and lasting friendships are unheard of. Educational needs cannot be met because no single teacher is in control of what is taught, thus completing a generational cycle of illiteracy. It is true, also, that small hands may be needed in the fields. Legally, children as young as ten years old may work as harvesters, side by side with adults. Molestation and sexual assault are very real threats and when they occur are often unreported crimes (*Reefer Madness* 85).   7

Jill Wheeler's book *Cesar Chavez* recounts one migrant child's difficulty attending school: "It was hard for the children of the farm   8 workers to get an education because they were working to help their families. They constantly moved from one job to the next. As a child, Cesar attended nearly forty different schools" (Wheeler 14). The bright migrant child, under this burden of transience and without the continuity of curriculum, has little hope of academic success. He or she will never fully advance with the class and indeed most migrant children do not continue their schooling beyond the sixth grade. With no high school diploma and no formal training, many barely able to speak English, they are ill-equipped for any work other than the fields. They cannot escape the patterns of the harvest, the same necessary and seasonal migration that trapped their parents before them. Similarly, without a decent wage earned, or credit history established, many farm-workers are without the means to live in private quarters. At the mercy of their employers, they are often left with no choice but to sleep out-side or in communal tents with strangers.

Journalist Carole Pearson notes: "A lack of adequate, affordable   9
housing forces many seasonal migrant workers to live in deplorable conditions. Because growers are not required to provide accommodations for their employees, it's not uncommon to see workers camped along the river banks or in the orchards, living in shelters of discarded cardboard and plastic tarps" (Pearson 4). Migrants are expected to work long hours, always outdoors, whether in pouring rain or blazing sunshine; they are also expected to sleep wherever they can. Some have roofs, but not all. Some have floors, but many do not. Most are in the midst of shanty towns where clean running water is not guaranteed, bathroom facilities may not be available, and nothing stops the spread of contagious diseases (Pearson 6).

The possibility of a spreading epidemic, created by ignorance   10
and poor hygiene among a mostly transient population, has fright-ening consequences for the general public. Estimates of the num-ber of migrants working in the United States during any one harvest period vary, but all studies agree there are at least 1.5 million people who work the fields under these circumstances. Some studies state that number may be as high as 5 million individuals; 5 million chances for a disease to move (Carrasco-Mendoza 2).

By contrast, according to a recent census, more than half of these   11
United States have less than 5 million residents (Facts and Figures). Colorado ranks as our twenty-second most populated state with a mere 4.7 million. Arkansas drops down to under 3 million. When added to-

gether, the populations of the states of Maine, Idaho, and Hawaii do not equal the estimated number of migrant workers. Even taking the more conservative estimate of 1.5 million leaves us with a migrant group larger than the populations of Delaware, Hawaii, Idaho, Maine, Montana, New Hampshire, Rhode Island, Vermont, and Wyoming (Facts and Figures).

Separated, unnoticed, and uncared for, this undeniably large group 12 of people is spread across every state's farmland. Touching every agricultural community, they bring their own risk factors with them. As Pat Hanson points out in the article "Migrant Farmers 'Suffering in Silence'": "Close to one third had never been to a doctor in their lives. Seventy-five percent had no health insurance" (Hanson 3). Without health insurance, money becomes the most important obstacle to healing. Very few doctors will treat undocumented workers unless they are able to pay cash or provide a billing address. Additionally, cultural, educational, and language differences, as well as prejudice and discrimination, are cited as barriers to obtaining health care (Carrasco-Mendoza 2). Without money, the ability to understand what care is needed, or the ability to speak English fluently, many migrants are treated as undesirable aliens who must be turned away.

Many would argue that doctors who will not treat indigent tran- 13 sient workers are simply protecting themselves and the entire health care industry from potentially hundreds of thousands of dollars or more in health care costs. For a system that is already overwhelmed by rising fees and an uncontrolled number of patients, adding the additional migrant population might cause a final catastrophic collapse, in effect leaving all Americans without proper care. Additionally, this argument holds, for an individual farmer to insure each of his migrant workers would nearly bankrupt an already fragile agricultural system.

Both of these points, while valid, are solely based on economic 14 payout and overlook the need for each system as it currently stands to be overhauled. In essence, they state that we cannot afford to help the migrant living in poverty because it would break an already broken system. According to Wikipedia, "the generally high cost of treatment has led to the concept of doctors completing their *pro bono* work, although in practice even serious conditions are left untreated. Health insurance is expensive and medical bills are overwhelmingly the most common reason for personal bankruptcy in the United States" ("Health Care in the United States"). By contrast, government-funded health care systems such as Canada's can provide an equal opportunity for treatment regardless of the patient's ability to pay. In America, however, it is still possible to die of an expensive disease.

Similarly, American agriculture is changing under severe pressure [15] from large corporations. Those who still own small family farms have difficulty raising and selling enough crops to stay competitive. Aggressive techniques are used to raise crop yields — bioengineering more hardy and weather-resistant varieties combined with multiple pesticide usage. In the center of this David-and-Goliath battle is the migrant farmworker. With a larger crop to harvest, smaller farms must turn to outside help or lose their investment. Eric Schlosser addresses this issue extensively in his book *Fast Food Nation:* "Family farms are giving way to corporate farms that stretch for thousands of acres. These immense corporate farms are divided into smaller holdings for administrative purposes, and farmers who are driven off the land are often hired to manage them" (118).

The argument, then, that paying for health care and providing [16] for the basic living needs of the harvesters would harm the individual farmer, doesn't apply if the real wealth behind agriculture belongs to large and often multinational corporations whose profits can be measured in the billions of dollars. While it may hurt the smallest independent farmer financially, it also follows that the least amount of acreage would require the least help to manage it. If five men can pick one hundred laden apple trees, only the largest orchard would find this requirement unduly burdensome.

Another argument raised against providing for the migrants simply [17] states that this kind of care and benefit should be reserved for United States citizens alone, and that to treat those who are illegal immigrants as equals is unjust to the American field hand. This point of view refuses to acknowledge the migrants' contribution to the American economy. The United States fruit and vegetable industry, worth 28 billion dollars annually, would lose both its function and its profitability without the work of the migrant harvester (Schlosser 230). The Thanksgiving table itself would have no harvest to celebrate; it would be empty of both food and spirit. Indeed, the migrants' contribution to America cannot be separated from the United States economy. Every day that is spent in the field supports this country and its citizens. It seems only fair, then, that migrant workers should receive something back.

Some writers state that to aid undocumented workers is to 18
reward them for breaking the law. This quote from William Triplett
puts forth that idea quite plainly: "Some farm bosses even have been
convicted in recent years of enslaving workers, most of whom are illegal aliens afraid to speak out for fear of deportation. Human rights
advocates say the only way to improve conditions is to give undocumented workers legal residency, but opponents say that would reward
illegals for breaking U.S. immigration laws and ultimately spark more
illegal immigration" (829).

This position implies that the United States is undeniably a better 19
place to live than anywhere else, and that given any reason to do so
many more immigrants would come here to live illegally. It does not
specifically address how that would be easier to do, or why many more
people would wish to do so. At its heart, this argument is a form of
national arrogance, but more than that, it too seems to miss the most
obvious point. Namely, the illegal immigrant as migrant worker has
toiled and bled as little more than slave labor for over sixty years and
should, indeed, be rewarded. It was the United States, after all, that
created the Bracero Program and in so doing created an artificial reli-
ance in both cultures, Mexican and American, on transient and low-
paid work. It is in the interest of international justice to acknowledge
our role in the creation and proliferation of our immigrant workforce,
legal or otherwise.

As Americans, many of us are far removed from our own food 20
chain. Most cannot grow enough to survive. Many have no idea how
to pick different kinds of produce when they are ready to harvest and
some do not even know how to prepare them. It cannot be wise, then,
to treat those who do have that knowledge so poorly. The migrant
workers among us are the silent, movable backbone of our agriculture.
Intricately tied to our ability to feed ourselves and by extension the
world, they play an irreplaceable role in our economy. Even so, their
lives are endangered daily by ignorance, prejudice, poverty, and disease. If the state population of Colorado cried out in one tormented
voice of great distress, thousands across the nation would hasten to
answer. It cannot be, and must not be, any different when the voices
come from the farms, in every direction, and speak in Spanish.

But ours is a land of nomad harvesters. 21
They till no ground, take no rest, are homed nowhere.
Travel with the warmth, rest in the warmth never;

Pick lettuce in the green season in the flats by the sea.
Lean, follow the ripening, homeless, send the harvest home;
Pick cherries in the amber valleys in tenderest summer.
Rest nowhere, share in no harvest;
Pick grapes in the red vineyards in the low blue hills.
Camp in the ditches at the edge of beauty.

— from "The Nomad Harvesters"
by Marie De L. Welch (Sackman, xii)

WORKS CITED

Carrasco-Mendoza, Rachel. "Migrant Farm Workers Significant to America's Way of Life." *La Voz* 27 Aug. 1997: 3. *ProQuest.* Web. 8 Nov. 2006.

"Facts and Figures, United States Populations by State." *FactMonster.com.* Fact Monster/Information Please Database, 2005. Web. 15 Nov. 2006.

Hanson, Pat. "Migrant Farmers 'Suffering in Silence': California Groups Look at Problems and Solutions." *The Hispanic Outlook in Higher Education* 12.17 (2002): 28–32. *ProQuest.* Web. 9 Nov. 2006.

"Harvest of Shame." Narr. Edward R. Murrow. *CBS Reports.* CBS. WCBS, 25 Nov. 1960. Fox Video, 1992. Videocassette.

"Health Care in the United States." *Wikipedia.* Wikipedia Foundation, Inc., 14 Nov. 2006. Web. 16 Nov. 2006.

Pearson, Carole. "A Case of Apples: Mexican Farm Workers in Washington." *Our Times* 20.6 (2002): 21. *ProQuest.* Web. 10 Nov. 2006.

Reynolds, Kathleen, and George Kourous. "Legislation and Regulation Favor Agribusiness: An Overview of Health, Safety and Wage Issues." *Border Lines* 6.8 (1998): n. pag. *ProQuest.* Web. 9 Nov. 2006.

Sackman, Douglas C. Foreword. *Factories in the Fields.* By Carey McWilliams. Archon: North Haven, 1969. Print.

Schlosser, Eric. *Fast Food Nation.* New York: Houghton, 2002. Print.

———. *Reefer Madness.* New York: Houghton, 2003. Print.

Triplett, William. "Migrant Farmworkers." *CQ Researcher* 14.35 (2004): 829–52. *CQ Researcher.* Web. 9 Nov. 2006.

Wheeler, Jill C. *Cesar Chavez.* ABDO & Daughters, 2003. Print.

Proposing a Solution 7

Problem solving requires a questioning attitude—a refusal to accept things as they are simply because they've always been that way. It invites creative effort—time spent imagining how things might be improved. When you identify a problem that has long existed or notice that old solutions are failing because they're outdated, you take a step toward positive change. As a student, you are in an enviable position to identify and solve problems. Studying and writing, you have been practicing a stance that problem solving requires—thinking skeptically and creatively. And you have the luxury of time to notice problems and think hard about solutions.

Don't be afraid to research problems that are new to you—an outsider's fresh, unbiased point of view is often very valuable. But remember to consider problems from an insider's perspective too: problems of your town and city, neighborhood and dormitory, athletic team and booster club. If you volunteer time and effort on behalf of political parties, religious and cultural groups, or gender and environmental organizations, this experience with specific groups uniquely qualifies you to examine their limitations. What's more, a proposal to solve a local problem may well have national implications.

In addition to giving you a say in your community, practice in presenting problems and proposing solutions will expand your professional-writing repertoire. If student writer Kati Huff pursues a career in management, applies for a job directing a nonprofit, or volunteers to work for a local political organization, she will have demonstrated her ability to notice and analyze problems and suggest ways to fix them, while acknowledging the concerns of the people who would have to carry them out—in this case, school administrators who create cafeteria policy and the cafeteria employees who would have to learn new rules and techniques if existing policies were changed.

It can be frustrating to work diligently on a proposal for a problem that you know you have little power to solve; no matter how well argued, many proposals are never carried out. People who are quite insightful about solving problems may be hampered or thwarted by economic constraints or aggressive opposition from prominent stakeholders. But this shouldn't deter you from proposing a solution to a problem, especially when you choose a local problem in which you have a personal interest. For example, a friend's account of her experience as a long-term-care nurse inspired Kim Spencer Kline and Dana Jordan to tackle the problem of poorly regulated nursing homes in their state. The students interviewed their friend, reviewed newspaper accounts of nursing home violations in Iowa, researched the laws regulating nursing homes in their state and in others, and set out to write "a real proposal, not just an assignment." Their hard work paid off. Kline reports: "Through a friend, we were able to share this paper with a candidate for governor in our state, who was quite impressed with our work and asked to keep a copy of it."

Don't underestimate the power of interviewing people affected by the problem you intend to solve and of approaching others who have the power to change it. Interviews with those who have firsthand experience with the problem can help you anticipate objections to your solution and will allow you to test it with an audience directly involved. Scheduling an interview with someone who has the power to solve the problem may help you anticipate and counter resistance to your proposal. Use these basic features of the genre as a guide for your own writing. Essays that propose a solution feature a focused, well-defined problem; a well-argued solution; an effective response to objections and alternative solutions; and a clear, logical organization.

You are ready to add your voice to the conversations about problems on your campus; in your town; at your job; or with college, government, or corporate officials, whose policies affect your life and the lives of your family and friends. If your proposal can convince readers to consider and perhaps implement your solution, you will have succeeded in altering the conditions of your world.

Use the guidelines in the Critical Reading Guide (below) to practice peer review using the essays in this chapter.

A Critical Reading Guide

A FOCUSED, WELL-DEFINED PROBLEM

Has the writer framed the problem effectively?

Summarize: Tell the writer what you understand the problem to be.

Praise: Give an example where the problem and its significance come across effectively such as where an example dramatizes the problem or statistics establish its significance.

Critique: Tell the writer where readers might need more information about the problem's causes and consequences, or where more might be done to establish its seriousness.

A WELL-ARGUED SOLUTION

Has the writer argued effectively for the solution?

Summarize: Tell the writer what you understand the proposed solution to be.

Praise: Give an example in the essay where support for the solution is presented especially effectively—for example, note particularly strong reasons, writing strategies that engage readers, or design or visual elements that make the solution clear and accessible.

Critique: Tell the writer where the argument for the solution could be strengthened—for example, where steps for implementation could be laid out more clearly, where the practicality of the solution could be established more convincingly, or where additional support for reasons should be added.

AN EFFECTIVE RESPONSE TO OBJECTIONS AND ALTERNATIVE SOLUTIONS

Has the writer responded effectively to objections or alternative solutions?

Summarize: Tell the writer what you understand to be the objections or alternative solutions that he or she is responding to.

Praise: Give an example in the essay where the writer concedes or refutes a likely objection to the argument effectively, and where reasons showing the limitations of alternative solutions are most effectively presented.

Critique: Tell the writer where concessions and refutations could
be more convincing, where possible objections or reservations
should be taken into account or alternative solutions should be
discussed, where reasons for not accepting other solutions need
to be strengthened, or where common ground should be sought
with advocates of other positions.

A CLEAR, LOGICAL ORGANIZATION

Is the proposal clearly and logically organized?

Summarize: Underline the sentence(s) in which the writer establishes the problem and proposes a solution. Also identify the
places where the writer forecasts the argument, supplies topic
sentences, and uses transitions or repeats key words and phrases.

Praise: Give an example of how the essay succeeds in being readable—for example, in its overall organization, its use of forecasting statements or key terms introduced in its thesis and
strategically repeated elsewhere, its use of topic sentences or
transitions, or an especially effective opening or closing.

Critique: Tell the writer where the readability could be improved.
For example, point to places where using key terms would help
or where a topic sentence could be made clearer, where the use
of transitions could be improved or added, or indicate whether
the beginning or ending could be more effective.

The Social Security Problem

Max Moore

University of California, Riverside
Riverside, California

In this essay, Max Moore takes a complex current issue—Social Security—and, based on his thoughtful research, effectively explains the subject to his audience and then offers one possible solution. For an issue that is the result of many factors, Moore acknowledges that his might not be a very popular solution; however, he has done such a thorough job of considering various aspects of the problem—smoothly weaving authoritative sources throughout—that the reader is inclined to grant his suggestion serious consideration. As you read, take heart in knowing that even the most complicated social issues become easier to manage when careful research guides your writing.

It is hard to be 19 years old and give any thought to retirement. Why would anyone begin saving money for a time that exists so far in the future? It can be easy to forget about retirement in the competitive and fast-paced world we live in today. This is why Social Security is such an important program for many Americans. President Franklin D. Roosevelt created Social Security in 1934 to protect the elderly and handicapped from the widespread poverty of the Great Depression (Glazer et al. 793). Each year, every working citizen in the United States pays a tax that helps finance Social Security checks for the elderly. Starting in the 1970s, various experts and officials began warning that the Social Security system was soon going to be bankrupt. Today, the U.S. Department of the Treasury predicts that if the Social Security program continues functioning the way it is, there will be insufficient funds by 2041 (7). It is clear that some type of action must be taken to save Social Security, or else the program will be lost within the next thirty years.

The concept of Social Security would have been quite difficult to explain to most people a hundred years ago. Until the twentieth century, most people worked until they died. Today, it is uncommon for a person to work past the age of 65 (Gendell 14), even if they are still healthy (Gendell 19). In the 1950s, the average age of retirement for men was 68.5; since then, it has dropped to 62.6 (Gendell 14). Social Security is faced with a larger burden as more people decide to leave the work force earlier. Most experts agree that demographic changes and the country's shrinking workforce are the main causes of the Social Security problem (Gruber and Wise 1). These two opposing factors are slowly creating a perfect storm that will quickly drain the money in the Social Security fund.

Based on various demographic trends, the elderly population will continue to increase for the next fifty years. When Social Security was created, the fertility rate in the United States was 3.7 children per woman (Brain 239). Today, the fertility rate is 2.1, and experts expect that it will continue to drop (Cox et al. 964). A declining fertility rate means that each future generation is smaller than the last, and with a smaller younger generation, there are proportionately more elderly people that must be paid for. Death rates have also been steadily declining (Brain 239). With declining fertility and death rates, the percentage of elderly people compared to the total population is rapidly increasing. One model estimates that by 2050 the elderly population will make up 20 percent of the total population, compared to 7 percent when Social Security was first created (Cliquet and Thienpont 28; Brain 240). Another factor attributing to the Social Security problem is the decreasing workforce. In the 1950s, there were 15 workers for every Social Security beneficiary; today there are only 3.3 workers for every beneficiary (Glazer et al. 788). In the years to come, each worker will have to support a larger fraction of retired elderly. Based on the population differences of the elderly and changed retirement trends, it is easy to see why the future budget of Social Security is in jeopardy. There is no way that the current tax structure can support the predicted increase in the number of elderly citizens.

Without reform, Social Security is clearly on a downward slope. However, solutions to the problem become complicated because there is no practical way to increase the birth and death rates. One popular proposed solution that has brought much debate came in 2001 when President George W. Bush boldly tried to tackle the growing financial issue facing Social Security. He was not alone in the debate over Social Security reform. In 1982, President Ronald Reagan had to call for an emergency commission to fix the impending Social Security deficit at hand (Benavie 15). The commission raised taxes and retirement age requirements, which solved the deficit problem only for the short term (Benavie 15). Ever since then, various reforms have been brought to the continuing debate, but most politicians are afraid that pushing Social Security reform would be committing political suicide (Benavie 37). Bush proposed that the best way to fix Social Security was to make it partially privatized.

Privatization of Social Security, under Bush's reform, is a system   5 in which younger workers have the choice to invest a portion of their payroll tax into a personal retirement account (Benavie 37). This retirement account would consist of various stocks that each person has chosen to invest in. In the long run, these retirement accounts would hypothetically accrue much higher returns than the present trust fund system does (President's Commission 26). The basic idea of privatization is that the higher returns made from the privately invested accounts would reduce the cash deficit of the Social Security trust fund. Bush has explained that over the long term the yields from a balanced stock portfolio are around 6 percent; he compares this yield to the return on retirement benefits, which is only around 2 percent (Benavie 40, 41). The current system in place now is referred to as the "pay as you go" system (U.S. Dept. of Treasury 6). This means that "each generation's taxes finance the benefits of the generation that preceded it" (U.S. Dept. of Treasury 6). Under privatization, each generation saves its own money for retirement (U.S. Dept. of Treasury 6). The differences between the two systems are quite large, which means that implementing a privatization system would mean a complete renovation of Social Security. This is where the first issue with Bush's reform comes into play.

If privatization is used to fix the Social Security problem, a large   6 "transition cost" will have to be paid by the first few generations using the new system (Benavie 42). In the initial stages of privatization, the government still has to pay benefits to prior generations that did not partake in the privately invested accounts. As the present workforce begins privatization, there is less money in the Social Security program (Benavie 42). The resulting deficit in the system is referred to as the transition cost. This large deficit in Social Security is largely unavoidable, and usually can be fixed only by more government spending (Cox Edwards and Edwards 9). The President's Commission to Strengthen Social Security, created by President Bush, tried to estimate the transitional cost needed to sustain a privatized system; the lowest cost was .4 trillion dollars and the highest was 1.1 trillion dollars (92). It appears privatization creates only a larger deficit in the near future. Supporters of privatization would argue that various taxes could be used to pay for the transition (Kotlikoff 19), but an increase in taxes is what people are trying to avoid. The higher yielding benefits received by the first few generations using the privatized system will significantly be diminished by the transitional cost they'll have to pay for (Benavie 42). In the end, there is no real advantage to higher yielding accounts if the government has to increase taxes anyway.

The personal accounts used in privatization are not only more risky, they contradict the ethics involving Social Security. Under this plan, people can choose to invest in more risky portfolios if they wish to receive a higher yield as privatization leaves it up to workers to exercise judgment with their retirement money (President's Commission 143). Is increased risk what U.S. citizens need for their retirement funds? Today, after market plunges and corporations abandoning their 401k plans, Social Security is the only source of retirement income for many Americans (Glazer et al. 784). It may not offer very high benefits, but it is fairly reliable. Franklin D. Roosevelt said that the Social Security program was meant to "give some measure of protection to the average citizen . . . against poverty-ridden old age" (U.S. Dept. of the Treasury 2). Bush's plan does not seem to protect the average citizen. By allowing citizens to invest in risky stocks, privatization creates a less safe environment for the average citizen's retirement plan (Benavie 43). Social Security is fundamentally intended to function as an insurance against poverty, not as a risk-involved retirement plan. Trying to privatize Social Security is economically and fundamentally illogical in our current situation. Privatizing Social Security would create a large transitional cost, and would also create a more unstable environment for citizens' retirement plans. It is clear that something must be done to fix Social Security, but President Bush's proposed reform is not the solution.

Solving the Social Security problem is certainly not easy: Factors such as demographic changes are very hard to maneuver around.

Also, radical changes to the existing structure of Social Security, like privatization, create more problems than originally existed. Therefore, the best way to keep Social Security solvent for the next few generations is to increase both taxes and the retirement age. Most Americans treat increased taxes like the plague, and the last thing senior citizens want is to wait longer to receive their retirement checks. Even though my proposed solution may have some negatives, this remains the best way to fix the Social Security problem.

Increasing the retirement age would better represent the economic and demographic structure of today. Currently, the age at which a person can start receiving full benefits is 66 (U.S. Dept. of the Treasury 3). Since 1935, the age requirement to receive benefits has only gone up one year. This does not correspond to the three-year increase in life expectancy since 1935 (Benavie 29). Social Security laws should stay consistent with the surrounding demographics. If government programs are to remain solvent for more than a century, updates must be made to keep the programs relevant to the times. The elderly are much different today than they were when Social Security was created. The amount of elderly living at the poverty level has dropped 20 percent since 1955 (Brain 242). 9

Society as a whole has changed dramatically since the Great Depression. Due to the automation of industry and globalization, the job structure in the United States is radically changing (Reich 214). Most people no longer find themselves unable to work at the age of 65 after a lifetime of hard manual labor. Today, many people can continue working as long as their mind permits it. We can predict only that these economic and demographic changes will continue into the twenty-first century. Increasing the retirement age would reflect only the current changes in the elderly today. There is no way that the workforce of the future can support the growing elderly population without help. By making the retirement age older, it is highly likely that people at the ages of 65 to 70 will remain in the workforce. This would ease the burden of Social Security payments. We cannot reduce the elderly population, but we can redefine what it means to be elderly. Raising the retirement age proportionate to the average life expectancy is the best way to keep Social Security afloat. Another factor that would complement an increased retirement age is increased taxes. No one likes raising taxes. On the other hand, no one likes elderly people living at the poverty level. As time goes on, people will decide a fair balance between age and tax increases. The 10 issue will continue to be a hot topic for debate in the years to come; although this solution is not perfect, it is the best possible option. Every generation that replaces the last must tackle the various hurdles Social Security poses. In the next fifty years, we will see if Franklin D. Roosevelt's progressive plan will survive or fail.

WORKS CITED

Benavie, Arthur. *Social Security Under the Gun*. New York: Palgrave Macmillan, 2003. Print.

Brain, Charles M. *Social Security at the Crossroads*. New York: Garland Publishing, 1991. Print.

Cliquet, Robert, and Kristiaan Thienpont. *Population and Development: A Message from the Cairo Conference*. Dordrecht: Kluwer Academic Publishers, 1995. Print.

Cox, Rachael S., et al. "Declining Birthrates." *CQ Researcher* 18.41 (2008): 961–84. CQ Researcher. Web. 3 June 2010.

Cox Edwards, Alejandra, and Sebastian Edwards. "Social Security Privatization Reform and Labor Markets: The Case of Chile." *The National Bureau of Economic Research*. N.p., May 2002. Web. 21 May 2010.

Gendell, Murray. "Retirement Age Declines Again in 1990s." *Bureau of Labor and Statistics*. N.p., Oct. 2001. Web. 3 June 2010.

Glazer, Sarah, et al. "Social Security Reform." *CQ Researcher* 14.33 (2004): 781–804. CQ Researcher. Web. 3 June 2010.

Gruber, Jonathan, and David A. Wise. "Social Security Programs and Retirement around the World: Fiscal Implications." *The National Bureau of Economic Research*. National Institute on Aging, Apr. 2005. Web. 15 May 2010.

Kotlikoff, Laurence. "Privatization of Social Security: How It Works and Why It Matters." *The National Bureau of Economic Research*. N.p., Sept. 1996. Web. 21 May 2010.

Presidential Statements: George W. Bush—2001. Social Security Online. Web. 21 May 2010.

President's Commission to Strengthen Social Security. *Strengthening Social Security and Creating Personal Wealth for All Americans*. By Lea Abdnor, et al. Washington D.C. 2001. Web. 21 May 2010.

Reich, Robert B. *The Work of Nations: Preparing Ourselves for the 21st Century Capitalism*. New York: Random House, 1991. Print.

U.S. Dept. of the Treasury. *Social Security Reform: The Nature of the Problem*. Washington D.C. 2007. Web. 3 June 2010.

Cracking Down on Lighting Up
Monica Perez
The Catholic University of America
Washington, D.C.

In a proposal essay, even the most well-publicized problem bears re-
peating, and Monica Perez does this well by solidifying the risks of
smoking and the benefits of quitting with statistics and expert testimony. Having readied readers for her proposal by refreshing their
memories about the horrors of the "nasty habit," Perez outlines a
three-part action plan to "help push smoking out of society," and
successfully responds to possible objections to her proposal from tobacco companies, states, and bar and restaurant owners. As you read,
pay attention to Perez's tone, which reveals both her disgust with
smoking and her determination to "crack down" on it. How effective is that tone as a call to action? Does it anger you? Inspire you?

On September 29, 2002, more than a thousand young people con-
verged on Louisville, Kentucky—the heart of tobacco country. They
brought some cameras; the media brought some more . . . and for
what? To drop dead. Where? In front of a major tobacco manufac-
turer. That's what it looked like, anyway, as the students—recruits
from nearby colleges and universities—fell to the ground in unison
for the filming of a commercial. The commercial, sponsored by the
American Legacy Foundation, is part of an antismoking campaign
called The Citizens' Commission to Protect the Truth, which joins a
decades-long movement to educate the public about the dangers of
smoking. 1

Smoking is a nasty habit that is the leading cause of many types of
cancer; these include cancer of the kidney, cervix, bone marrow, pan-
creas, and stomach, to name a few. Some of the more obvious diseases 2

caused by smoking include lung, oral, and throat cancers, along with chronic lung disease. Studies have also linked smoking to heart disease, osteoporosis, and cataracts. Secondhand smoke is another side effect of smoking, but this affects not smokers but the bystanders who happen to be around smokers. According to the Environmental Protection Agency, secondhand smoke is a "Class A carcinogen," meaning that it causes cancer and that it is not safe to be exposed to at any level or for any amount of time. One estimate stated that environmental tobacco smoke kills "53,000 Americans every year" (Clark).

Thankfully, many of the harsh effects of smoking can be reversed. By quitting smoking, you can reap the healing benefits. According to About.com, after twenty-four hours of not smoking, blood pressure decreases, body temperature increases, carbon monoxide and oxygen levels return to normal, and the chance of a heart attack decreases. After two days, nerve endings begin to regrow, and there is an improvement in one's ability to taste and smell. Soon, former smokers may have a new lease on life: in as little as a month, there is significant improvement in coughing, fatigue, shortness of breath, and sinus congestion ("Quit Smoking Benefits"). The question isn't, however, why should someone quit smoking, but how do we get them to do so? How do we help change society's mentality on smoking? We should start with continuing prevention and treatment programs, implementing clean-air laws and smoke-free policies, and continuing to increase cigarette sales taxes.

The best way to get people to quit smoking is to make sure that they never start. "Prevention is a far better investment" than treatment simply because it is so much harder to rid people of an addiction than it is to keep them from falling victim to one ("Smoking Kills"). When it comes to prevention, education is key. We must continue to target younger audiences and teach them the risks of lighting up. If we start to educate children as soon as they enter the schooling system, there is a much better chance they will not be influenced later on. We must also focus our attention on teens. As a group, teenagers and young adults have one of the highest growth rates of new smokers, with three thousand young people beginning every day ("Smoking"). To reduce the number of teens who start smoking, we need to change smoking's image. It doesn't help that our society is bombarded by continual advertisements and positive images of smoking in movies and television shows. An internal tobacco company marketing report from 1989 said, "We believe that most of the strong, positive images for cigarettes and smoking are created by cinema and television" ("Facts"). We must teach the next generations to filter out these false images. There are thousands of different organizations, like The Truth, that can help. But it must be a cooperative effort; parents must speak to their kids, and teachers must act as role models and continue to stress the dangers of cigarette smoking. We also cannot forget that young smokers need extra support and encouragement to quit.

Implementing or strengthening clean-indoor-air laws and smoke- 5
free policies state-by-state is another way to help reduce smoking nationwide. These policies include prohibitions against smoking in public places, such as bars, restaurants, and the workplace. It is important that the public know that clean-indoor-air laws "prompt more smokers to try to quit; increase the number of successful quit attempts; reduce the number of cigarettes that continuing smokers consume," and have a strong, documented "positive impact . . . on preventing children and adolescents from ever starting" to smoke (Barry, "Clean Indoor Air"). *The American Journal of Public Health* reviewed nineteen studies on smoke-free workplaces and found that all reported either declines in daily cigarette consumption by continuing smokers or reductions in smoking prevalence after bans on smoking in the workplace were introduced (Barry, "Clean Indoor Air"). Smoke-free homes and workplaces also significantly lower adolescent smoking rates. And smoke-free policies are also good for nonsmokers. According to Charles S. Clark, "88% of Americans find cigarette smoke annoying." Some people have even developed allergies to smoke, especially those with asthma. Others just plain don't like the smell and certainly don't want to taste the smoke in their food. According to a report by the Campaign for Tobacco-Free Kids, "People are speaking up for their right to breathe clean, smoke-free air" ("Smoke-Free Laws"). Smoke-free policies will help protect nonsmokers and smokers alike, although perhaps for different reasons.

Like implementing smoke-free policies, raising the sales tax on 6
cigarettes is another indirect way to encourage people to quit or to at least cut down on smoking. If you are a smoker, then you know just how expensive packs are becoming these days. As of 2003, the average price per pack, with all taxes, was about $4.12. And that average is rising, with cigarette taxes in many states going up. Virginia raised its tax to 35 cents per pack from 2.5 cents in February 2004. Alabama followed Virginia's lead by increasing its tax by about 26 cents per pack in May 2004. Results from recent surveys conclude that teen smoking

decreases by 7 percent and overall smoking goes down by 3–5 percent for every 10 percent increase in the price of cigarettes ("Update from the States").

Opposition can be seen from every corner. The tobacco compa- 7 nies, the states, and bar and restaurant owners all have something to say. Tobacco companies are upset for the obvious reason that if measures such as these are taken, sales will go down and the number of new smokers will decline — which really isn't such a bad thing. One of the biggest misconceptions about smoke-free laws is that they harm business for restaurants and bars. Not only will these laws "help protect restaurant and bar employees and patrons from the harms of second-hand smoke," but there is overwhelming evidence — dozens of studies and hard economic data — that smoke-free laws can do this without harming business (Barry, "Smoke-Free Laws"). In March 2003, New York passed a citywide comprehensive smoke-free law. A year later, the city reported that "business receipts for bars and restaurants have increased, employment has risen, and virtually all establishments are complying with the law." Moreover, the 2004 Zagat Survey found that while 4 percent of New Yorkers surveyed were eating out less often because of the smoke-free law, a whopping 23 percent were eating out *more* often because of the law (Barry, "Smoke- Free Laws"). There will be the occasional bar that hurts because they "relied on customers who spent a majority of their day there smoking and drinking," but overall the positive effects far outweigh the negative effects. States worry about the loss of cigarette revenues and the fate of the tobacco farmer. I say, in this day and age, a health-savvy trend is sweeping the nation and especially the younger generations. It is only a matter of time before the number of new smokers drops so significantly that they cannot support the tobacco industry. States that rely on tobacco revenues should start switching their areas of income now. Tobacco farmers can help this transition by growing soybeans or corn instead. For those wary states, why not at least pursue a trial period of passing smoke-free laws or flat out banning smoking to see the results for yourselves? There will hardly be a "negative economic impact, so there are no valid reasons for . . . states not to pass similar laws" ("Profile: New Study").

According to Terry Martin, "Smoking remains the leading pre- 8 ventable cause of death in this country." Thousands of lives will be taken this year. Perhaps by implementing these suggested measures, a few may be saved. I can't think of a logical reason not to do everything within states' power to help push smoking out of society. The American community as a whole needs to join together in a collective effort to rid our country of the maladies smoking brings. Neither one person nor one state can do it alone.

WORKS CITED

Barry, Matt. "Clean Indoor Air Laws Encourage Smokers to Quit and Discourage Youth from Starting." *Campaign for Tobacco-Free Kids.* Campaign for Tobacco-Free Kids, 1 July 2004. Web. 10 Apr. 2005.

————. "Smoke-Free Laws Do Not Harm Business at Restaurants and Bars." *Campaign for Tobacco-Free Kids.* Campaign for Tobacco-Free Kids, 1 July 2004. Web. 10 Apr. 2005.

Clark, Charles S. "Crackdown on Smoking." CQ Researcher Online. CQ Press, 1992. Web. 8 Apr. 2005.

"Facts." *truth.* Truth.com, n.d. Web. 8 Apr. 2005.

Martin, Terry. "The Health Consequences of Smoking." *Smoking Cessation.* About.com, 8 Sept. 2004. Web. 8 Apr. 2005.

————."Quit Smoking Benefits—One to Nine Months." *Smoking Cessation.* About.com, 8 Sept. 2004. Web. 8 Apr. 2005.

McMahon, Katie. "State Cigarette Tax Rates & Rank, Date of Last Increase, Annual Pack Sales & Revenues, and Related Data." *Campaign for Tobacco-Free Kids.* Campaign for Tobacco-Free Kids, 18 Mar. 2005. Web. 10 Apr. 2005.

"Profile: New Study Shows Effect of Statewide Smoking Ban in Massachusetts." Narr. Steve Inskeep. *Morning Edition.* National Public Radio, 5 Apr. 2005. Transcript. *Proquest.* Web. 8 Apr. 2005.

"Smoke-Free Laws: Protecting Our Right to Breathe Clean Air." *Campaign for Tobacco-Free Kids.* Campaign for Tobacco-Free Kids, 5 July 2004. Web. 8 Apr. 2005.

"Smoking Kills Millions Each Year." *Australian Nursing Journal* 12.7 (2005): 27. Proquest. Web. 8 Apr. 2005.

"Smoking: U.S. Won't Meet Smoking Goals." *Medical Letter on the CDC & FDA,* 10 Jan. 2000: 11. *Proquest.* Web. 8 Apr. 2005.

"Update from the States: Tobacco Taxes and Smoke-Free Policies in Action." *American Heart Association.* American Heart Association, 28 Mar. 2005. Web. 8 Apr. 2005.

Adapting to the Disappearance of Honeybees

James Benge

University of California, Riverside
Riverside, California

Sometimes students who specialize in math and science don't always recognize that the techniques they've mastered in a composition course provide them with the structure and tools they need to support effective research in other disciplines. James Benge provides an excellent example of a more technical style that still maintains a clear purpose—solving a specifically defined problem—and a well-argued solution (while also considering potential flaws in the plan). Despite the scientific subject matter, Benge engages his readers with a clever introduction and relatable tone as he considers several potential causes for the global decline in honeybees and then offers the best possible solution. As you read, consider who Benge assumes his audience to be: Are they laypeople unfamiliar with his subject, biologists knowledgeable about the issue, or some combination of the two? How might his tone or approach change with a different audience?

Let's talk about honeybees. They're loud, they sting, and they make honey. The end. If only it were that easy. Honeybees are probably the single most important component in almost all of agriculture. To get a grasp of the impact these little guys have, we just need to examine any one foodstuff and follow the trail it leaves. We spin the wheel and land on almonds. Every August, billions of farm-grown honeybees are released onto the California Central Valley almond orchards by being deceived that it is springtime. The almonds are exported worldwide, bringing in billions of dollars, the husks are sold as topsoil, and the rest is sold as cattle feed, all thanks to the honeybee (Agnew). An article from *Annals of Botany* states that "70 percent of crops that account for about 35 percent of all agricultural production depend to varying extents on pollinators" (Aizen et al., "How Much" 1585).

Unfortunately, a disturbing phenomenon is cropping up over the globe that is sending not only farmers, but economists, into a frenzied panic as this money-making godsend drops dead. Recent studies have shown a severe drop in honeybees around the world, and in the United States alone losses have increased from "30 to 60 percent on the West Coast" to "as much as 70 percent in parts of the East Coast and Texas" (Sylvers). Scientists are not entirely sure as to what the source of the problem is, but accusations have ranged from "mobile telephones" to "nanotechnology" (Neumann and Carreck 3). Most of these claims have been debunked and much of the drivel has been weeded out as scientists have narrowed the biggest causes down to three: stress, mites (Bjerga), and disease (Neumann).

The scientific community has coined a term for this phenomenon, calling it "colony collapse." The article "Does Infection by *Nosema ceranae* Cause 'Colony Collapse Disorder' in Honey Bees (*Apis mellifera*)?" presents at least one of the possible scenarios that could cause this problem and Robert J. Paxton has analyzed and theorized that the pathogen *Nosema ceranae* is "potentially serious on the individual [honeybee] and the colony." He admits that his hypothesis is unlikely to be the main cause of CCD (colony collapse disorder) in North America, but possibly is in Spain. *N. ceranae* are a microsporidia (impossible to detect without a microscope) that infect hives within about eighteen months, in turn leading to colony collapse (Paxton). Climate change is moving this once temperately isolated pathogen to farther regions of the globe. So the problem may not seem as widespread as the next suspect for CCD, but it is worth further observation (Paxton).

Mites pose what could be a more serious threat to CCD. *Varroa destructor*, a mite capable of rendering honeybees flightless, is the second biggest factor of colony collapse. Though not globally ferocious enough to be the leading cause of CCD, they could prove to be the longest-lasting progenitor of this catastrophe. As mentioned in the article "The Almond and the Bee," "Mite treatments only work for a while before the mites reproduce resistant strains, and render the chemicals useless" (Agnew). While pathogens like *N. ceranae* and the

Israeli virus can be eliminated through pesticides, mites are far more adaptive, and need to be handled more locally, as each case of mite-caused CCD could be different.

Unfortunately, *Nosema ceranae* and *Varroa destructor* are just two 5 of many speculated contributors factoring into the cause of CCD. The biggest suspect, by far, is the Israeli acute paralysis virus. The United States Department of Agriculture (citing several studies done on the virus) found that 96.1 percent of hives that suffered from CCD also were found to have been infected with the Israeli virus. They also discovered that the Israeli virus can also be carried by the Varroa mite. Despite the compelling evidence, in a quote from USDA's cited article "Genetic Survey Finds Association Between CCD and Virus," Jeffery S. Pettis admits that "what we have found is strictly a strong correlation of the appearance of IAPV and CCD together. We have not proven a cause-and-effect connection" (Kaplan).

Let us pretend for a moment that all of the honeybees have dis- 6 appeared from the face of the earth. Disease, a declination of local habitat (Winfree et al.), and millions of years of nonstop work have finally caught up to the honeybees. Without them, the world as mankind knows it teeters on the brink of collapse as orchards can no longer be pollinated, thus leaving no fruits, vegetables, or nuts for people to eat, no husks or shells to supply to farms for food, potentially eliminating both the meat and the dairy departments. Fortunately, that is not something we have to endure (as far as honeybees are concerned), for we have alternatives.

If we wanted to go down the route of flat-out replacing the hon- 7 eybee, then its relatives are the first place to look. *Hymenoptera,* the order name for bees and wasps, along with ants and termites, is the largest order of anything to ever crawl, walk, scuttle, swim, or fly on Earth since day naught. The blue orchard bee, the wild squash bee, and a wild berry pollinator called the *osmia agalia* are seen as the next in line for desperate beekeepers (Bjerga). They are just as reliable, and the diversity would be vital. However, as the exchange rate goes, blue orchard bees, along with most of the other wild bees, are a more expensive property than the honeybee, even with their own rising price, but that is a short-term wall that could be overcome through proper management.

Bees alone are not the only viable successors that scientists are 8 looking at. Oddly enough, crickets, from a different order entirely, are being examined for their pollination abilities. The discovery is recent, but as *Annals of Botany* shows, a nocturnal and undescribed species of raspy cricket is capable of pollinating orchids (Micheneau et al.). This may seem a little too niche for anyone to care, but there is potential for domestication, expanding its pallet for what it can pollinate. This could take years, and since there is no natural colony mind-set in crickets, there will need to be managerial techniques for managing the crickets as well.

The United States Department of Agriculture started its action 9 plan to combat Colony Collapse Disorder back in 2007. Enclosed in the document is a scientifically driven, 7.7 million dollar investigation (*Colony Collapse* 3). The USDA is attacking the heavyweight causes head-on, despite the proposed causes being simply correlative at the moment. Under "Topic 4: Mitigative and Preventative Measures," several immediately accessible and financially reasonable solutions are presented to fight these known causes, such as high concentrations of ozone sprayed into hibernating beehives during winter to kill pathogens and pesticides, localizing honeybees to reduce stress, and studying local bumblebees, due to their similar ancestry, to determine local causes for CCD (*Colony Collapse* 23).

These are well-reasoned and intelligent solutions to the disappear- 10 ance of the honeybees, but it is hiding the real problem at hand, and that is the homogeny of the pollinator industry. Honeybees are not going to be around forever, yet the agricultural industry is becoming more dependent on pollinators every year. Since 1961, the American honeybee hive has been in decline by about 1.79 percent per year even before the outbreak of CCD (Aizen et al., "Long Term" 915). The only viable solution for beekeepers and other farmers dependent on the honeybee is to expand resources to cover multiple species of bees, as well as other pollinators. If the true cause of CCD does lie somewhere with the Varroa mite, the Israeli virus, or stress, the honeybee's salvation will not come overnight, if it even comes at all, and while the USDA's proposal can help to preserve currently living honeybees, diversity is the key to the survival of the industry.

WORKS CITED

Agnew, Singeli. "The Almond and the Bee." *The San Francisco Chronicle* 14 Oct. 2007. *United States Department of Agriculture National Agriculture Library.* Web. 20 May 2010.

Aizen, Marcelo A., Lucas A. Garibaldi, Saul A. Cunningham, and Alexandra M. Klein. "How Much Does Agriculture Depend on Pollinators? Lessons from Long-Term." *Annals of Botany* 103 (2009): 1579-88. Web. 21 May 2010.

Aizen, Marcelo A., Lucas A. Garibaldi, Saul A. Cunningham, and Alexandra M. Klein. "Long-Term Global Trends in Crop Yield and Production Reveal No Current Pollination Shortage But Increasing Pollinator Dependency." *Current Biology.* Oct. 28 2008. Web. 14 May 2010.

Bjerga, Alan. "Blue Orchard Bees Find Favor in Colony Collapse Disorder Peril." *Bloomburg.com.* 19 Oct. 2007. United States Department of Agriculture National Agriculture Library. Web. 20 May 2010.

Colony Collapse Disorder Action Plan. N.p.: United States Department of Agriculture, 2007. Web. 24 May 2010.

Kaplan, Kim. "Genetic Survey Finds Association Between CCD and Virus." 6 Sept. 2007. United States Department of Agriculture National Agriculture Library. Web. 21 May 2010.

Micheneau, Claire, Jacques Fournel, Ben H. Warren, Sylvian Hugel, and Anne Gauvin-Bialecki. "Orthoptera, a New Order of Pollinator." *Oxford Journals* 105.3 (2010): 335-64. Web. 21 May 2010.

Neumann, Peter, Norman L. Carreck. "Honey Bee Colony Losses." *Journal of Apicultural Research.* 2010. Web. 14 May 2010.

Paxton, Robert J. "Does Infection by *Nosema ceranae* Cause 'Colony Collapse Disorder' in Honey Bees (*Apis mellifera*)?" *Journal of Apicultural Research.* 2010. Web. 14 May 2010.

Sylvers, Eric. "Case of the Disappearing Bees Creates a Buzz." *The New York Times* 22 Apr. 2007. United States Department of Agriculture National Agriculture Library. Web. 24 May 2010.

Winfree, Rachel, Ramiro Aguilar, Diego P. Vasquez, Gretchen LeBuhn, and Marcelo A. Aizen. "A Meta-Analysis of Bees' Responses to Anthropogenic Disturbance." *Ecology* 90.8 (2009): 2068-76. Web. 21 May 2010.

Quality Long-Term Care: Our Elderly Deserve It

Kim Spencer Kline and Dana Jordan

Des Moines Area Community College
Des Moines, Iowa

Kim Spencer Kline and Dana Jordan begin their essay by briefly recounting several sad and gruesome incidents, including the choking death of an elderly Des Moines woman. These stories get readers' attention and create a framework for the students' proposal, which aims to protect some of Iowa's most vulnerable citizens: men and women in nursing homes. But if stories interest and orient, it is often drier details—laws and regulations, for example—that tip interest into motivation. This is as true for writers as it is for readers: Kline's friend's experience as a long-term-care nurse got the cowriters interested in their topic, but it was the students' research into Iowa's laws and the laws of other states that motivated them to "write a real proposal, not just an assignment," and address not only their teacher and fellow students but also lawmakers and lobbyists. As you read, notice the range of interest- and motivation-generating strategies Kline and Jordan use to win their audience's ear—from asking rhetorical questions and telling stories to citing graphs and legislation.

———————

During your lifetime, you or someone in your family will probably   1
need to be placed in a nursing home. One of your grandparents or
parents may already be in a long-term care facility. But have you ever
considered whether that facility neglects or abuses its patients? Are patients' lives in jeopardy simply because the facility is short on staff? Far
too often, the answer is yes. For instance, between March and April
2004, the *Des Moines Register* printed more than seven articles advising the public of the numerous noncompliance issues at the Abbey
Nursing Home (Kauffman; Kauffman and Leys). On April 4, 2004,

the Department of Inspections and Appeals declared the forty-one residents of the Abbey in "immediate jeopardy." Indeed, the residents were in jeopardy. In one recorded incident, a female resident died from choking on food while unattended in the dining area. Former Abbey employee Joanie Grace, a long-term care nurse of fifteen years, recounted another incident in which the Abbey staff could not locate an oxygen tank to resuscitate a patient. Dangerous situations like these stem from inadequate staffing. To prevent similar problems at long-term care facilities across Iowa, we propose that the Iowa legislature implement specific nursing-staff requirements and implement laws to enforce penalties for noncompliant facilities.

INADEQUATE STAFFING ISSUES

Incidents of abuse, neglect, and accidental death occur all too often in Iowa's care facilities. A shortage of qualified LPN and RN nurses and certified nursing assistants on each shift causes most of these tragedies. And the staffing problem is only getting worse: Over the past three years, complaints to Iowa's ombudsman's office have increased (see Figure 1). 2

Many patients require extensive care from skilled nurses. Joanie Grace reflects, "If I am responsible for fifty-eight patients on a shift and some of them require G-tube feedings, trach care, and vent monitoring, a sick patient down the hall may not get assessed until he or she is acutely ill and needing hospitalization. We may have been able to 3

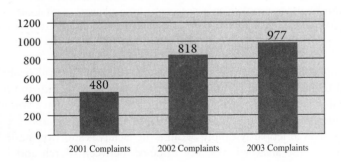

Percent Increase 2002–2003: 19% Percent Increase 2001–2003: 103%

Figure 1. Iowa State Ombudsman Complaint Activity, 2001–2003

treat the patient at the facility if he or she had been assessed sooner." She continues, "This adds to the burden of financing health care. We need more staff. The inability to provide necessary care is scary for the patient and for the nurse whose license is on the line."

Unfortunately, Joanie's experience in the long-term care field is   4 not uncommon. Understaffing at many hospitals means that most nurses must cover three shifts, including holiday and weekend shifts. When a licensed practical nurse or CNA does not report for work, the staff must scramble to find someone to cover his or her shift, often requiring another nurse to pull a double shift.

Inadequate staffing poses risks for patients and nurses alike. Residents may be unattended at crucial times, which can result in falls or choking incidents. Calls for assistance to the bathroom or shower may go unanswered for long periods of time, leaving residents lying in their own waste for hours. Important information in medical charts may be overlooked or omitted by overburdened nurses, resulting in incorrect dosing of medications or improper diets that could lead to serious medical complications. The nurses are directly affected since they are held accountable for any mistakes or oversights in patient care. Proper staff-to-patient ratios could prevent many of these problems.

CURRENT LEGISLATION

The state of Iowa currently requires "adequate staffing" but does not   6 suggest actual minimums—based on facility size and resident acuity (care) levels—to fulfill this requirement (State of Iowa House File 2990). In fact, none of the regulations are well-defined. The ambiguity of the law's language makes appealing noncompliance fines all too easy. What's more, extended care facilities are excluded from the adequate staffing requirement:

> A health facility, *other than an extended care facility,* shall ensure that it is staffed in a manner that provides sufficient, appropriately qualified direct-care nurses in each department or unit within the facility in order to meet the individualized care needs of its patients and to meet the requirements specified in this section. Bill: H.J.259.2, Sect. 4, 135M.4, 5:4–9.

This leaves the staffing requirements for long-term care facilities in the hands of individual facilities. Inadequate staffing has often been the result.

THE FLAWED PROCESS OF THE DEPARTMENT OF INSPECTIONS AND APPEALS

The Iowa Department of Inspections and Appeals annually inspects   7
care facilities, issuing fines to those they find noncompliant. As stated
above, facilities can appeal these fines and be exonerated. In addition
to being fined, a facility that has been noncompliant for six months
or more can lose its Medicaid/Medicare certification. This means the
facility is unable to receive additional Medicare patients until the facility has reached the "reasonable assurance" period and is eligible to
apply for recertification (Wood).

The use of fines and penalties has proven to be ineffective in   8
most cases because, when faced with thousands of dollars in fines,
many long-term care facility owners will voluntarily close their business and sell it to the highest bidder. Some reopen facilities under a
new name or declare bankruptcy. Many facilities are owned by corporations or partnerships that, upon being closed down in one state,
simply open another facility in another state and proceed to run that
facility into the ground.

Though fines and penalties are aimed at punishing the owners and   9
administrators of facilities, in the not-so-long run, staff and residents
suffer the consequences. A facility that owes huge debts for noncompliance has less money to spend operating the facility efficiently. The
result is inadequate staffing, poor wages, inadequate management, or
lack of resources, all elements that directly affect patients. A reform in
the law regulating long-term care facilities is desperately needed. The
health, safety, and financial well-being of the people who live in these
facilities are at stake.

GIVING OUR ELDERLY THE QUALITY CARE THEY DESERVE

First, we propose that the law clearly define staffing requirements   10
for long-term care facilities, mandating specific staff-to-patient ratios
that take into account the number of residents and level of acuity in
a facility, just as staff-to-patient ratios are mandated for other health-
care facilities. For example, a reasonable ratio for patients requiring
intermediate care would be 7:1, seven patients to one staff member.
In addition, each facility should be required to contract with a private
nursing pool to provide staffing in emergency situations.

Furthermore, each facility must develop a state-mandated man- 11
agement team that includes not only the facility's administrator and
selected staff, but also a state administrator from the Iowa Department of Inspections and Appeals, who interacts with this management team monthly. A state administrator team member should
oversee no more than fifteen local facilities to ensure that he or she
devotes an adequate amount of time to problem solving in any one
facility. The management team would be responsible for overseeing
and maintaining proper staffing ratios, ensuring efficient resource
management, problem solving for quality-care issues, and implementing incentive programs to encourage good employee attendance
and quality work. The state administrator would be responsible for
offering alternative solutions to specific problems, such as finding reliable staff.

Next, we propose that the Iowa state legislature implement laws 12
to enforce penalties for noncompliant facilities. Our proposal requires
that any long-term care facility that does not meet 90 percent compliance following two consecutive inspections loses its Medicaid/
Medicare certification as well as its license to own and operate a long-
term care facility in the state of Iowa. Fines based on level of noncompliance would be issued, and the facility would have thirty days
to transfer its residents and close its doors.

To prevent chronically noncompliant owners from reopening 13
elsewhere, the existing public registry needs to provide state licensing
agencies with a detailed history of all owners/corporations of long-
term care facilities, complete with each company's noncompliance issues, penalties, and fines. Serious complaints should be noted in this
registry. This registry needs to be accessible on a national scale and
should make use of a grading scale for easier deciphering of information. Information should be graded on a scale of 1–4, mirroring
the grading scale of the inspections department. Implementation of a
complete public registry will help prevent other long-term care facilities from being opened by the same people who ran shoddy, unsafe
operations elsewhere.

THE OTHER SIDE

Some may argue that current Iowa regulations as stated in House File 14
2290 are sufficient. But the current regulations leave the responsibil-

ity for maintaining adequate staffing in the hands of the individual facilities; there is no accountability. The management teams we suggest would provide the accountability and the resources necessary to provide quality care in a safe and positive environment.

Other options have been suggested, such as cameras in residents' 15 rooms to monitor the level of care (Huggins). Not only are cameras an infringement of a citizen's right to privacy, but they also "institutionalize" the atmosphere of long-term care facilities.

The state has considered incentive programs to hire better qual- 16 ity nurses, but this does not solve inadequate staffing problems.

Facility administrators may argue that they cannot afford more 17 nurses, but the management team we have proposed would look at time-management issues within the existing staff to better allocate responsibilities. Also, funds that are currently spent on the lengthy inspection and appeals process could be used in the management of facilities.

THE BOTTOM LINE

With the increase in complaints about elder care in Iowa, the time 18 has come for Iowa lawmakers and citizens to set a higher standard for quality of life for our elderly generation. Iowa standards in long-term care should set the example for the rest of the nation. Our proposal eliminates staffing problems, distributes funds more efficiently, and encourages quality health care in a positive environment. Happy, healthy residents are the best advertisers for long-term care facilities, and a positive work environment promotes loyal and competent employees. The focus in long-term care facilities needs to be directed back to the residents, where it belongs.

WORKS CITED

Grace, Joanie. Personal interview. 17 Mar. 2005.

Huggins, Charnicia E. "States Consider Allowing Cameras in Nursing Homes." *Global Action on Aging*. N.p., 23 Aug. 2004. Web. 1 Apr. 2005.

Kauffman, Clark. "Care Center Investigated Again." *Des Moines Register.* Des Moines Register, 19 Mar. 2004. Web. 19 Mar. 2005.

Kauffman, Clark, and Tony Leys. "D. M. Facility's Residents Removed over Safety Fears." *Des Moines Register.* Des Moines Register, 3 Apr. 2004. Web. 19 Mar. 2005.

Office of the State Long-Term Care Ombudsman. Iowa Department on Aging, n.d. Web. 28 Mar. 2005.

State of Iowa. House of Rep. *House File* 2290. H.J. 259.2. Des Moines: Iowa State Legislature. Web. 20 Mar. 2005.

Wood, Erica F. "Termination and Closure of Poor Quality Nursing Homes." *American Association of Retired Persons.* AARP Public Policy Institute, Mar. 2002. Web. 19 Mar. 2005.

Unhealthy Lunchrooms: Toxic for Schoolchildren and the Environment

Kati Huff

Lake Michigan College
Benton Harbor, Michigan

Kati Huff takes on two problems in this essay: unhealthy food and the generation of excessive waste. Two solutions in one essay is a tall order, but Huff shows the link between these issues. Both the food and the waste are unhealthy—for us and for the environment—and unsustainable for the future. Huff cites her sources in APA style and provides an annotated bibliography at the end of her essay, where, instead of just listing her references, she describes each source briefly, telling what information it contains and who produced it.

America's waistline is bulging over its belt, and the environment is slowly wasting away. The cause of both of these problems lies in the most unlikely of places. This is a place where all schoolchildren have roamed, gossiped, and played, and where they have been conditioned to gorge themselves with fat-ridden food while at the same time disregarding Mother Nature. Where is this nightmare taking place? In tens of thousands of elementary, junior, and senior high cafeterias across the nation. Fried foods and foam trays are prevalent in almost all public schools. Schoolchildren, especially in elementary schools, are oblivious to what they are putting into their bodies and into the garbage cans that fill up landfill after landfill. Feeding children deep-fried corn dogs and grease-saturated French fries on non-biodegradable trays is doing nothing for two of the biggest concerns this country has: obesity and the environment. By using reusable trays and being provided with healthy food, students may become more environmentally conscious as well as aware of what they are putting into their bodies. Landfills and the ozone layer will be less impacted by the production and disposal of thousands of foam trays and students will get the nutrition their growing bodies need.

As an elementary school student, my friends and I used to have   2
contests to see who could squeeze the most grease out of their cheese pizza on pizza Fridays. Usually, whoever ended up with the juicy middle piece of the pizza won. Because we were children, and we were hungry, we would set the grease puddle aside and continue to eat the pizza. This is not the type of food that should be infecting future school kids' stomachs. Schools need to change the way kids eat. In a *Newsweek* article published in 2005, it becomes apparent that the meals schools serve often consist of French fries, breaded patties, and some sort of canned vegetable. This, in turn, makes kids want to buy cookies and other snacks that the a la carte section of the cafeteria may offer instead (Tyre & Staveley-O'Carroll, 2005). Though public schools are now offering healthier items, some of the schools still have too many unhealthy foods weighing them down (Ramirez, 2007).

Unfortunately, the cost of healthy food is skyrocketing. In a   3
2005 article in the *Food Service Director* (2007), C. Atwell, a director from California, says that he supports the use of healthy foods and making the transition to them is not the problem. California schools are required to ban fatty and sugary foods from their schools. And a state program gives school districts 10 cents per meal served when the lunchroom offers two vegetable and fruit options (Shalfi, 2007). However, the cost of food has "risen 25% over the last four years while [funding] increases from the state and federal governments came in at about 13%. The difference seems to grow wider every year" (qtd, Shalfi, 2007, p. 24). Even with some help from the government, schools have trouble affording healthy food for all their students.

If students could choose healthier foods at lunch, they would still   4
be putting the food on foam lunch trays. The food might be better, but what about the environment? Schools need to change the food they serve, and also the kind of trays they are serving food on. Though the foam trays are often called Styrofoam trays, the name Styrofoam is a trademark of Dow Chemical Company. Dow.com (2007a) states that Styrofoam is not the substance used for these foam trays, cups, or containers. Polystyrene, a substance much like Styrofoam but less

durable and less insulating, is used for school lunch trays (Dow.com, 2007b). According to an editorial written by members of the Committee for the Preservation of Wildlife of Northern Illinois University (2005), 1,369 tons of products made with polystyrene are carelessly dumped in our landfills every day in the United States. This number is only increasing due to the excessive use of polystyrene trays in schools. For example, there are approximately 600 students at Berrien Springs High School, a public school in Southwestern Michigan. Every day the cafeteria serves lunch to roughly 400 students. If they used 400 trays a day for five days a week, that would be 2,000 polystyrene foam trays waiting to be dumped somewhere at the end of the week. This number is only for the high school. The elementary schools and junior high in the Berrien Springs School district also use foam trays. The number of foam trays being dumped every day is astronomical.

P. Evans, the food service director for Berrien Springs Public   5 Schools, stated that almost every school district in the area uses polystyrene foam trays. The reason, she says, is that using foam trays is more economically feasible. "We buy foam trays in cases of 500 that are about three to four cents apiece," said Evans. "Buying these disposables [trays] is much cheaper than the labor we would have to pay for employees to wash dishes" (personal communication, November 15, 2007).

Another benefit to the disposable polystyrene trays is that they are   6 sanitary. With disposable trays, districts do not have to worry about cleaning trays two or three times to make sure they are up to code to serve food on again. However, an article by the Committee for the Preservation of Wildlife (2005) reports that polystyrene is made with petroleum and benzene. Both of these are known cancer-causing elements. In 1986 the EPA National Human Adipose Tissue Survey said that they had found styrene residues in 100% of samples of human tissues. Styrene (a part of polystyrene) exposure has been found to cause fatigue, low hemoglobin values, carcinogenic effects, and nervousness (Committee for the Preservation of Wildlife, 2005). If these side effects from styrene exposure have been proven, why do schools continue to serve children food on trays made from those very elements? Schools must come up with a better solution.

One solution would be to use disposable trays that are better   7 for the environment. Unfortunately, this plan has many problems. P. Evans said that the Berrien Springs School District had looked into buying more ecologically friendly trays. However, "Go Green" lunch trays cost three to four times as much as the foam trays, and few districts could afford that. The Boise, Idaho, schools tried to use trays made of sugar cane fiber, even though the trays cost three times as much as the foam ones. This school district was willing to stretch the extra penny and try them. However, the trays needed to be composted in humidity and high heat, which is not likely weather in Idaho (Allen, 2007).

To reduce the number of trays in landfills, the foam trays that schools use now could be recycled. However, recycling polystyrene is not an easy process and is extremely costly (Myron, 1995). Schools would lose money trying to recycle every single tray they use. P. Evans stated that if the Berrian Springs School District were to recycle the foam trays, they would need to be washed and cleared of food debris before the recycling company would take them. This would defeat the purpose of using the trays — they would still need people to wash them. And the process to make polystyrene produces chemicals that pollute the ozone, so it would still be bad for the environment (Myron, 1995).

Extra labor, special facilities, and healthy foods are certainly not cheap. Though these costs seem outrageous, they can be managed. When using reusable trays, schools have to pay once for the trays and also for occasional replacement trays. There are ways to eliminate extra labor as well. Berrien Springs School District food service program is trying out touch screens that will let students order their meal. This will eliminate the time it takes for cafeteria workers to fill out an order slip for each student. With this extra time, cafeteria workers will have time to wash dishes without going into overtime (personal communication, November 15, 2007). According to M. Shalfi of *Food Service Director* (2007), a school district in Ohio is looking at investing in a combi-oven. The oven cooks with steam and adds crispness without deep frying. Since they won't be deep frying, the school will not have to pay for oil or wash out fryers. They say that the oven will pay itself off in time because they will be saving about $3,000 a year. Another option for washing the trays would be to use students. Students at the high school level are, in most states, required to complete a certain number of community service hours. What better way to get those hours in than during the lunch period without taking the time to leave campus? Also, incentives for helping, such as a free lunch, can be used to get students to help wash the trays. In this way, there would be no extra cost for cafeteria labor.

While food service directors are trying to find a cost-effective, 10 "green" approach to the trays, they must also try to get students to eat healthier. Sneaking new ingredients into foods is one option. Unfortunately, students sometimes turn away from foods that look the same as the unhealthy ones but taste different. According to a Liberal Democrat report, 250,000 fewer meals are eaten in secondary schools after mandating nutrition guidelines (Druce, 2007). Requiring a course on nutrition might help students make better food choices at lunch, but hiring and training new teachers would be costly, and students might not make the right decisions anyway.

There is, however, a light at the end of this toxic tunnel. It is sim- 11 ple to get students to eat healthier food. Slowly introducing fresh fruits and vegetables is a great way to start. Offering a well-balanced meal with a touch of the old food is the way to get the students to eat new foods. Children do not like change, so the transition to healthier foods needs to be a slow and continual process. Skim milk, fresh fruits and vegetables, and whole grains should be easily accessible at each meal. The main course does not have to be made of soybeans, but healthy options need to be available for students to fill up their reusable trays with. If done properly, at a slow and steady pace, healthy foods will catch on and become just as popular as grease-pizza Friday.

By implementing this simple and effective plan, several groups of 12 people will benefit. Food services will save money and time for not having to buy foam trays or pay for labor. Schoolchildren will be making the right food choices and will have less chance of becoming obese in the future. Finally, the environment will be cleaner and less impacted by millions of polystyrene foam trays polluting it. Although these solutions would require some changes to the current school food system, they would be worth it for their benefit to students and to the environment.

ANNOTATED BIBLIOGRAPHY

Allen, A. (2007, October 30). Boise schools pushing for eco-friendly lunch trays: Community urges schools to use materials that can be recycled or composted. *Idaho Statesman*. Retrieved from http://www.idahostatesman .com

The Boise Idaho school district shows their concern about foam trays used in the school cafeteria. Some of the schools in the district are equipped with facilities to use plastic trays while others tried a new tray made of sugarcane fiber that can be composted. Although these trays cost three times as much as the foam ones, students seemed to prefer them. Problems like recycling or composting the fiber trays arose. PTO groups are now offering to put dishwashers into the schools. Alternatives to the foam trays are still being discussed.

American Chemistry Council Plastics Food Processing Group (PFPG). (2007). *Polystyrene facts.* Retrieved from http://www.americanchemistry.com

The Plastics Food Processing Group is a business group of the American Chemistry Council and supplies the public with resin and polystyrene while responding to inquiries from the public. PFPG explains why polystyrene is sanitary, sturdy, efficient, economical, and convenient. The PFPG advocates the use of polystyrene products while relating them to our daily lives. The arguments for using polystyrene products are clearly stated here.

Committee for the Preservation of Wildlife. (2005, February 11). Students should choose Styrofoam alternative. *Northern Star.* Retrieved from http://www .star.niu.edu

This article, written by members of the Committee for the Preservation of Wildlife, explains some dangers of the use of polystyrene. The article ties in the dangers of its use with students' lives at the Northern Illinois campus. This article also reflects students' views of the foam trays.

Dow Chemical Company. (2007a). *What is STYROFOAM?* Retrieved from http://www.dow.com

Dow Chemicals explains that Styrofoam is not used in plates or trays that are commonly used in school cafeterias. Styrofoam is a trademarked name.

Dow Chemicals Company. (2007b). *Polystyrene.* Retrieved from http://www .dow.com

Dow Chemical explains what polystyrene is and what it is used for.

Hackes, B., and W. Shanklin. (1999). Factors other than environmental issues influence resource allocation decisions of school food service directors. *Journal of the American Dietetic Association, 99*(8), 944–46. Retrieved from http://www.adajournal.org

Respondents to an extensive survey give insight into school food service recycling programs. Also, recommendations are made to conserve environmental resources and cut down on pollution.

Myron, H. (1995). *Polystyrene foam recycling.* Retrieved from http://www .newton.dep.anl.gov/newton/askasci/1995/environ/ENV138.HTM

"Ask a Scientist" offers some insight into recycling and alternatives to polystyrene (used for foam trays in school cafeterias). Recycling the foam is costly and not many companies are interested in buying back the recycled material. Also, ozone-destroying chemicals are used to make foam products.

Ramirez, E. (2007, August 16). Do school cafeterias make the grade? *U.S. News & World Report.* Retrieved from http://www.usnews.com

Creative ways to bring in more healthy foods to schools and the expenses of those healthy foods are discussed.

Shalfi, M. (2007, August 15). Taking back school lunch: Operators meet the challenges of the increased costs of healthier foods with creative solutions and an outcry for federal funding. *Food Service Director, 20*(8), 24–27. Retrieved from http://www.fsdmag.com

Transitioning to healthier lunch items is something that all schools agree on, but healthy food is expensive and not all school districts get the funding for it. "Sneaking" healthy foods into entrees has proven successful but nutrition education in the schools is still missing. Creative solutions such as buying combi-ovens, bringing back salad bars, creating more ethnic cuisines, and using whole grains are presented.

Tyre, P., and S. Staveley-O'Carroll. (2005, August 8). How to fix school lunch: Celebrity chefs, politicians, and concerned parents are joining forces to improve the meals kids eat every day. *Newsweek, 146,* 50.

As the number of children who are obese or have diabetes grows, it is becoming apparent that school kitchens need to be reevaluated. Meals provided by untrained workers in understaffed cafeterias do not give children the nutrition they need. Also, money from vending machine sales has declined because of the implementation of healthy foods; therefore, schools find it hard to pay for fresh fruits and vegetables.

Justifying an Evaluation 8

You are already very familiar with evaluations. In fact, if you're like most of us, you depend on evaluations on a daily basis. Before spending money to dine out, you probably ask for suggestions from friends who know the local restaurant scene or read restaurant reviews online or in your local newspaper. And you probably don't watch movies cold; instead, you're more likely to go to the theater on a friend's recommendation or read brief descriptions of what's playing on a movie-review site before buying a ticket. For a major purchase like a car or truck, cell phone, digital camera, or even a pair of running shoes, you're likely to look for a recent, authoritative review of the product, perhaps in *Consumer Reports*—a magazine whose comprehensive evaluations have catapulted its parent organization, the Consumers Union, into the national consciousness.

Obviously, reviews are wide ranging. Student writers in this chapter evaluate quite different subjects: a painting, a movie, a book, and even satellite radio. However, each writer employs the same basic features to justify his or her evaluation: a well-presented subject; a well-supported judgment; an effective response to objections and alternative judgments; and a clear, logical organization. Like any reviewers, these writers judge their subjects, but they go well beyond giving them just a thumbs-up or -down: They give reasons for their judgments and then support each reason with definitions, examples, descriptions, and comparisons to similar subjects. They may even anticipate readers' reservations or alternative judgments.

Judgments are easy to make—so much so that they are sometimes referred to as "snap judgments." When you evaluate, you test your snap judgments, turning them into reasoned evaluations. In doing so, you develop your powers of attention to details and the ability to discriminate among them. When evaluating a subject and writing up your evaluation of it, you must look closely and attentively, think hard and rethink, and justify—all the while extending and refining your understanding of subjects like the one you are evaluating. To evaluate, then, is to engage in thoughtful, responsible, discriminating work—work that is worth your time.

Use the guidelines in the Critical Reading Guide (below) to practice peer review using the essays in this chapter.

A CRITICAL READING GUIDE

A WELL-PRESENTED SUBJECT

Has the writer presented the subject effectively?

Summarize: Tell the writer what you understand the subject of the evaluation to be, and identify the kind of subject it is.

Praise: Point to a place where the subject is presented effectively—for example, where it is described vividly and accurately, where it is named, or where it is clearly placed in a recognizable genre or category.

Critique: Tell the writer where readers might need more information about the subject, and whether any information about it seems inaccurate or possibly only partly true. Suggest how the writer could clarify the kind of subject it is, either by naming the category or by giving examples of familiar subjects of the same type.

A WELL-SUPPORTED JUDGMENT

Has the writer supported the judgment effectively?

Summarize: Tell the writer what you understand the overall judgment to be, and list the criteria on which it is based.

Praise: Identify a passage in the essay where support for the judgment is presented effectively—for example, note particularly strong supporting reasons, appeals to criteria readers are likely to share, or especially compelling evidence.

Critique: Let the writer know if you cannot find a thesis statement or think the thesis is vague or overstated. Tell the writer where the evaluation could be improved—for example, suggest another reason that could be added; propose a way to justify one of the criteria on which the evaluation is based; or recommend a source or an example that could be used to bolster support for the judgment.

AN EFFECTIVE RESPONSE TO OBJECTIONS AND ALTERNATIVE JUDGMENTS

Has the writer responded effectively to objections and alternative judgments?

Summarize: Choose an objection or alternative judgment about the subject, and explain it in your own words.

Praise: Identify a passage in the essay where the writer responds effectively to an objection or alternative judgment. An effective response may include making a concession—for example, agreeing that a subject the writer is primarily criticizing has some good points, or agreeing that the subject has weaknesses as well as strengths.

Critique: Tell the writer where a response is needed or could be made more effective—for example, suggest a likely objection or alternative judgment that should be taken into account, help the writer understand the criteria behind an alternative judgment, or offer an example that could be used to refute an objection.

A CLEAR, LOGICAL ORGANIZATION

Is the evaluation clearly and logically organized?

Summarize: Summarize: Briefly describe the strategies used to make the essay clear and easy to follow.

Praise: Give an example of where the essay succeeds in being readable—in its overall organization, in its clear presentation of the thesis, in its effective opening or closing, or by other means.

Critique: Tell the writer where the readability could be improved. Can you, for example, suggest a better beginning or a more effective ending? If the overall organization of the essay needs work, make suggestions for rearranging parts or strengthening connections.

Watchmen

Matthew Fontilla

Chaffey College
Rancho Cucamonga, California

Watchmen, a 2009 movie based on Alan Moore's graphic novel by the same name, is about a group of superheroes in an alternate-reality version of New York City in 1985. In this brief, exuberant review, Matthew Fontilla expresses his admiration for the style, characters, and overall intensity of the film. His review is designed for an audience who might see the movie based on his enthusiasm, and perhaps also for one that will identify as either "intellectual" or "geek." As you read, notice how Fontilla supports his judgment in each paragraph of his essay. Does it succeed in making you want to see *Watchmen*?

The film *Watchmen* is a "must see" for intellectuals and geeks alike; 1 its visual style surpasses that of all other comic book films. There is never a dull moment during the film because the cinematography is phenomenal and the philosophy, although slightly arcane, is scathingly profound; your eyes will never leave the screen and your mind will never stop deciphering the meaning of the film. A second viewing is highly recommended if you wish to grasp all the information and the metaphors; the only problem with this is the fact that you will have spent six hours and twelve minutes watching it twice. However, if you take a lesson from Doctor Manhattan, you should be able to regard time as meaningless, which will allow you to appreciate this film without worrying about the hours passing by. *Watchmen* is a masterpiece because of its elucidation of the plight of society, the pains of superiority, and the limits of time. The characters illustrate these points by their vigilance, noncompliance with authority, and wisdom.

Watchmen alludes to fear in society being like a wildfire; it spreads   2
rapidly and the masses do nothing to impede its spread. Only a few
vigilantes will, sometimes foolishly, put their lives on the line in an
effort to put a stop to something bigger than themselves. The Watchmen are these few vigilantes in a fire that is the fear of, among many
other issues, a seemingly inevitable nuclear war. Vigilantes are not
always heroes, though. This moral complexity is one of the reasons
why *Watchmen* is such a great film. While the Watchmen are superheroes, their actions aren't always justifiable. A recurring theme in the
film is the question: "Who watches the Watchmen"? This suggests
that the public is not always grateful for the actions of the Watchmen.
They are frequently violent, occasionally destroy public property, and
cannot always help the society they are a part of.

A brilliant aspect of the film lies underneath the costumes; a cer-   3
tain degree of noncompliance is at the heart of all vigilantes. Each one
is reluctant to follow the rules of society or even to follow a leader
within the group. Although the Watchmen have a history as a public
group, they are not always willing to comply with the public's demands.
At the time the film is set, their superpowers have been made illegal;
only two Watchmen are active, with government approval. However,
each member of the Watchmen exemplifies this noncompliance in his
or her own way. Rorschach, the member of the Watchmen who narrates the film, is perhaps the least compliant of the group. He is an independent, hardly a member of the group at all. His bitterness about
the immorality of society leads him to kill those whom he considers im-
moral; the viewer must consider whether his actions are morally just.

A notable quote from the film that will give some insight on the   4
wisdom of each character is: "My father was a watchmaker. He aban-
doned it when Einstein discovered time is relative. I would only agree
that a symbolic clock is as nourishing to the intellect as a photograph
of oxygen to a drowning man." (The "symbolic clock" in the quote
is the nuclear doomsday clock, which indicates symbolically how close
the world is to nuclear war.) The Watchmen have cultivated wisdom
by analyzing the malice of society, and the people who contribute to
it, throughout their decades of existence. Thus, fearful symbols like
the doomsday clock mean little to them. They each hold steadfast beliefs on how to remake a malevolent society, even if that means destroying it.

If you are looking to view an intellectually stimulating thriller, a   5
compelling superhero action film, or both, watch *Watchmen*. The deep

symbolism throughout the film will leave you in awe, and the action sequences will have your palms sweaty in no time. Your imagination will be grateful, as long as you are willing to dedicate your undivided attention to the screen for almost three hours.

Evaluation of Nickel and Dimed

Jane Kim

University of California, Riverside
Riverside, California

For this essay, Jane Kim chose to evaluate *Nickel and Dimed*, Barbara Ehrenreich's firsthand investigation into the lives of the working poor. In her very first paragraph, Kim presents the reader with enough information about the book to understand her position on the book and its argument. Then Kim easily leads us through her well-organized argument, using relevant quotations from the book to support her judgments. As you read, notice the criteria Kim sets up for evaluating Ehrenreich's work.

Barbara Ehrenreich, a journalist with a PhD in biology, reports her experience in the world of the working poor in her book *Nickel and Dimed*. As an investigative reporter and scientist, she creates an experiment, sets some limits, takes a few necessities, and detaches herself from the upper-class world, which she is familiar with, and inserts herself into the society of the impoverished. She gains firsthand experience in what it feels like to live on a barely livable wage, always hoping to have shelter and nourishment the next day. She works as a waitress, a maid, a dietary aide, and an employee of Wal-Mart, while trying to sustain herself off just what she makes at these jobs, minus the advantages she came in with in her experiment (car, extra cash, and health). Ehrenreich, through her hands-on experience, evinces the difficulty and almost impossibility of living off the wages such workers make (as of 2001). Overall, Ehrenreich does a fair job of revealing the situation of the working poor and making it clear that something must be done to relieve this "state of emergency" (Ehrenreich 214).

Ehrenreich presents her argument that it is very difficult to "live   2
on the wages available to the unskilled" as "many people earn far less
than they need to live on" through excellent uses of supporting evidence (Ehrenreich 1, 213). Furthermore, to persuade her readers that
her claim is important, Ehrenreich shows the wage rise over the years,
saying "wages at the bottom are going up, [but] they're not going
up very briskly" and "they have not been sufficient to bring low-wage
workers up to the amounts they were earning twenty-seven years ago,
in 1973" (Ehrenreich 203). The author clearly presents her position
and argument through effective diction and by revealing the seriousness of the issue, which should not be ignored, as the experiences of
low-wage workers "are not part of a sustainable lifestyle, even a lifestyle of chronic deprivation and relentless low-level punishment" (Ehrenreich 214).

By doing firsthand field research to add to her extensive library   3
and Internet research, the author makes an especially convincing argument. Describing the daily lives of low-wage workers makes her evidence authoritative. For example, in the second chapter, Ehrenreich
shares the experience she went through working two jobs: a weekend
position as a dietary aide at a nursing home ($7 an hour) and a 40-
hour per week maid position ($6.65). Even when working two jobs
and being thrifty, she reveals the difficulty of managing to pay for rent
and food. In terms of rent, she explains that "when the rich and the
poor compete for housing on the open market, the poor don't stand a
chance" and essentially "the poor have been forced into housing that is
more expensive, more dilapidated, or more distant from their places of
work" (Ehrenreich 199). Furthermore, to increase the effectiveness of
her argument that wages must be higher, the author reveals that even
when the low-wage worker receives aid, it is difficult to get it. When
she tried to obtain food from food pantries and emergency aid, it took
her seventy minutes of calling and driving to get around seven dollars
worth of food, with limited choices (Ehrenreich 103).

In addition to her personal experience, Ehrenreich uses other   4
authoritative sources to enhance her reliability, integrating statistical
sources within her text and citing those sources in footnotes. For example, to explain why wages don't rise, Ehrenreich refers to a report
by Louis Uchitelle in the *New York Times* on how "many employers
will offer almost anything — free meals, subsidized transportation,
store discounts — rather than raise wages" (Ehrenreich 204).

Without Ehrenreich's investigative reporting, it would be hard for   5
people outside of the low-wage working class to grasp the reality of the
problem. Through firsthand experience, Ehrenreich effectively reveals
the dark world of the daily life of the low-wage worker. She acknowledges that some readers could argue that she didn't truly experience
"poverty," as she went in with some advantages: a car (her own) or
a rental vehicle (paid with credit card instead of earned wages), the
cushion of relying on her credit card for food if she ever thought she
wouldn't have food the next day, and knowing she could end the
project at the particular location if she ran out of money for rent (Ehrenreich 5–6). Ehrenreich concedes this objection to her experiment,
explaining that "there was no way [she] was going to 'experience
poverty' or find out how it 'really feels' to be a long-term low-wage
worker" (Ehrenreich 6). Furthermore, she makes it clear that there
are people who endure much worse conditions than she does during
her experiment: "this is in fact the best-case scenario: a person with
every advantage that ethnicity and education, health and motivation
can confer attempting, in a time of exuberant prosperity, to survive in
the economy's lower depths" (Ehrenreich 10). Ehrenreich lets readers
know through such comments that she is not portraying herself as having experienced exactly what the impoverished face every day.

Another kind of objection Ehrenreich anticipates is that she   6
should not speak for others, but let them speak for themselves.
Although she concedes it would be better if they did speak and act
for themselves, Ehrenreich provides some information to support her
speaking out on behalf of the low-wage workers. She makes the point
that workers are often hesitant to form unions for fear of getting fired
because "the poorer they are, the more constrained their mobility usually is." She also notes that "help-wanted signs and want ads coyly re-
frain from mentioning numbers" so workers can't compare wages, and
of course their employers may "make it hard to air [their] grievances
to peers or to enlist other workers in a group effort to bring about
change" (Ehrenreich 205, 206, 209). Ehrenreich effectively argues
that low-wage workers do not have many opportunities to safely speak
for themselves, so she is justified in attempting to speak for them.

Overall, Ehrenreich's *Nickel and Dimed* is well written and effec-   7
tively enlightens readers on a situation facing members of their own
community. The author's use of personal experience and authoritative
resources gives her argument strength and believability. Her inclusion

of personal ethical indignation combined with effective rhetoric gives her argument an intensity that has the potential to move readers to action. She may not provide solutions to the problem she so vividly presents, but Ehrenreich achieves her goal of opening readers' eyes to the hardship of those who make the lives of others more comfortable at the expense of their own well-being.

WORK CITED

Ehrenreich, Barbara. *Nickel and Dimed*. New York: Metropolitan Books, 2001. Print.

May I Have This Dance?

Robert Nava

Riverside Community College
Riverside, California

We have all had the experience of coming away disappointed from an art exhibition or performance. After attending several "dreary and uninspiring" exhibits at his college's art gallery, Robert Nava was beginning to tire of such disappointments. Then one show—and one painting in particular—caught him pleasantly by surprise. Justifying an evaluation means more than just pointing out what you did or didn't like about a work. Evaluative authors should also provide reasons for their opinions and be able to support those reasons, and that means knowing their subject well. Experience helps, as do close or repeated viewings and, in some cases, additional research. Nava establishes his authority as an evaluator by noting his past experience at his college's art gallery. But he has also done his homework. Much of his essay is devoted to an examination of how color and texture work together in the painting to create the impression of movement. That examination required both a sustained viewing of the piece and an understanding of color theory, a concept Nava explains to his readers. We come away from Nava's essay with both a desire to see the painting in person and a new appreciation for color theory and its usefulness as an artist's strategy. It is a gift to the reader when an evaluation combines critique with insight or instruction.

A visit to the Riverside Community College art gallery can sometimes be dreary and uninspiring. Having seen the faculty art show before, I have found that the pieces on display become repetitive and tiresome, with the same artists displaying new pieces with the same style and technique they've used every year before. However, this year the faculty artists have produced quite a few surprises, one of which is *Dance VII* by Gina Han. At first glance, I disregarded the oil painting, thinking little or no effort had gone into creating it. What could be so special about a canvas covered in random blotches of color? On a second look, I discovered what was so exciting about *Dance VII*: the creation of movement through color, placement, and texture.

But to better appreciate *Dance VII*, a brief explanation of color theory is necessary. An important tool for any artist is the color wheel, an arrangement of primary (red, yellow, and blue) and secondary (orange, green, and violet) colors that logically blend into one another in a circle, or wheel. From the combination of the primary and secondary colors, all other colors are created. The primary colors, those colors that cannot be created by mixing other colors, are equidistant from one another on the wheel. Secondary colors are those colors created by mixing two primary colors—for example, combining red and blue to create violet. There are also tertiary colors, which are made by mixing a primary color with its adjacent (on the color wheel) secondary color—for example, red (primary) mixed with orange (secondary) will create red-orange (tertiary). The color wheel in Figure 1 shows primary, secondary, and tertiary colors.

With the color wheel, we can also identify different color combinations that, oddly and without any notable explanation, are pleasing

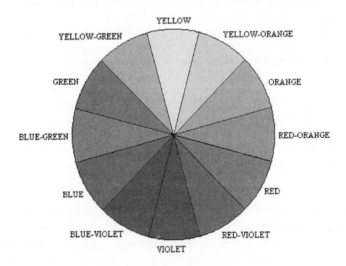

Figure 1. The color wheel.

to the eye. One of these combinations is called *complementary,* which is a pairing of two opposing or contrasting colors—such as red and green, blue and orange, or yellow and violet—that are positioned directly across from each other on the color wheel. These complementary relationships also extend to secondary colors, so that red-orange, for example, is complementary to blue-green. Another relationship on the color wheel involves harmonious colors, which are colors in the same section of the color wheel. The closest relationship, however, exists between a primary color and its secondary color.

Initially, *Dance VII* strikes the viewer as merely a colorful piece, but one of its functions is as a testing ground for color theory, creating radical—but acceptable—color combinations. In Figure 2, the majority of the color blotches are purple, violet, pink-violet, and red-violet, all of which are harmonious colors. The complementary color to violet is yellow, hence the background color. Another use of complementary colors is in the color blotches themselves. Each blotch consists of two "disks" of color, one overlapping the other. On occasion, these colors are complementary: green on top of red, violet on top of yellow, etc. On other occasions, however, the complementary colors are implied or less direct. For example, a little bit of green can be mixed into red to produce a new, toned-down version of red that complements green in an interesting and fresh way. 4

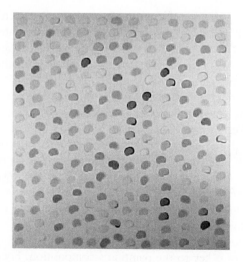

Figure 2. *Dance VII* by Gina Han. Oil on canvas (Han).

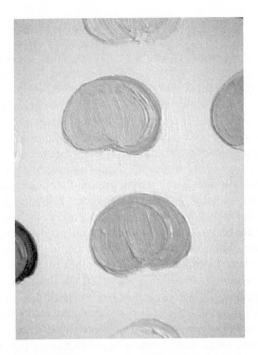

Figure 3. A visual relationship can be found between adjacent blotches (Han).

Another noticeable element in *Dance VII* is that each color blotch 5
is in some way related to one or more color blotches immediately surrounding it. The two blotches in the center of Figure 3 have a color
in common: pink. Han uses exactly the same pink for the top "disk"
of the lower blotch as she does for the bottom "disk" of the upper
blotch. The upper blotch relates to the one above it because Han has
used the same greenish color on each blotch's top "disk." The uppermost blotch in Figure 3 is linked to the blotch on the right because
Han has used harmonious violet colors for the uppermost blotch's
bottom "disk" and the right-hand blotch's top and bottom "disks."
The violet-on-violet right-hand blotch is linked to the lower blotch because the lower blotch's bottom "disk" is also a shade of violet. These
playful relationships appear throughout the entire piece, creating paths
of color for the viewers' eyes to follow.

In addition to the clever use of color, the placement of the indi- 6
vidual blotches is key to the painting's composition. Focusing on the
perimeter of *Dance VII*, we see that the blotches are, for the most part,

lined up neatly. Toward the center of the painting, the blotches begin to break up and "move around," forcing our eyes to wander around without focusing on any single blotch. Once the orderly relationship of blotches begins to break down, the color relationships come into play, bringing order to a largely chaotic environment.

Texture also contributes to movement. The entire piece is smothered in thick applications of paint, and the brushes' bristles carved deep grooves as they were dragged across the canvas. The most noticeable elements of the painting are the blotches, which have the densest application of paint (see Figure 4), but in the negative space, or background, we can see peaks and valleys in the thick layers of paint. These textured strokes intentionally flow around the blotches like ocean currents sweeping against a collection of islands, suggesting movement. The background's fluid-like texture keeps viewers' eyes moving, cunningly redirecting them, again and again. 7

Dance VII is an exciting surprise. The painting disguises itself as an unexciting, effortless piece and then jumps out at the viewers if they dare to examine it more closely. The exploration of color relationships initially draws in the viewers, inviting them to participate. But over time, the viewers will begin to see the relationships between the blotches of color. Their eyes begin to move, and they are swept 8

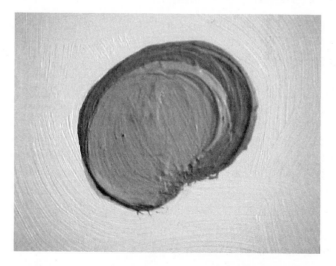

Figure 4. Thick applications of paint create texture, adding to the suggestion of movement (Han).

away in a whirling assortment of color and texture. As suggested by the painting's title, *Dance VII* conveys a fluid, harmonious movement among its colors, well-placed blotches, and textures.

WORK CITED

Han, Gina. *Dance VII*. N. d. Oil on canvas. Riverside Community College Art Gallery, Riverside, CA.

Satellite Radio
Julie Plucinski

Triton College
River Grove, Illinois

Julie Plucinski offers an evaluation from a consumer's viewpoint; she explains the benefits of satellite radio, considers potential concerns, and provides readers with details that allow them to make an informed decision. She begins by telling her audience about the merits the company boasts on its Web site, then provides reasons and support for this judgment based on her personal experience. This essay can, at times, read like a professional advertisement. As the reader, does this form of consumer enthusiasm attract you to a potential product or service, or are you wary of what might come across as a sales pitch? What other methods does Plucinski employ to justify her evaluation?

It's 4:23 in the afternoon, and I am stuck in bumper-to-bumper traffic on the way home from work. Flipping through the local radio stations to ease my tension yields little release from the aggravation. Commercials hawking the new blockbuster movie or cell phone sale with a local wireless company blare through my speakers. Is it too much to ask for some actual music? Satellite radio to the rescue!

"It's like nothing you've ever heard before" boasts the SiriusXM Web site (SiriusXM.com). That statement couldn't be any more accurate. A subscription to SiriusXM satellite radio grants a consumer immediate access to over 130 channels including 71 commercial-free music broadcasts. If you aren't in the mood for music you can always turn to one of the many comedy, sports, kid-friendly, weather, or news channels offered for your listening pleasure. Content on SiriusXM radio is static-free (due to its transmission via satellite) and uncensored (Guttenberg and Moskovciak). Additionally, the listener is able to view a song's title and artist on the face of the radio, which can be noted for future downloads to your iPod. A vast array of static-free, clearly displayed channels that are uncensored, and all of the songs played in their original format. What's not to love?

Prior to purchasing a subscription you must obtain a car radio capable of receiving a satellite radio. (Lucky for us, most foreign and domestic vehicles produced over the past few model years are technologically advanced and automatically equipped with satellite capable radio systems as standard.) If your existing vehicle does not come equipped with a receiver capable of obtaining satellite radio, one may be purchased at a cost ranging anywhere from $90 to $249.   3

Some may wish to forgo satellite radio in exchange for a "cheaper" option such as an iPod adapter wire or wireless transmitter. These devices would allow an individual with an iPod to stream previously downloaded music through their car stereo. However, there would be cost involved in purchasing an iPod and additional hardware required to stream music that had previously been downloaded for $0.99 on iTunes. If a consumer downloaded 500 songs on their $200 iPod, the total cost would add up to almost $700! Any perceived savings are eliminated and, actually, far exceed the cost of a satellite receiver and subscription to SiriusXM satellite radio. I had personally tested both the wired and wireless music streaming devices. The wired option works well but has one major flaw. If the driver does not want to hear a song that begins to play, the user would need to physically pick up the iPod and navigate the various, tiny display screens in search of another tune. All of this manual activity would be highly difficult to do while driving and could lead to an accident. The wireless adapter does not work at all as reception is fuzzy and wanes in and out in search of a signal. Leave the iPod for the office or gym, and avoid the risk of having an avoidable collision. Get a SiriusXM receiver and subscription!   4

Once you have made the decision to purchase a SiriusXM radio subscription, I strongly urge you to write down your satellite radio number. This information will be required to activate your subscription. I purchased a car in 2009 that came with a free six-month trial subscription. When it came time for me to purchase a SiriusXM subscription package I encountered quite a bit of difficulty finding the radio number. In fact, finding the radio number was the most difficult part of the entire process.   5

I would recommend purchasing a subscription via their Web site. 6
Their site is very easy to navigate and provides the user with channel
information, pricing details, and user testimonials. Once a user has decided on the desired package content, he or she can simply click on the
"Subscriptions" tab at the top of the page. The screens walk the future
satellite-radio listener through the steps of entering billing data and the
radio number, choosing a term length, and activating the subscription.
Activating the account does take a few minutes as SiriusXM must trans-
mit a signal from a satellite to the radio, but the wait is well worth it.

For those who may be initially overwhelmed by the wide vari- 7
ety of content, a channel guide will be mailed to you once you have
subscribed and will be an invaluable resource when programming all
of your preset channels. When in doubt, you can always visit the SiriusXM Web site for up-to-date information on channel content and live
concert events. These resources are capable of introducing the listener
to a whole new genre of music, providing years of future enjoyment.

The question you are surely asking yourself is "Why would I 8
pay for radio that I can get for free through my local channels?" My
number one response to that inquiry would be that satellite radio is
commercial-free! There is virtually no need to change the channel to
find worthwhile listening content. Yes, you must purchase a plan, which
will be automatically renewed until the time in which you cancel your
subscription. If you wish to cancel your subscription you must contact
SiriusXM within three business days to incur no additional charges. I
spend a considerable amount of time in my car and would gladly pay
around $15 per month to avoid commercials. Many other consumers
appear to be following this trend as SiriusXM recently raised their projected revenue outlook for 2012 from $3.3 billion to approximately
$3.4 billion (SiriusXM). Almost 1.6 million vehicular and Internet sub-
scribers can't be wrong.

Another key feature I like about satellite radio is that the channels 9
are broken down by genre. One day I may need a quick cure for the
morning doldrums and blare the '80s channel on the way to the office. On my way home, I may want to be transported back to my high
school years and yearn for some grunge rock. Yes, some local radio
stations do provide commercial-free radio. However, the channels are
few and far between and do not offer the extensive variety SiriusXM
satellite radio provides. Occasionally, SiriusXM will even offer specialty
stations premiering the work of one specific artist for an entire month.
Some friends and family may think that I am a little too old, but a pack

of wild horses couldn't tear me away from the Metallica channel in March of 2009. I have not yet found a local commercial-free channel with this advantage. You can always find a genre or artist channel to suit your mood on SiriusXM satellite radio.

Want to take your favorite channels with you on a road trip? Sat- 10
ellite radio offers coast-to-coast coverage spanning over 3,717,792 square miles (SiriusXM). The days of driving over the Illinois border and losing a radio signal are long gone! SiriusXM satellite streaming ensures that you will be discoing all the way to California. An article from *Travel & Leisure* magazine contradicts my view on this topic. In this review the author feels that the local music heard over regular radio frequencies connects him to the state or area in which he travels; he cites radio as "one way the world around you gets into the cocoon of your car" (Torkells). Some individuals may prefer listening to country music while coasting through Texas or Bluegrass while driving through Louisiana. I am not one of those people.

SiriusXM satellite radio continually improves their service by 11
launching new satellites into space. However, the listener can expect one minor drawback. Your SiriusXM radio signal will wane a bit when passing through enclosed spaces such as a viaduct, bridge, or heavily wooded area. The signal from the satellite cannot pass through these types of enclosures. These outages are usually very brief, lasting no more than a few seconds.

Another item that diehard morning show fans may miss is impor- 12
tant or trending local news updates. You can listen to a Chicago-based news station on satellite but will likely be put to sleep by the broadcast-er's monotone, sociology lecture, teacher-from-hell simulcast. Sleeping and operating heavy machinery is never a good combination! A few of the pop music channels do offer some of the morning show banter you may have come to love from your local channels, but the listener is constantly reminded of the fact that the broadcast is produced in a New York-based studio. So long as you do not come to expect Rod Blagojevich jokes or happenings in the Chicagoland area, your longing for a locally based morning show crew will be short-lived.

Consumers are no longer forced to listen to countless hours of 13
commercials while waiting to hear the latest pop music hit song. Advancements in technology have given us the gift of an alternate means for obtaining entertainment on the road. While SiriusXM satellite radio is not without some minor flaws, the aforementioned nuances

are a small price to pay for the sheer variety of listening entertainment offered and commercial-free convenience.

WORKS CITED

Guttenberg, Steve, and Matthew Moskovciak. "CNET's Quick Guide to Satellite Radio." *CNET.* CBS Interactive Inc., 1 March 2005. Web. 14 July 2012.

"Sirius XM Radio Raises Revenue Outlook." *CNBC.* CNBC, 9 July 2012. Web. 12 July 2012.

Siriusxm.com. Siriusxm.com, n.d. Web. 12 July 2012.

Torkells, Eric. "XM and SIRIUS Satellite Radio." *Travel & Leisure.* American Express Publishing Corporation, April 2001. Web. 12 July 2012.

9 *Speculating about Causes*

Beginning your day, you wonder why your car is increasingly hard to start. Driving to campus, you puzzle over why you seem unable to make better use of your study and homework time. Circling the parking lot looking for a space, you fret about what could be holding up ground breaking for the promised multistory parking structure. This kind of thinking is so natural that your brain does it for you, without any urging or pushing. You couldn't really stop yourself from thinking about the whys and hows of things—even if you wanted to.

But fretful and even obsessive as this kind of thinking may be sometimes, you wouldn't want to shut it off because it could save you time if it inspires you to remove some obstacle; it could make you wiser if it leads to new understanding about yourself, other people, or the world at large; it could make you happier if it results in reaching a long-sought goal. Nevertheless, this daily causal thinking—about how something you notice came to be the way it is, or why something happened or continues to happen— is idle and unsystematic.

Yet this is the basis for a more demanding, sustained kind of causal thinking, the kind you will find in the essays of this chapter—essays that speculate about the possible causes of phenomena or trends. (To *speculate* means to conjecture, wonder, or guess, or even to hypothesize or theorize. It can imply risk, play, uncertainty, and chance. A *phenomenon* is something noticeable that occurs or happens. This kind of essay can also speculate about a *trend*—something that has changed or is changing over time.) The student essay writers in this chapter speculate about these phenomena: Why are more people right-handed than left-handed? Why would an immigrant to the United States choose not to learn English? What could motivate a person to commit serial murder? These phenomena are the students' subjects, which are well defined and described in the essays. But that's usually the easy part.

The hard part is speculating about the causes of these phenomena. Instead of idle speculation, you are trying to convince readers that your proposed causes are plausible or likely. As you read the essays in this chapter, note the basic features of the genre used to influence readers: a well-supported causal analysis; an effective response to objections and alternative causes; and a clear, logical organization. The causes you propose may come from your own experience, from research, or both. The writing engages you in sustained, systematic thinking to answer a significant social, cultural, or political question—sustained because it's going to take you awhile; systematic because you will need to select the most likely of many possible causes, sequence them logically, and support them so that they seem plausible, all with the aim of convincing particular readers to take your speculations seriously.

The rewards are great. Along with the other kinds of argument writing in this book, speculating about causes enables you to become the kind of person who confidently inquires deeply into events. You expect there is usually more to know than first appears. Adopting this stance, you join a new culture of debate, reflection, initiative, and knowledge seeking. Gaining confidence, you shake off old constraints and limits.

Use the guidelines in the Critical Reading Guide (below) to practice peer review using the essays in this chapter.

A Critical Reading Guide

A WELL-PRESENTED SUBJECT

How effectively does the writer present the subject?

Summarize: Tell the writer what you understand the subject to be and why he or she thinks it is important and worth analyzing.

Praise: Give an example of something in the draft that you think will especially interest the intended readers and help them understand the subject.

Critique: Tell the writer if you have any confusion or uncertainty about the subject. What further explanation, examples, or statistics do you need to understand it better? If you can think of a more interesting way to present the subject, share your ideas with the writer.

A WELL-SUPPORTED CAUSAL ANALYSIS

How plausible are the proposed causes, and how well does the writer support the causal analysis?

Summary: Identify the possible causes the writer argues are the most plausible and interesting.

Praise: Tell the writer which cause seems most convincing. Point to any support (such as a particular example, a statistic, a research study, or a graph) that you think is especially strong.

Critique: Tell the writer if any of the causes seem too obvious or minor, and if you think an important cause has been left out. Where the support seems lacking or unconvincing, explain what is missing or seems wrong. If the reasoning seems flawed, what makes you think so?

AN EFFECTIVE RESPONSE TO OBJECTIONS AND ALTERNATIVE CAUSES

How effectively does the writer respond to readers' objections and alternative causes?

Summary: Identify the objections or alternative causes to which the writer responds.

Praise: Point out any response you think is especially effective, and tell the writer what makes you think so. For example, indicate where the support is especially credible and convincing.

Critique: Point to any objections or alternative causes that the writer could have responded to more effectively, and suggest how the response could be improved. Also indicate if the writer has overlooked any serious objections.

A CLEAR, LOGICAL ORGANIZATION

How clear and logical is the causal analysis?

Summary: Underline the thesis statement and topic sentences.

Praise: Give an example of where the essay succeeds in being especially clear and easy to follow—for example, in its overall organization, its use of key terms and transitions, or its use of visuals.

Critique: Point to any passages where the writing could be clearer, where topic sentences or transitions could be added, or where key terms could be repeated to make the essay easier to follow. Try suggesting a better beginning or a more effective ending.

Left Out

Virginia Gagliardi

Lebanon Valley College
Annville, Pennsylvania

As you begin to conduct research for your essay, you may discover that an issue doesn't always have one clear cause. When this happens, how do you ensure that your discussion of the topic is strong? For Virginia Gagliardi, the biggest challenge was incorporating the various causes she had discovered. She solved this problem by organizing them into three main subject areas: genetics and physiology, general influences, and local influences. As you read, you'll notice that Gagliardi relies on research for both her proposed causes and her support of those causes. Altogether, she makes good use of six different sources for this short essay. Instead of merely patching the sources together, she imposes her own plan and selectively paraphrases and quotes the sources only as they are relevant to the three main causes she addresses.

Behavioral differences that cause one limb or sense organ to be preferred for certain activities, despite the apparently insignificant differences in their morphology, constitute a problem that . . . has fascinated scientists and laymen for centuries. (Coren 2)

Opening a can, drawing a straight line, and writing a sentence are three basic activities that display our *handedness*, or the "differential or preferred use of one hand in situations where only one can be used" (Coren 2). Handedness presents itself in two well-known categories—right- and left-handedness. But what causes each of us to be either right- or left-handed? Why are there so many fewer left-handed people than right-handed people? For years, scientists thought handedness was genetic; however, no genetic theory accounts for the ratio

1

of right- to left-handers, and the exact contribution of factors to predisposition to one side remains unknown. Genetic models propose many different ideas about the roles of genes in handedness, but as McManus writes in *Right Hand, Left Hand: The Origins of Asymmetry in Brains, Bodies, Atoms and Cultures,* "what they cannot do is tell us exactly what it is that makes us right- or left-handed" (163). A combination of factors in physiology, history, and society explains why genetics plays only a minor role in a Western bias toward one side—the right side—of the body.

Perhaps the most basic explanation of handedness is the initial genetic theory, which states that genetics determines handedness through a specific gene inherited from parents. If both parents have the right-handed gene, the children will all become right-handed; in contrast, if both parents have the left-handed gene, the children would all become left-handed. Since there are fewer lefties in the world than right-handed people, the model appears to fulfill conceptions for why handedness occurs and why left-handedness occurs less often than right-handedness. In the book *Left Brain, Right Brain,* however, Sally P. Springer and Georg Deutsch elaborate on the extensive biological studies of this genetic model. The biologists who conducted these studies quickly discovered that in comparison with obtained data about handedness, "this [genetic] model cannot account for the fact that 54 percent of the offspring of two left-handed parents are right-handed" (108). So how does this possible cause fail? If the genetic model were accurate, reported data would show that two left-handed parents would have only left-handed children. Therefore, new studies began in an attempt to repair this theory with a complementary, yet more complex, model.

After many studies attempting to salvage this basic genetic theory, the idea of "variable penetrance" arose. Variable penetrance means "that all individuals with the same genotype [pattern of genes] may not express that genotype in the same way" (Springer and Deutsch 108). Simply put, the statement suggests that although the genes make the parents left-handed, the combination that passes to the child may not cause left-handedness in the child. This speculation provides the explanation for two left-handers having right-handed children; however, "even with variable penetrance built into the [allele] model, the [variable penetrance] model's 'goodness of fit' to actual data is less than satisfactory" (Springer and Deutsch 108). The probability of left-handedness increases as the number of left-handed parents increases.

However, the real-life data does not coincide with the theory. According to McManus, the fact that handedness "runs in the family" (156) remains distinguishable, but exactly how remains a mystery.

A third theory suggests that nurture determines handedness, 4 not nature—or genetics—itself. Scientists base the theory on how handedness appears, not on which side it appears. In this case, genetics would determine handedness, just not a particular side to the handedness. Simplified, the design suggests, "If your mother and father are strongly handed [very reliant on one side], although we can't predict on the basis of their handedness whether you will be right- or left-handed, we can predict that you will be strongly handed. It is the strength . . . that is genetically variable" (Coren 91). Of all the theories, this idea proves the most plausible.

While genetics undoubtedly participates in determination of hand- 5 edness, the suggestion that nurture more likely decides the side of handedness continues as the most logical "genetic" explanation. As McManus explains, "there are many things that run in families that are not inherited through genes" (157), such as parents' influence on their children in the development of handedness. The explanation lies in the fact that parents "convey basic pattern[s] of behavior to children" (Porac and Coren 108). Probably the most fundamental behavior learned is in the use of utensils. Parents "teach them [children] to use their first tools, such as spoons, knives, and pencils . . ." (Porac and Coren 108), so if the child's predisposition favors left-handedness but he continually learns right-handed motions, he will essentially develop into a right-handed child. This situation provides yet another example of the formation of handedness and how right-handedness forces itself into culture. The most easily defined reason for handedness presents itself every day in society: Many people adopt right-handedness for ease of life and teach their children to do the same. This thought about the influence of nurture extends into the fact that handedness incorporates history into its origins.

Religion, which tends to be derived from nurture, is one of the 6 most controversial historical justifications for handedness in Western culture. This idea is obviously seen in biblical illustrations. Followers of many Christian religions resort to right-handedness as a result of beliefs or traditions. The notion that left-handedness engages the devil explicates this fact. Passages from the Bible further reinforce these principles, such as the verses found in Matthew 25:34–41 in the New Testament:

> Then shall the King say unto them on His right hand, "Come ye blessed
> of my Father, inherit the kingdom prepared for you from the foundation
> of the world." . . . Then shall He say also unto them on the left hand,
> "Depart from Me, ye cursed, into everlasting fire, prepared for the devil
> and his angels." . . . And these shall go away into everlasting punishment;
> but the righteous into life eternal. (qtd. in Springer and Deutsch 105)

The Creator's association with the right hand strongly biases Chris-
tians toward the right hand, or the right side in general. Thus, this
preference flows into other aspects of Christian culture. The most
prominent example is in the sign of the cross, performed only with
the right hand; using the left hand is sacrilegious. Another example appears during Communion, when the communicant receives the wafer
in the left hand so that the clean, right hand can transfer the wafer to
the mouth (Fincher 32).

The bias, though, does not limit itself to the church; it also ex- 7
tends into portraits concerning religion. Why, then, is there a "marked
tendency in classical renderings of the Madonna and child" (Fincher
30) to illustrate Mary holding Jesus on her left side? Analysts propose
several reasons. According to Fincher, some analysts of the portraits
suggest that the cause lies in the idea of freeing the "right hand for
other, better things" (30). On the contrary, Fincher himself distin-
guishes the motive as something else: "Putting the child on Mary's
left puts Him on the viewer's—and the art work's—right, clearly the
place of honor" (31). Essentially, religion provides incentive for left-
handers to become right-handers; however, religion remains just one
aspect of history that influences this partiality for one side of the body.

For those people who lack a religious affiliation, the simple act of 8
speaking holds an effect equivalent to the effect of religion on handedness because language places a stigma on left-handedness. Consistently,
favorable connotations referring to right-handedness emerge in several
languages. Fincher illustrates this idea from the word "riht, Anglo-
Saxon for straight, erect, or just" (37). He also uses the "French word
for right, droit, [which] also means 'correct' and 'law'" (37), to further
demonstrate the point of language as a root of favoritism in handedness. Springer and Deutsch point out that "the French word for 'left,'
gauche, also means 'clumsy'" and that "mancino is Italian for 'left' as
well as for 'deceitful'" (104). They also explain that the Spanish phrase
"no ser zurdo," which means "to be clever," translates directly as "to
not be left-handed" (104). As terrible as those definitions appear, most
Western languages have them—including the English language.

In English the term "left-handed" has derogatory classifications. 9
For example, *Webster's Third International Dictionary* lists several definitions of the adjective "left-handed," including the following:

> a: marked by clumsiness or ineptitude: awkward; b: exhibiting deviousness or indirection: oblique, unintended; c: obs.: given to malevolent scheming or contriving: sinister, underhand. (qtd. in Springer and Deutsch 104)

Similarly, analysis of the English language reveals common phrases filled with bias. "For instance, a *left-handed compliment* is actually an insult. A *left-handed marriage* is no marriage at all. To be about *left-handed business* is to be engaged in something unlawful or unsavory" (Coren 2). On the contrary, "to be someone's *right-hand man* means to be important and useful to that person" (Coren 2). Over time, this tainting of a certain handedness carries over into everyday life and remains one of several reasons why left-handers may try to become right-handers or at least ambidextrous. Other motives to switch revolve around the impressions and pressures of social traditions.

One of the largest-scale examples lies in written language. The 10
system of the written English language solely supports right-handed people because "[written] alphabetic languages . . . were designed for right-handers" (Ornstein 83). Coren explains the differences in the mechanics of left- and right-handed writing as:

> Our left-to-right writing pattern is set up for a right-handed writer. The most comfortable and controlled hand movement is a pull across the body. For the right-hander it is a left-to-right movement, and for the left-hander it is reversed. (230)

Due to the way a left-hander pulls across his body, his hand will rub over words he has already written, whereas a right-hander always moves his hand away from the words he has already written. This problem forces left-handers into unnatural hand positions during writing; most primary school teachers attempt to persuade left-handed children into writing right-handed. In fact, the "Victorians even invented a vicious leather device with a belt and buckles for strapping the left hand firmly behind the back" (McManus 268). Writing, although the most obvious of problems, remains just one of many issues for a left-hander in a right-handed society.

Every day, left-handers encounter issues with common tools that 11
right-handers take for granted. A simple household item, such as a can opener, can become the most complex of items for a leftie. Because a

can opener "is designed to be held with the left hand while the cutting gear is operated by rotating a handle with the right hand" (Coren 223), using the instrument left-handed "forces the left-hander into a set of ungainly contortions" (Coren 223). Another example surfaces in the use of knives, typically beveled on only one side—the right side. Having the knife designed as such aids the "right-hander by producing a force which holds the blade upright" (Coren 227), causing the slice to peel outward from the material, rather than toward it. Still other issues outside of household items exist only for lefties.

More problems affecting left-handers reside in locations such as school and work. The simple process of using a ruler becomes a difficult task for a left-handed individual. The ruler, designed with right-handers in mind, presents numbers in a left-to-right fashion, much like the written English language. "This [style] makes sense for the right-hander because the motion of drawing the line usually begins at the 'zero inch' location on the far left and continues . . . until it reaches the mark indicating the desired length, somewhere to the right" (Coren 231). For a leftie, however, this system poses several problems:

> [This process] requires the left-hander to cover the numbers while drawing the line with a pulling motion across the body from right to left. The left-hander also covers the end of the ruler . . . causing a tendency for the pen to suddenly drop off the end of the ruler if the line is drawn too quickly and the unseen "zero inch" point is reached before the pen is stopped. (Coren 231)

Saws create problems by exposing body parts dangerously close to the blade. "When the right hand is used, the arm and elbow flare out to the side, safely away from the saw blade" (Coren 237), protecting a right-handed person from injury. Yet "if a left-hander wants to use this equipment, he must either use his right hand to hold the work . . . or cross his body with his left hand which places his arm directly in line with the saw blade" (Coren 237). This design forces a left-hander to resort to right-handedness temporarily or even permanently in many factory and workshop settings. However, these mechanical influences cannot solely explain the phenomena of left-handedness.

The combination of these factors forms a basis for handedness in the world. Right- and left-handedness appear as common expressions in everyday life, but the existence of both presents a misconception. Due to factors in physiology, history, and society, handedness appears in two forms, but not in right- and left-handedness. Rather, handed-

12

13

ness categorizes into right-handedness and ambidextrous handedness for the sole reason that "to survive in this right-sided world, left-handers soon learn to do with the right hand many things that the right-hander could never and will never do with the left. The end result is a degree of ambidexterity" (Porac and Coren 95). Perhaps only one form of handedness exists, since, according to Porac and Coren, essentially "the left-hander must become more right-handed" (95). This idea reinforces the reason why right-handedness appears more often than left-handedness. Therefore, even though the exact cause of handedness remains unknown, the residue of known facts points not toward a right- and left-handed world, but in the direction of a world that completely relies on one-sided handedness.

WORKS CITED

Coren, Stanley. *The Left-Hander Syndrome: The Causes and Consequences of Left-Handedness.* New York: Macmillan, 1992. Print.

Fincher, Jack. *Lefties: The Origins and Consequences of Being Left-Handed.* New York: Barnes and Noble, 1993. Print.

McManus, Chris. *Right Hand, Left Hand: The Origins of Asymmetry in Brains, Bodies, Atoms and Cultures.* Cambridge: Harvard UP, 2002. Print.

Ornstein, Robert. *The Right Mind.* New York: Harcourt Brace, 1997. Print.

Porac, Clare, and Stanley Coren. *Lateral Preferences and Human Behavior.* New York: Springer-Verlag, 1981. Print.

Springer, Sally P., and Georg Deutsch. *Left Brain, Right Brain.* San Francisco: W. H. Freeman, 1981. Print.

Hispanic Pride vs. American Assimilation

Stephanie Cox

Metropolitan Community College
Omaha, Nebraska

Stephanie Cox takes a stand on a hot-button social and political issue: a growing trend among Hispanic immigrants to choose not to learn English. Many Americans would be unsympathetic to a flat refusal to learn English. Cox too admits some preconceived notions on the matter; however, she keeps an open mind. She wants to know more about the subject before she judges the decision. To engage her readers' interest and provide a concrete example they will identify with, Cox first relates the story of a Spanish-speaking mother who loses her little girl and is unable to communicate. Cox then defines the phenomenon of acculturation and forecasts three causes, or explanations, that she will argue for. Her plan is simple and visible, and because her research is motivated by curiosity rather than preconceived ideas, her essay is effective.

My heart ached for the woman. She was visibly distressed and seemed to grow more agitated by the minute. Tiny beads of perspiration were beginning to form on her brow, and the black purse she carried shook in her trembling grasp. She was desperately trying to tell me something, but I was unable to understand. She spoke Spanish and I didn't. After many awkward attempts at communication, the woman's ten-year-old English-speaking son was located. His translation revealed her worry over her missing toddler. It seems the child had wandered off while her mother was visiting a pastor of the church I work for. With the woman's son's help, we gathered enough details about her daughter's disappearance to locate the child, who had been playing in an empty classroom.

Even though the situation seemed to have ended happily, I was   2
still troubled by it. If only the woman had known some English. The
church offered several excellent programs to help immigrants learn
about American culture and practice the English language. Had she
taken the help offered by the church, she would have been able to
communicate effectively enough to convey her message and prevent
unnecessary frustration and possibly dangerous delay. When I presented my concerns to one of the church pastors, I was surprised by his
response. This woman was at the church to pick up her son from an
English class. When she had been given the same opportunity, she quietly refused. While she felt strongly about the importance of English
for her son, she herself was proud of her Mexican heritage and had no
desire to become an English speaker.

I was shocked. Why would immigrants want to make their lives   3
more complicated by having to rely on others to communicate for
them? This woman must surely be an exception, I thought, but to my
surprise, she is among many Hispanic immigrants in the United States
who are acculturating rather than assimilating into American culture
(Grow et al.). Many Americans still view the United States as an ideal
nation, a model for the world, and assume everyone must surely want
to "be like us," but there is a new phenomenon among many U.S.
immigrants: active pride in their home cultures. This cultural pride is
especially evident among Hispanic immigrants who choose to adapt to
American culture without losing the traditions and values of their native countries.

Hispanics are one of the fastest growing and largest minority   4
groups in the United States, and they are developing their own version of the "true" American. Nearly nine out of ten Hispanics have
accepted the importance of adapting to American culture, while nearly
nine out of ten also believe it is extremely important to continue to
uphold the values and traditions of Latin America (Artze). This phenomenon of Hispanic acculturation rather than assimilation can be
witnessed in several cities and towns in the United States.

Perhaps one of the best examples of how Hispanics are striving   5
to maintain their own culture can be seen in Los Angeles. As early as
1950, Los Angeles contained the largest Hispanic population in the
country, and the conflict between assimilation and acculturation was
already beginning. Immigrants were forced to choose between American cultural traditions and the distinctive values of Latin America.
Today, you will find groups of new immigrants along with second- and

third-generation Hispanics all with the same goal in mind: to success-fully thrive in an ethnocentric culture without losing their own identity (Rodriguez).

While there may be quite a few reasons immigrants are reluctant to assimilate, forgetting old traits and adopting new ones, three are most prominent. First is the strong feeling of pride Hispanics have for their native countries and cultural values, and the security they feel when segregated from American society. Second is the close proxim-ity of Hispanics, especially Mexican Americans, to their native country. Third, and most startling, is the seeming lack of support from many Hispanic Americans to help new immigrants assimilate.   6

With the ever-increasing number of immigrants from Latin Amer-ica, it is not uncommon to find exclusively Hispanic communities within American towns and cities. These communities help to rein-force cultural traditions and pride, and make it unnecessary for immi-grants to adopt new cultural traits or learn the English language. Many Hispanic Americans feel not only comforted by their segregation but also are wary of the negative influences American society may have on their families (Branigin).   7

The self-segregation of many Hispanic immigrants in America can be compared to that of Americans who live and work abroad but re-main quite isolated from their host culture. A classmate of mine de-scribed living in Japan while her husband was stationed at a military base there. Day-to-day life revolved around American customs. Her children attended American schools on the military base; she shopped at military stores geared toward the wants and needs of Americans; and her family socialized with a close-knit group of American friends. On the rare occasions that she and her family left the military base, she was startled by the numerous stares and suspicious glances she and her family received from Japanese citizens. While confident that she and her family had done their best to adhere to Japanese societal norms, the reaction of the Japanese left her with the acute feeling that she was still very different, and the isolation of the military base offered her family a feeling of security.   8

My classmate's experience is mirrored by the experiences of many Hispanics living in the United States. In response to unsubstantiated fears of America becoming "Mexicanized," some politicians and gov-ernment officials are being urged to speak out against Hispanic im-migration. Most notably, border states such as California and Arizona are openly opposing immigration from Latin America by developing   9 new anti-immigration bills. California's Proposition 187 and Arizona's Proposition 200 would limit the public benefits received by illegal immigrants, and politicians acting on public support of these bills and hoping to seek reelection are motivated to develop even more anti-immigrant legislation (Judis). While these propositions are much more aggressive than suspicious stares, the message is the same: If you are different, you must be a threat.

In addition to feeling more comfortable within their own com- 10 munities, many Hispanic immigrants see isolation as a way to hold on to their cultural values. In California, where bilingual education is no longer the norm, children from Hispanic families are immediately submerged into the English language and thus into American culture. Many Hispanics feel that this immersion forces their children to choose between the values taught by their parents—such as the importance of family—and those of their new country (Rifkin).

Reluctance to assimilate is strengthened even more when tradi- 11 tional, conservative Hispanic families witness their children adopting negative aspects of American culture. Many Hispanics cite American gang violence when defending their decision to keep their children away from American culture. Alarmingly, Hispanic youth may actually be propelled toward gang life by the attitudes and stereotypes of Americans who mistakenly assume that most Latinos are illegal immigrants (Branigin). A quest for group identity and a sense of belonging can be a strong lure for Hispanic teens trying to find their place in an unsympathetic society.

Fear of negative influences impacting traditional cultural values 12 is not the only reason Hispanics have hesitated to adopt American culture. Unlike the majority of immigrants from other locations, Hispanics—especially Mexican Americans—have the privilege of living fairly close to their native country. It is not uncommon for many Hispanics to travel between their native and adopted countries on a regular basis. These frequent visits help reinforce the customs, values, and language of Latin America (Grow et al.).

This reinforcement of Hispanic customs and values is evidenced 13 not only by immigrants' attitudes toward American society but also by the many cultural traditions Hispanics bring to the United States. One tradition that is growing in popularity in America is the Quinceanera, the celebration of a Latina girl's fifteenth birthday. Historically rooted in Aztec and Roman Catholic customs, the Quinceanera is a time to celebrate a young girl's entrance into adulthood. While this lavish celebration is primarily a Hispanic one, which begins with a Roman Catholic Mass and ends with a reception in which the girl performs a dance with her father and members of her court, it is also showing signs of adaptation to American society. This can be seen in the celebrations held by Hispanics who are not members of the Roman Catholic Church, and who tend to invite friends of different ethnic heritages (Miranda). Once primarily a closed ceremony for family and close friends, the Quinceanera is expanding beyond its Latin American roots and replanting itself into Hispanic American culture.

Another example of a Hispanic cultural tradition celebrated in the United States is Cinco de Mayo. Celebrated on the fifth of May, this holiday commemorates the 1862 Battle of Puebla, one of the most glorious victories in Mexico's military history. When France attempted to take control of Mexico by force, a poorly equipped Mexican army was able to halt the invasion of the French powerhouse despite being outnumbered by thousands. This celebration, with its message of success despite overwhelming obstacles, inspires Hispanics to be proud of their heritage (Vargas). 14

Finally, many new immigrants to the United States may feel more comfortable within their own cultural group and hesitate to adapt to American culture because of discouragement from their own peers. Mexican Americans born and raised in the United States, called Chicanos, often humiliate new immigrants who are attempting to learn English. One immigrant teen, who despite three years in an English as a second language course still did not speak fluent English, believed the other students were laughing at her when she attempted to speak English (Branigin). This kind of teasing can lead to feelings of insecurity among newly arrived immigrants. 15

Not only are Hispanic children and teens experiencing discouragement from Mexican Americans, but so are many new immigrant adults who are seeking jobs in the United States. An immigrant named Antonio experienced this harsh reality when he found himself assigned to do one of the most laborious jobs in a meatpacking plant, while his cultural counterpart, a Chicano, was displaying the title of supervisor and taunting immigrant workers like him. In fact, in this particular meatpacking plant, it was quite common to see new immigrants from Mexico performing arduous tasks while enduring snide comments from their Chicano supervisors, who would make statements such as 16

"Go back to Mexico, wetback!" or "Chicanos numero uno!" (Campo-Flores). Humiliation like this can cause many immigrants to stay within their own communities, where they feel accepted.

The feelings of isolation felt by the immigrant teen and the feel-   17
ings of frustration felt by the immigrant worker Antonio shed new light on the complexities Latin American immigrants must face every day. Distrust of an unfamiliar culture mixed with strong pride in their own heritage has led to immigrants' longing to maintain the traits of their native country. As I remember the distraught woman who quietly yet proudly refused the pastor's offer to help her learn English, I can now respect her decision. She was quoted as saying, "I was Mexican at birth, I am Mexican today, and I will be Mexican forever."

WORKS CITED

Artze, Isis. "To Be and Not to Be." *Hispanic* Oct. 2000: 32–34. *EBSCOhost*. Web. 22 Jan. 2006.

Branigin, William. "Immigrants Shunning Idea of Assimilation." *Washington Post* 25 May 1998: A1+. Print.

Campo-Flores, Arian. "Brown against Brown." *Newsweek* Sept. 2000: 49–50. *EBSCOhost*. Web. 25 Jan. 2006.

Grow, Brian, Ronald Grover, Arlene Weintraub, Christopher Palmeri, Mara Der Hovenesian, and Michael Eidam. "Hispanic Nation." *Business Week* Mar. 2004: 58–70. *EBSCOhost*. Web. 10 Jan. 2006.

Judis, John B. "Border War." *The New Republic* 16 Jan. 2006: 15–19. Print.

Miranda, Carolina A. "Fifteen Candles." *Time* July 2004: 83. *EBSCOhost*. Web. 27 Jan. 2006.

Rifkin, Jane M. "Locked in Conflict with Mainstream America." *Hispanic Times* Dec. 1998–Jan. 1999: 40–41. *EBSCOhost*. Web. 22 Jan. 2006.

Rodriguez, Gregory. "Don't Mistake the Parts for the Whole in L.A." *Los Angeles Times* 6 July 2001: B15. Print.

Vargas, Roberto. "Cinco de Mayo: An Opportunity to Inspire Courage." *Hispanic* May 1999: 48. *EBSCOhost*. Web. 25 Jan. 2006.

What Makes a Serial Killer?

La Donna Beaty

Sinclair Community College
Dayton, Ohio

In most essays speculating about causes, conclusions must be tentative. However, don't let this scare you away from discussing phenomena that may not have obvious causation. La Donna Beaty approaches a topic—serial killers—that would seem to most to be an unsolvable mystery and systematically examines potential causes she uncovered in her research. Though it may not solve the problem, speculating about the reasons serial killers develop may be our best approach: the scientists and psychologists who continue such speculative work may one day find a humane way to treat potential killers. Beaty offers several possible triggers that, taken together, might turn a child into a serial killer, including psychological abuse, frequent moves, and genetic abnormalities, and she manages to discuss them without sensationalizing. As you read, notice how visibly Beaty signals her move from one cause to the next as the argument progresses.

1   Jeffrey Dahmer, John Wayne Gacy, Mark Allen Smith, Richard Chase, Ted Bundy—the list goes on and on. These five men alone have been responsible for at least ninety deaths, and many suspect that their victims may total twice that number. They are serial killers, the most feared and hated of criminals. What deep, hidden secret makes them lust for blood? What can possibly motivate a person to kill over and over again with no guilt, no remorse, no hint of human compassion? What makes a serial killer?

2   Serial killings are not a new phenomenon. In 1798, for example, Micajah and Wiley Harpe traveled the backwoods of Kentucky and Tennessee in a violent, yearlong killing spree that left at least

twenty—and possibly as many as thirty-eight—men, women, and children dead. Their crimes were especially chilling, as they seemed particularly to enjoy grabbing small children by the ankles and smashing their heads against trees (Holmes and DeBurger 28). In modern society, however, serial killings have grown to near epidemic proportions. Ann Rule, a respected author and expert on serial murders, stated in a seminar at the University of Louisville that between 3,500 and 5,000 people become victims of serial murder each year in the United States alone (qtd. in Holmes and DeBurger 21). Many others estimate that there are close to 350 serial killers currently at large in our society (Holmes and DeBurger 22).

Fascination with murder and murderers is not new, but researchers in recent years have made great strides in determining the characteristics of criminals. Looking back, we can see how naive early experts were in their evaluations: in 1911, for example, Italian criminologist Cesare Lombrosco concluded that "murderers as a group [are] biologically degenerate [with] bloodshot eyes, aquiline noses, curly black hair, strong jaws, big ears, thin lips, and menacing grins" (qtd. in Lunde 84). Today, however, we don't expect killers to have fangs that drip human blood, and many realize that the boy next door may be doing more than woodworking in his basement. While there are no specific physical characteristics shared by all serial killers, they are almost always male, and 92 percent are white. Most are between the ages of twenty-five and thirty-five and often physically attractive. While they may hold a job, many switch employment frequently, as they become easily frustrated when advancement does not come as quickly as expected. They tend to believe that they are entitled to whatever they desire but feel that they should have to exert no effort to attain their goals (Samenow 88, 96). What could possibly turn attractive, ambitious human beings into cold-blooded monsters?

One popular theory suggests that many murderers are the product of our violent society. Our culture tends to approve of violence and find it acceptable, even preferable, in many circumstances (Holmes and DeBurger 27). According to research done in 1970, one out of every four men and one out of every six women believed that it was appropriate for a husband to hit his wife under certain conditions (Holmes and DeBurger 33). This emphasis on violence is especially prevalent in television programs. Violence occurs in 80 percent of all prime-time shows, while cartoons, presumably made for children, average eighteen violent acts per hour. It is estimated that by the age of eighteen, the average child will have viewed more than 16,000 television murders (Holmes and DeBurger 34). Some experts feel that children demonstrate increasingly aggressive behavior with each violent act they view and become so accustomed to violence that these acts seem normal (Lunde 15, 35). In fact, most serial killers do begin to show patterns of aggressive behavior at a young age. It is, therefore, possible that after viewing increasing amounts of violence, such children determine that this is acceptable behavior; when they are then punished for similar actions, they may become confused and angry and eventually lash out by committing horrible, violent acts.

Another theory concentrates on the family atmosphere into which   5 the serial killer is born. Most killers state that they experienced psychological abuse as children and never established good relationships with the male figures in their lives (Ressler, Burgess, and Douglas 19). As children, they were often rejected by their parents and received little nurturing (Lunde 94; Holmes and DeBurger 64–70). It has also been established that the families of serial killers often moved repeatedly, never allowing the child to feel a sense of stability; in many cases, they were also forced to live outside the family home before reaching the age of eighteen (Ressler, Burgess, and Douglas 19–20). Our culture's tolerance for violence may overlap with such family dynamics: with 79 percent of the population believing that slapping a twelve-year-old is either necessary, normal, or good, it is no wonder that serial killers relate tales of physical abuse and view themselves as the "black sheep" of the family (Holmes and DeBurger 30; Ressler, Burgess, and Douglas 19–20). They may even, perhaps unconsciously, assume this same role in society.

While the foregoing analysis portrays the serial killer as a lost,   6 lonely, abused little child, another theory, based on the same information, gives an entirely different view. In this analysis, the killer is indeed rejected by his family but only after being repeatedly defiant, sneaky, and threatening. As the child's lies and destructiveness increase, the parents give him the distance he seems to want in order to maintain a small amount of domestic peace (Samenow 13). This interpretation suggests that the killer shapes his parents much more than his parents shape him. It also denies that the media can influence a child's mind and turn him into something that he doesn't already long to be. Since most children view similar amounts of violence, the argument goes, a responsible child filters what he sees and will not resort to criminal activity no matter how acceptable it seems to be (Samenow 15–18).

In 1930, the noted psychologist Alfred Adler seemed to find this true of any criminal. As he put it, "With criminals it is different: they have a private logic, a private intelligence. They are suffering from a wrong outlook upon the world, a wrong estimate of their own importance and the importance of other people" (qtd. in Samenow 20).

Most people agree that Jeffrey Dahmer or Ted Bundy had to be "crazy" to commit horrendous multiple murders, and scientists have long maintained that serial killers are indeed mentally disturbed (Lunde 48). While the percentage of murders committed by mental hospital patients is much lower than that among the general population, it cannot be ignored that the rise in serial killings happened at almost the same time as the deinstitutionalization movement in the mental health care system during the 1960s (Lunde 35; Markman and Bosco 266). While reform was greatly needed in the mental health care system, it has now become nearly impossible to hospitalize those with severe problems. In the United States, people have a constitutional right to remain mentally ill. Involuntary commitment can only be accomplished if the person is deemed dangerous to himself or others or is gravely disabled. However, "[a]ccording to the way that the law is interpreted, if you can go to the mailbox to pick up your Social Security check, you're not gravely disabled even if you think you're living on Mars"; even if a patient is thought to be dangerous, he cannot be held longer than ninety days unless it can be proved that the patient actually committed dangerous acts while in the hospital (Markman and Bosco 267). Many of the most heinous criminals have had long histories of mental illness but could not be hospitalized due to these stringent requirements. Richard Chase, the notorious Vampire of Sacramento, believed that he needed blood in order to survive, and while in the care of a psychiatric hospital, he often killed birds and other small animals in order to quench this thirst. When he was released, he went on to kill eight people, one of them an eighteen-month-old baby (Biondi and Hecox 206). Edmund Kemper was equally insane. At the age of fifteen, he killed both of his grandparents and then spent five years in a psychiatric facility. Doctors determined that he was "cured" and released him into an unsuspecting society. He killed eight women, including his own mother (Lunde 53–56). The world was soon to be disturbed by a cataclysmic earthquake, and Herbert Mullin knew that he had been appointed by God to prevent the catastrophe. The fervor of his religious delusion resulted in a death toll of thirteen (Lunde 63–81). All of these men had been treated for their mental disorders, and all were released by doctors who did not have enough proof to hold them against their will.

Recently, studies have given increasing consideration to the genetic makeup of serial killers. The connection between biology and behavior is strengthened by research in which scientists have been able to develop a violently aggressive strain of mice simply through selective inbreeding (Taylor 23). These studies have caused scientists to become increasingly interested in the limbic system of the brain, which houses the amygdala, an almond-shaped structure located in the front of the temporal lobe. It has long been known that surgically altering that portion of the brain, in an operation known as a lobotomy, is one way of controlling behavior. This surgery was used frequently in the 1960s but has since been discontinued as it also erases most of a person's personality. More recent developments, however, have shown that temporal lobe epilepsy causes electrical impulses to be discharged directly into the amygdala. When this electronic stimulation is re-created in the laboratory, it causes violent behavior in lab animals. Additionally, other forms of epilepsy do not cause abnormalities in behavior except during seizure activity. Temporal lobe epilepsy is linked with a wide range of antisocial behavior, including anger, paranoia, and aggression. It is also interesting to note that this form of epilepsy produces extremely unusual brain waves. These waves have been found in only 10 to 15 percent of the general population, but over 79 percent of known serial killers test positive for these waves (Taylor 28–33). 8

The look at biological factors that control human behavior is by no means limited to brain waves or other brain abnormalities. Much work is also being done with neurotransmitters, levels of testosterone, and patterns of trace minerals. While none of these studies are conclusive, they all show a high correlation between antisocial behavior and chemical interactions within the body (Taylor 63–69). 9

One of the most common traits that all researchers have noted among serial killers is heavy use of alcohol. Whether this correlation is brought about by external factors or whether alcohol is an actual stimulus that causes certain behavior is still unclear, but the idea deserves consideration. Lunde found that the majority of those who commit murder had been drinking beforehand and commonly had a urine alcohol level of between .20 and .29, nearly twice the legal level of intoxication (31–32). Additionally, 70 percent of the families that reared serial killers had verifiable records of alcohol abuse (Ressler, Burgess, and Douglas 17). Jeffrey Dahmer had been arrested in 1981 10 on charges of drunkenness, and before his release from prison on sexual assault charges, his father had written a heartbreaking letter pleading that Jeffrey be forced to undergo treatment for alcoholism—a plea that, if heeded, might have changed the course of future events (Davis 70, 103). Whether alcoholism is a learned behavior or an inherited predisposition is still hotly debated, but a 1979 report issued by Harvard Medical School stated that "[a]lcoholism in the biological parent appears to be a more reliable predictor of alcoholism in the children than any other environmental factor examined" (qtd. in Taylor 117). While alcohol was once thought to alleviate anxiety and depression, we now know that it can aggravate and intensify such moods; for serial killers, this may lead to irrational feelings of powerlessness that are brought under control only when the killer proves he has the ultimate power to control life and death (Taylor 110).

"Man's inhumanity to man" began when Cain killed Abel, but   11 this legacy has grown to frightening proportions, as evidenced by the vast number of books that line the shelves of bookstores today—row after row of titles dealing with death, anger, and blood. We may never know what causes a serial killer to exact his revenge on an unsuspecting society, but we need to continue to probe the interior of the human brain to discover the delicate balance of chemicals that controls behavior; we need to be able to fix what goes wrong. We must also work harder to protect our children. Their cries must not go unheard; their pain must not become so intense that it demands bloody revenge. As today becomes tomorrow, we must remember the words of Ted Bundy, one of the most ruthless serial killers of our time: "Most serial killers are people who kill for the pure pleasure of killing and cannot be rehabilitated. Some of the killers themselves would even say so" (qtd. in Holmes and DeBurger 150).

WORKS CITED

Biondi, Ray, and Walt Hecox. *The Dracula Killer.* New York: Simon, 1992. Print.

Davis, Ron. *The Milwaukee Murders.* New York: St. Martin's, 1991. Print.

Holmes, Ronald M., and James DeBurger. *Serial Murder.* Newbury Park: Sage, 1988. Print.

Lunde, Donald T. *Murder and Madness.* San Francisco: San Francisco Book, 1976. Print.

Markman, Ronald, and Dominick Bosco. *Alone with the Devil.* New York: Doubleday, 1989. Print.

Ressler, Robert K., Ann W. Burgess, and John E. Douglas. *Sexual Homicide—Patterns and Motives.* Lexington: Heath, 1988. Print.

Samenow, Stanton E. *Inside the Criminal Mind.* New York: Times, 1984. Print.

Taylor, Lawrence. *Born to Crime.* Westport: Greenwood, 1984. Print.

10 *Analyzing Stories*

Analyzing a story requires you to make inferences, something you do in your everyday life when you arrive at insights about people and relationships, whether in real life or in fiction. You make inferences when you gossip with one friend about a mutual friend, or judge the motives of a TV or movie character. Rather than being final verdicts, your judgments in these situations are more likely to be invitations to further discussion. The same goes for story interpretations, which can be logical and even insistent without being final or comprehensive. In a classroom in which every student offers a different interpretation of the same story, no one student need be right; sharing and discussing the interpretations will result in a fuller understanding of the story for everyone.

Using your gossiping and character-judging experience as a starting point, analyzing a short story can lead you someplace different and, to be honest, harder to get to. After all, unlike gossiping or discussing a movie, interpreting a short story is a solitary experience, not a social one. It's textual, not conversational. And it is unbending in its demands on your time because it's usually associated with a deadline and requires that you choose every word, shape every phrase and sentence, and visibly and logically connect every sentence to the one before and after it. Writers who analyze stories generally use the same basic features of the genre: an understandable, arguable thesis; a well-supported argument; and a clear, logical organization.

Though it may seem daunting, this kind of writing can bring great satisfaction. It teaches you strategies that enable you to deepen and extend any interpretation you wish to make, whether in real life or in the arts, and to support your insights in ways your readers or listeners will find plausible and enlightening. It gives you more confidence in asserting and supporting your insights about anything at all with different kinds of people in various kinds of situations. Most important to you personally, it will help you decide which of your insights are worth keeping—which insights, added to your store of hard-won personal knowledge, will lead you to a place of greater understanding of yourself and your world. Along with the other kinds of argumentative writing in Chapters 6–9, thesis-centered interpretations—logically organized and well supported—can take you there.

Use the guidelines in the Critical Reading Guide (below) to practice peer review using the essays in this chapter.

A Critical Reading Guide

A CLEAR, ARGUABLE THESIS

How well does the writer present the thesis?

Summarize: Tell the writer what you understand the essay's thesis to be and what its key terms are.

Praise: Tell the writer what seems most interesting to you about his or her main claim about the story, whether you agree with it or not.

Critique: If you cannot find the thesis statement or cannot identify the key terms, let the writer know. Evaluate the thesis statement on the basis of whether

- it makes an interesting and arguable assertion (rather than making a statement of fact or an obvious point);
- it is clear and precise (neither ambiguous nor vague);
- it is appropriately qualified (neither overgeneralized nor exaggerated).

A WELL-SUPPORTED ARGUMENT

How well does the writer develop and support the argument?

Summarize: Underline the thesis statement and the major support for it. (Often, the major support appears in the topic sentences of paragraphs.)

Praise: Give an example in the essay where support for a reason is presented especially effectively—for instance, note where brief quotations (words and short phrases), a longer quotation, or summaries of particular events are introduced and explained in a way that clearly illustrates a particular point that is being argued.

Critique: Tell the writer where the connection between a reason and its support seems vague, where too much plot is being relayed with no apparent point, or where a quotation is left to speak for itself without explanation. Let the writer know if any part of the argument seems to be undeveloped or does not support the thesis.

A CLEAR, LOGICAL ORGANIZATION

Has the writer clearly and logically organized the argument?

Summarize: Underline the sentence(s) in which the writer forecasts supporting reasons, and circle transitions or repeated key words and phrases.

Praise: Give an example of something that makes the essay especially easy to read—where, for example, the key terms introduced in the thesis recur throughout the essay in topic sentences and elsewhere, or where transitions are used logically.

Critique: Tell the writer where readability could be improved. For example, point to places where key terms could be added or where a topic sentence could be made more clearly to indicate where the use of transitions might be improved, or note where transitions are lacking and could be added.

Synopsis: D. H. Lawrence's "In Love"

D. H. Lawrence's story "In Love" was published in *The Woman Who Rode Away and Other Stories* in 1928. You can search for the book in your college library or, better yet, access it online through Google Books Search (books.google.com). When you have the book in your browser, simply enter the keyword "Hester" into the search bar to skip ahead to "In Love" on page 138. Or, for a quick orientation to the story, read the synopsis below.

***

"In Love," a short story by D. H. Lawrence, opens with twenty-five-year-old Hester anxiously fretting about a weekend visit to the farm cottage of her fiancé, Joe. On this day a month before the wedding, Hester's younger sister, Henrietta, confronts her and tells her point-blank that she needs to snap out of her pout and "either put a better face on it, or . . . don't go." Although Hester does make the trip, she is never comfortable with her decision.   1

The crux of Hester's problem is that she and Joe had been good friends for years before she finally promised to marry him. Hester had always respected Joe as a hardworking, "decent" fellow, but now that they are to marry, she finds him changed. What she detests is the fact that, in her view, he seems to have made "the wretched mistake of falling 'in love' with her." To Hester, this notion of being in love, accentuated by all of Joe's "lovey-dovey" attempts to cuddle and snuggle and kiss, is completely idiotic and ridiculous.   2

After she arrives at Joe's farm cottage, Hester avoids his advances by asking him to play the piano. As he concentrates on his fingering, she slips outside into the night air and, when Joe comes looking for her, remains hidden in a tree. Alone in the dark, Hester falls into a fit   3

205

of internal questioning, doubt, and upset concerning "the mess" her life seems to have become. Then suddenly, in the midst of her anxiety, who should arrive but Henrietta, claiming she is in the neighborhood on a visit to a friend down the road. Hester leaps at the chance to join Henrietta and thus escape her entrapment with Joe. When Joe hears this, however, he responds angrily, accusing the two sisters of playing a "game."

In the confrontation that follows, Hester and Joe, for the first 4 time, speak honestly of their feelings. Hester tells Joe she detests his "making love" to her. Joe responds that she's mistaken, that he was in fact not "in love" with her but was behaving in such a manner only because he thought that "it was expected." In the conversation, Joe goes on to reveal his dilemma and his true feelings about Hester: "What are you to do," he says, "when you know a girl's rather strict, and you like her for it?"

In speaking the truth of their hearts to each other for the first 5 time, the couple is able to reveal the depth of their feelings. They recognize that they've betrayed the intimacy of their relationship because they've acted on the basis of expectations rather than on the basis of genuine emotion. By acknowledging these facts, the couple is able to reach a new understanding. Seeing Joe's honest love, Hester feels herself responding to him and, in the end, decides to stay with him. She will accept whatever he does, she says, as long as he really loves her.

In Love
Sarah Hawkins
University of California, San Diego
La Jolla, California

By the end of her third paragraph, Sarah Hawkins's interpretation of D.H. Lawrence's "In Love" is clear; in the last paragraph, she repeats it. In between, she focuses on details of the relationship between Hester and Joe, with Henrietta speaking for the predictable social expectations and constraints Hester and Joe must struggle against. Hawkins stays extremely close to the story throughout her essay, following through consistently with what is called a "close reading" to support her interpretation. The story offers only a small cast of characters and a small scene, and only a few hours pass; yet Hawkins has more than enough material to select from to support her interpretation. As you read, notice that Hawkins is not merely retelling the story. Instead, she's organized her essay around the stages of the argument supporting her interpretation. The first sentences of her paragraphs—where readers look for cues to the staging or sequence of an argument—keep readers focused and on track. Notice also Hawkins's careful choice of words to help readers understand the personal and social conflicts at the center of the story.

For most people, the phrase *in love* brings many rosy pictures to mind: 1
a young man looking into the eyes of the girl he loves, a couple walking along the beach holding hands, two people making sacrifices to be together. These stereotypes about what love is and how lovers should act can be very harmful. In his short story "In Love," D. H. Lawrence uses the three main characters to embody his theme that love is experienced in a unique way by every couple and that there isn't a normal or proper way to be in love.

Hester; her fiancé, Joe; and her sister, Henrietta, all approach and 2 respond to love in different ways. Hester is unwilling to compromise what she really feels for Joe, but she is pressured by her own notions of how a young woman in her situation should feel. Joe appears to be the typical young man in love. He seems at ease with the situation, and his moves are so predictable they could have come straight from a movie script. But when he is confronted and badgered by Hester and Henrietta, he admits that he was only putting on an act and feels regret for not being honest with Hester. Henrietta is the mouthpiece for all of society's conceptions of love. She repeatedly asks Hester to be normal and secretly worries that Hester will call off the wedding. Henrietta is like a mother hen, always making sure that Hester is doing the right thing (Henrietta's opinion of the right thing, anyway).

Hester and Joe are, in a sense, playing a game with each other. 3 Both are acting on what they feel is expected of them now that they are engaged, as if how they really feel about each other is unimportant. It is only when Hester and Joe finally talk honestly about their relationship that they realize they have been in love all along in their own unique way.

Hester, ever the practical one, becomes more and more frustrated 4 with "Joe's love-making" (650). She feels ridiculous, as if she is just a toy, but at the same time she feels she should respond positively to Joe, "because she believed that a nice girl would have been only too delighted to go and sit 'there'" (650). Rather than doing what she wants, enjoying a nice, comfortable relationship with Joe, Hester does what she feels she ought to. She says that she ought to like Joe's love-making even though she doesn't really know why. Despite her practical and independent nature, Hester is still troubled by what society would think.

Lawrence seems to be suggesting a universal theme here. If Hester, with such firm ideas about what she wants, is so troubled by what society dictates, then how much more are we, as generally less objective and more tractable people, affected by society's standards? Hester's is a dilemma everyone faces.

At the heart of Hester's confusion is Joe, whose personality was 6 so different before they became engaged that Hester might not have gotten engaged if she had known how Joe would change: "Six months ago, Hester would have enjoyed it [being alone with Joe]. They were so perfectly comfortable together, he and she" (649). But by cuddling and petting, Joe has ruined the comfortable relationship that he and

Hester had enjoyed. The most surprising line in the story is Hester's assertion that "[t]he very fact of his being in love with me proves that he doesn't love me" (652). Here, Hester makes a distinction between really loving someone and just putting on an act of being in love. Hester feels hurt that Joe would treat her as a typical girl rather than as the young woman she really is.

Hester is a reluctant player in the love game until the end of the story when she confronts Joe and blurts out, "I absolutely can't stand your making love to me, if that is what you call the business" (656–57). Her use of the word *business* is significant because it refers to a chore, something that has to be done. Hester regards Joe's lovemaking as if it were merely a job to be completed. When Joe apologizes, Hester sees his patient, real love for her, and she begins to have the same feelings for him again. When she says, "I don't mind what you do if you love me really" (660), Hester, by compromising, shows the nature of their love for each other.   7

Lawrence uses Joe to show a typical response to society's pressures. Joe obediently plays the role of the husband-to-be. He exhibits all the preconceived images one may have about a man about to be married. In trying to fit the expectations of others, Joe sacrifices his straightforwardness and the honesty that Hester valued so much in him. Although Joe's actions don't seem to be so bad in and of themselves, in the context of his relationship with Hester, they are completely out of place. His piano playing, for example, inspires Hester to remark that Joe's love games would be impossible to handle after the music he played. The music represents something that is pure and true—in contrast to the new, hypocritical Joe. Joe doesn't seem to be aware of Hester's feelings until she comes forward with them at the end of the story. The humiliation he suffers makes him silent, and he is described several times as wooden, implying stubbornness and solidness. It is out of this woodenness that a changed Joe appears. At first the word suggests his defensiveness for his bruised ego, but then as Joe begins to see Hester's point about being truly in love, his woodenness is linked to his solidness and stability, qualities that represent for Hester the old Joe. Once Joe gets his mind off the love game, the simple intimacy of their relationship is revealed to him, and he desires Hester, not in a fleeting way but in a way that one desires something that was almost lost.   8

Henrietta serves as the antagonist in this story because it is through her that society's opinions come clear. In almost the first line of text,   9

Henrietta, looking at Hester, states, "If I had such a worried look on my face, when I was going down to spend the weekend with the man I was engaged to—and going to be married to in a month—well! I should either try and change my face or hide my feelings, or something" (647). With little regard for Hester's feelings, Henrietta is more concerned that Hester have the right attitude. Although Henrietta herself is not married, the fact that Hester, who is twenty-five, is soon to be married is a relief to her. Not wanting her sister to be an old maid, Henrietta does all she can to make sure the weekend runs smoothly. She acts as though Hester were her responsibility and even offers to come with Hester to take the "edge off the intimacy" (648). Being young, Henrietta hasn't really formed her own views of life or love yet. As a result, she easily believes the traditional statements society makes about love. When Hester says that she can't stand Joe's being in love with her, Henrietta keeps responding that a man is supposed to be in love with the woman he marries. She doesn't understand the real love that Joe and Hester eventually feel but only the "ought-tos" of love imposed by society. It is unclear at the end of the story if Henrietta really recognizes the new bond between Hester and Joe.

What society and common beliefs dictate about being in love isn't   10
really important. In order to be happy, couples must find their own unique bond of love and not rely on others' opinions or definitions. Joe and Hester come to this realization only after they are hurt and left unfulfilled as a result of the love game they play with each other. Hester knew how she really felt from the beginning, but pressure about what she ought to feel worried her. Joe willingly went along with the game until he realized how important their simple intimacy really was. In the end, Hester and Joe are in love not because of the games they play but because of an intimate friendship that had been growing all along.

WORK CITED

Lawrence, D. H. "In Love." *The Complete Short Stories.* Vol. 3. New York: Penguin, 1977. 540–47. Print.

Synopsis: Susan Glaspell's "A Jury of Her Peers"

You can read Susan Glaspell's story "A Jury of Her Peers" online through the electronic text center at the University of Virginia library. Go to etext.lib.virginia.edu/modeng and look under "G" for "Glaspell." Or, for a quick orientation to the story, read the synopsis below.

Susan Glaspell's short story "A Jury of Her Peers" begins when three men and two women—Mr. Peters, the county sheriff; Mr. Henderson, the county attorney; and Mr. Hale, a farmer; along with two wives, Mrs. Peters and Mrs. Hale—begin to investigate the death of a farm neighbor, John Wright, who they believe was murdered the previous day by his wife, Mrs. Wright. Although there is no direct evidence linking her to the crime, Mrs. Wright is nevertheless jailed on suspicion of murder.

At the Wright farmhouse, the county attorney asks Mr. Hale, the man who by chance discovered the murder, to recount his experience at the farmhouse. Mr. Hale describes how he found Mrs. Wright sitting in a rocking chair as she calmly told him that Mr. Wright was upstairs dead with a rope around his neck.

As the three men search the farmhouse for evidence that might establish a motive for the crime, Mrs. Peters and Mrs. Hale sit in Mrs. Wright's kitchen. With attentive eyes, they keenly observe domestic details that begin to reveal a pattern of meaning that the men overlook. As they continue to look around, the details begin to speak volumes about the emotional lives and marital relationship of Mr. and Mrs. Wright. Mrs. Peters and Mrs. Hale notice the uncharacteristic dirty pans and towels in the kitchen, neither of which fit Mrs. Wright's character as a careful housekeeper. They note a half-full bag of sugar

211

that, again, is uncharacteristic, suggesting an interrupted task. They find a single square on Mrs. Wright's quilt that is raggedly sewn—just one, amid a field of perfectly sewn pieces—which suggests the seamstress had to be out of sorts.

As these domestic details add up, they gain significance for the 4 women while the men scoff and dismiss their concerns as simplistic and typical of women. Finally, when the women discover a birdcage with its door broken and then—at the bottom of the sewing basket—a dead canary wrapped in silk, its neck wrung, they realize they have stumbled upon the motive for the murder. Bound up in the details of violence and dishonor—the husband killed the wife's canary—Mrs. Peters and Mrs. Hale discover the joyless horror Mrs. Wright endured in her marriage to her hard, uncaring husband. They realize John Wright was the man who killed not only a canary but also the spirit of his wife, a woman who had been a beautiful singer—a songbird—in her youth. Mrs. Peters and Mrs. Hale draw on personal experiences to empathize with Mrs. Wright. Mrs. Peters recalls the raging desire to hurt the boy who killed her kitten when she was a girl, and Mrs. Hale recalls the stillness she felt when her first baby died, likening it to the stillness that Mrs. Wright must have endured in her loveless marriage.

In the end, Mrs. Peters's and Mrs. Hale's empathy for Mrs. Wright 5 is so deep that when the men return to collect them to leave, the women look at each other quickly and Mrs. Hale stuffs the dead bird into her coat pocket. Without concrete evidence to establish a motive for murder, they know a jury will not convict the woman. Mrs. Peters and Mrs. Hale act as Mrs. Wright's first jury—a true jury of her peers, relying on experience, intuition, and empathy rather than legal reasoning to find justice in their world.

Irony and Intuition in "A Jury of Her Peers"

Margaret Tate

DeKalb College
Decatur, Georgia

Margaret Tate begins by briefly establishing the historical context and setting of "A Jury of Her Peers"—the early years of the twentieth century in the U.S. Midwest. Her key terms are *intuition* and *irony,* her theme, the differences between men's and women's intuitions. She does not leave you waiting for her thesis: you will find it at the end of her first paragraph. As you read, notice how she selectively and repeatedly quotes and paraphrases the story without retelling it. Instead, she uses the details of the story to support each stage of her argument.

Though men and women are now recognized as generally equal in 1 talent and intelligence, when Susan Glaspell wrote "A Jury of Her Peers" in 1917, it was not so. In this turn-of-the-century, rural midwestern setting, women were often barely educated and possessed virtually no political or economic power. And being considered the weaker sex, there was not much they could do about it. Relegated to home and hearth, women found themselves at the mercy of the more powerful men in their lives. Ironically, it is just this type of powerless existence, perhaps, that over the ages developed into a power with which women could baffle and frustrate their male counterparts: a sixth sense—an inborn trait commonly known as women's intuition. In Glaspell's story, ironic situations contrast male and female intuition, illustrating that Minnie Wright is more fairly judged by women than by men.

"A Jury of Her Peers" first uses irony to illustrate the contrast be- 2 tween male and female intuition when the men go to the farmhouse looking for clues to the murder of John Wright, but it is the women who find them. In the Wright household, the men are searching for something out of the ordinary, an obvious indication that Minnie has been enraged or provoked into killing her husband. Their intuition does not tell them that their wives, because they are women, can help them gain insight into what has occurred between John and his wife. They bring Mrs. Hale and Mrs. Peters along merely to tend to the practical matters, considering them needlessly preoccupied with trivial things and even too unsophisticated to make a contribution to the investigation, as illustrated by Mr. Hale's derisive question, "Would the women know a clue if they did come upon it?" (289).

Ironically, while the men are looking actively for the smoking   3
gun, the women are confronted with subtler clues in spite of themselves and even try to hide from each other what they intuitively know. But they do not fool each other for long, as Glaspell describes: "Their eyes met—something flashed to life, passed between them; then, as if with an effort, they seemed to pull away from each other" (295). However, they cannot pull away, for they are bound by a power they do not even comprehend: "We all go through the same things—it's all just a different kind of the same thing! . . . why do you and I understand? Why do we know—what we know this minute?" (303). They do not realize that it is intuition they share, that causes them to "[see] into things, [to see] through a thing to something else . . ." (294). Though sympathetic to Minnie Wright, the women cannot deny the damning clues that lead them to the inescapable conclusion of her guilt.

If it is ironic that the women find the clues, it is even more   4
ironic that they find them in the mundane household items to which the men attribute so little significance. "Nothing here but kitchen things," the men mistakenly think (287). Because of their weak intuition, they do not see the household as indicative of John's and Minnie's characters. They do not see beyond the cheerless home to John Wright's grim nature, nor do the dilapidated furnishings provide them with a clue to his penurious habits. Minnie's depression and agitation are not apparent to them in the dismal, half-cleaned kitchen; instead, they consider Minnie an inept, lazy housekeeper. Oddly, for all their "snoopin' round and criticizin'" (290), the three gentlemen literally do not have a clue.

The women, on the other hand, "used to worrying over trifles"   5
(287), do attach importance to the "everyday things" (299), and look-

ing around the cheerless kitchen, they see many examples of the miserably hard existence of Minnie Wright. Knowing the pride a woman takes in her home, they see Minnie's kitchen not as dirty but as half-cleaned, and the significance of this is not lost on them. And upon discovering the erratic quilt stitching, they are alarmed. Also, they cannot dismiss the broken birdcage as just a broken birdcage. They instinctively know, as the men do not, that Minnie desperately needed a lively creature to brighten up such a loveless home. Upon finding these clues, ironically hidden in everyday objects, the women piece them together with a thread of intuition and create a blanket of guilt that covers the hapless Minnie Wright.

Though there is irony in the fact that the women, not the men, find the clues, and irony in the fact that they are found in everyday household things, most ironic is the fact that John Wright meets the same fate he has inflicted on the poor bird, illustrating that he is perhaps the least intuitive of all the men in the story. John Wright never sees beyond his own needs to the needs of his wife. He does not understand her need for a pretty creature to fill the void created by her lonely, childless existence. Not content to kill just Minnie's personality ("[s]he was [once] kind of like a bird herself. Real sweet and pretty" [299]), he kills her canary, leaving her with the deafening silence of the lonesome prairie. Minnie has endured many years of misery at the hands of John Wright, but he pushes her too far when he kills the bird. Then, ironically, he gets the "peace and quiet" (283) he values over her happiness.

John Wright lacks the intuition to understand his wife's love of her bird, but the two women do not. They understand that she needed the bird to fill the still air with song and lessen her loneliness. After discovering the dead bird, they do not blame her for killing John. The dead bird reminds Mrs. Peters of a traumatic episode from her childhood:

> "When I was a girl," said Mrs. Peters, under her breath, "my kitten — there was a boy took a hatchet, and before my eyes — before I could get there . . . If they hadn't held me back, I would have . . . hurt him." (301–02)

The women see the reason for Minnie's murderous impulse, but they know that the men lack the insight to ever fully understand her situation or her motivation; therefore, in hiding the bird, by their silence, they acquit Minnie Wright.

Through the ironic situations in "A Jury of Her Peers," Glaspell   8
clearly illustrates a world in which men and women vary greatly in
their perception of things. She shows men as often superficial in
the way they perceive the world, lacking the depth of intuition that
women use as a means of self-preservation to see themselves and the
world more clearly. Without the heightened perspective on life that
this knowledge of human nature gives them, women might not stand
a chance. Against the power and domination of men, they often find
themselves as defenseless and vulnerable as Minnie's poor bird.

WORK CITED

Glaspell, Susan. "A Jury of Her Peers." *Lifted Masks and Other Works.* Ed. Eric
    S. Rabkin. Ann Arbor: U of Michigan P, 1993. Print.

A Note on the Copyediting

We all know that the work of professional writers rarely appears in print without first being edited. But what about student writing — especially essays that are presented as models of student writing? Do these get edited too?

While it's easy to draw an analogy with professional writing and simply declare that "all published writing gets edited," there are some important differences between student and professional writing. For one thing, student writing is presented as student writing. That is, it's offered to the reader as an example of the kind of writing students can and do produce in a writing class. And since most students don't have the benefit of a professional editor, their work may not be as polished as the models they see in textbooks.

For another, unlike professional writers, students rarely have the opportunity to participate in the editorial process. Companion readers like this one are compiled while the main text is being revised, at a time when the authors and editors are immersed in the work of the text and don't have time to also supervise twenty-five or more student writers. For this reason, students are usually simply asked to sign a statement transferring to the publisher all rights to their essays, subject to final editing, and don't see their work again until it appears in print. For these reasons, editing student writing is problematic.

But publishing student essays without editing is equally problematic. Every composition teacher knows that even the best papers, the A+ essays, aren't perfect. But readers of published prose, accustomed to the conventions of edited American English, aren't always so generous. The shift in tense that may be seen as a simple lapse in a student narrative becomes a major distraction in a published piece. Rather than preserve that tense shift in the interest of absolute fidelity to the student's work, it is more in keeping with the spirit and purpose of the enterprise to edit the passage. After all, the rest of the evidence indicates that the student is a strong writer and that he or she would likely accede to the change if it were called to his or her attention.

The editing of a student essay is not a violation of the student's work, then, but really a courtesy to the writer. True, some essays require more editing than others—perhaps because some students did not have much opportunity to revise—but none in this collection has been altered significantly. In fact, every attempt has been made to respect the students' choices.

To give you an inside look at the editing process, we reproduce here the originally submitted version of Sheila McClain's essay from Chapter 4, "Proxemics: A Study of Space and Relationships," along with the Bedford/St. Martin's editor's changes. You might use this sample as an opportunity to consider the usefulness and necessity of editing. What changes were made, and why? Which of them improved the essay? Were all of them necessary? If you are a writer whose work has undergone editorial revision—perhaps as part of peer review—you might think about how the process felt to you. Did you appreciate your editor's work? Resent it? What did you learn from it? If you're like most of us, you probably realized that it's natural to resist, but necessary to accept, criticism. In other words, you learned to think like a writer.

Sample Copyediting

Proxemics: A Study of Space and Relationships

by

Sheila McClain

#

Everyday we interact and communicate, sometimes without even saying a word. Body language, more **formally** ~~correctly~~ known as nonverbal communication, speaks volumes about who we are and how we relate to others. As ~~noted by~~ **Lester** Sielski, an associate professor at the University of West Florida, **writes** "Words are beautiful, exciting, important, but we have over estimated them badly $\frac{1}{m}$ since they are not all or even half the message." He also asserts that "beyond words lies the bedrock on which human relationships are built $\frac{1}{m}$ nonverbal communication" (Sielski). ~~As related by author Roger E. Axtell~~ **A group of** psychology students at the University of Texas recently ~~discovered~~ **demonstrated** just how profound ~~and~~ an effect nonverbal communication can have

on people. ~~They~~ The students conducted an experiment to test the

unspoken rules of behavior on elevators. Boarding a

crowded elevator, the students stood facing and grinning at ~~and~~

~~facing~~ the other people on board. Understandably, the

people became ~~upset and~~ uncomfortable; ~~and~~ one person

~~was~~ even ~~heard~~ suggesting-ed that someone ~~should~~ call

911 (5-6). Why all the fuss? ~~Normal~~ Unspoken elevator etiquette

dictates that one should turn and face the door in a

crowded elevator, being careful not to touch anyone

else and honoring the sacred personal space of each

individual by staring at the floor indicator instead

of looking at anyone else. Although they are not

written down, strict rules govern our behavior in

public situations. This is especially true when

space is limited as on elevators, buses, or ~~the~~ subway

~~the~~ trains (Axtell 5-6).

Patricia Buhler, ~~A~~an expert in business management and associate

professor at Goldey-Beacon College, confirms the large

role nonverbal communication plays. She asserts that

as little as 8 percent of the message we communicate

is made up of words. We communicate the rest of our

message, a disproportionately large 92 percent,

with ~~utilizing~~ body language and other nonverbal forms of

communication (Buhler). ~~According to a professor of~~

~~social work.~~ while researchers have long known that
nonverbal cues play a large role in communication, for
many years they made no efforts to learn more about
them (Sielski).
~~this component of language.~~ Amid rising public
interest, several scientists pioneered new research in
the field of nonverbal communication in the 1950s.
Among these experts was anthropologist Edward T. Hall.
He ~~pioneered research~~ focused on a specific type of nonverbal
communication called _Proxemics._ Proxemics ~~defined as~~ is
the study of how people use personal space to
communicate nonverbally, plays a major role in
our everyday interactions with others, whether we are
conscious of it or not, our use of space

and
appreciate
just how
much our
use of
space
affects
our

A review of some of Hall's main terms will help us
~~Proxemics carries great importance because it
affects our relationships with others. To~~ better
understand ~~the impact~~ proxemics ~~can have on~~
relationships, For example, ~~we need to know the meanings of two key~~
according to ~~terms used by~~ Hall, in our everyday interactions, we choose
to position ourselves to create either "sociopetal" or "sociofugal" space.
~~A professor from University of
St. Thomas summarizes Dr. Hall's terms. The first term~~
"sociopetal space" invites communication. ~~The second
term~~ "sociofugal space" is the opposite ~~of the first.~~
It separates people and discourages interaction
(Jordan). ~~For example,~~ a student in a school lunchroom
may ~~choose to~~ sit alone at an empty table in ~~the~~
corner, away from the ~~others~~ students ("creating sociofugal space"),

or ~~he may choose to sit~~ **creating** directly across from a person he would like to befriend ("sociopetal space"). ~~As the examples show, our use of space could greatly impact our social relationships.~~

Hall identifies
~~Falling under both "sociopetal" and "sociofugal space,"~~ three ~~main types of space~~ **kinds of general spaces with** in which we ~~interact~~ **can create either sociofugal or sociopetal space. These are** ~~are defined by Dr. Hall. These include~~ "fixed-feature space," "semi-fixed feature space," and "informal space" (Jordan). "Fixed-feature spaces are hard, if not impossible, for us to control or change. ~~"Fixed feature" refers to the permanent aspects of the space in which we interact. A "fixed-feature" problem exists in~~ **For example, because** my college English class ~~where the room~~ is too small for the number of students attending, ~~Consequently,~~ **positioning ourselves so that** we have a hard time ~~finding a place where~~ we can ~~see~~ **all** the overhead projections. We cannot make the walls of the classroom bigger or the ceiling higher, and the overhead screen is likewise "fixed" in place. We must work within the constraints of th~~is~~**e** space. A "semi-fixed feature space" is ~~somewhat adjustable allowing for space to be~~ **usually** defined by ~~more~~ mobile objects**, such as furniture. The c**~~C~~ouches and chairs in a living room may ~~be oriented to~~ **for example** face only the television, thus discouraging conversations and relationship building. ~~Reorientation of the couch and chairs, so that they face each other, may~~ **But we are able to reposition the furniture to** create a

more social and conversational environment. Informal space is by far the easiest to manipulate. We each control our personal "bubble," and we can set distances between ourselves and others that reflect our relationships with them. Take, for example, the way that people approach their bosses. A man who is afraid of or dislikes his boss may communicate with her from as far away as possible. He might stand in her doorway to relay a message. Conversely, a woman who has known her boss for many years and is good friends with him may come right in to his office and casually sit down in close proximity to him. Individually, we have a great deal of control over our informal space, and how we use this space can speak volumes about our relationships with others.

after observing many interactions, Hall broke down informal space, further identifying four distances commonly used by people in their interactions with others: "intimate distance," zero to one and a half feet;

"personal distance," one and a half to four feet;
"social distance," four to twelve feet; and "public
distance," twelve feet and beyond ~~all distinguish zones we use for different interactions~~ (Beebe, Beebe,
and Redmond 231). "Intimate distance," as the name
suggests, is generally reserved for those people
closest to us. Lovemaking, hugging, and holding small
children all occur in this zone. The exception to this
rule comes when we extend our hand to perfect
strangers in greeting, allowing them to briefly enter
our intimate space with a handshake. "Personal
distance," while not as close as intimate, is still
reserved for people we know well and with whom we feel
comfortable. This zone ~~is~~ usually occupies an area
relatively close to us. It can at times be applied,
however, to include objects we see as extensions of
ourselves. For instance, while driving we may feel ~~that someone is invading~~ our personal space being invaded ~~when we are driving a car if the~~ by a car (behind us) follows our own too closely. We see ~~the~~ ing
car as an extension of ourselves and extend our
"personal bubble" to include it. "Social distance" is
often considered a respectful distance and is used in
many professional business settings as well as in
group interactions. There is a ~~To, illustrate~~ "public distance," ~~we might think of the distance used when~~ between a lecturer ~~a~~

and a class, or someone ~~large group or~~ speaking publicly from a podium and his or her audience. ~~This distance can also include speakers who are not physically present, such as watching the President address the nation on television.~~

In positioning ourselves in relation to others, especially in choosing nearness or distance, we communicate respect or intimacy, fear or familiarity. ~~As we have seen, proxemics, or how we use the space around us, has some impact on the multitude of interactions we have with others everyday.~~ We can improve ~~or damage our social~~ a friendly relationships simply by using a "warm, personable" distance, ~~with friends.~~ or ~~we may~~ drive potential friends away by seeming "cold and distant," or getting quite literally "too close for comfort." We can put people at ease or make them uncomfortable just by our proximity to them. The study of nonverbal communication, and specifically proxemics, demonstrates the truth of the old adage, "actions speak louder than words."

Submission Form

We hope that this collection is one of many, and that we'll be able to include more essays from more colleges and universities in the next edition. Please let us see the best essays you've written using *The St. Martin's Guide to Writing; The Concise Guide to Writing; Reading Critically, Writing Well;* or *Sticks and Stones.* Send them with this submission form and copies of the agreement form on the next page (one for each essay you submit) to English Editor—Student Essays, Bedford/ St. Martin's, 33 Irving Place, 10th Floor, New York, NY 10003. You can also submit essays online at **bedfordstmartins.com/theguide**, or by emailing **SubmitAnEssay@bedfordstmartins.com**.

Student's Name _____

Instructor's Name _____

School _____

Department _____

Course Text (circle one)

The St. Martin's Guide to Writing   *The Concise Guide to Writing*

Reading Critically, Writing Well   *Sticks and Stones*

Writing Assignment (circle one)

Remembering Events   Proposing a Solution

Writing Profiles   Justifying an Evaluation

Explaining a Concept   Speculating about Causes

Finding Common Ground   Interpreting Stories

Arguing a Position

Other: _____

Agreement Form

I hereby assign to Bedford/St. Martin's ("Bedford") all of my right, title, and interest throughout the world, including, without limitation, all copyrights, in and to my essay, _____ , and any notes and drafts pertaining to it (the sample essay and such materials being referred to as the "Essay").

I understand that Bedford in its discretion has the right but not the obligation to publish the Essay in any form(s) or format(s) that it may desire; that Bedford may edit, revise, condense, or otherwise alter the Essay as it deems appropriate in order to prepare the same for publication. I understand that Bedford has the right to use and to authorize the use of my name as author of the Essay in connection with any work that contains the Essay (or a portion of it).

I represent that the Essay was completely written by me, that I have cited any sources I relied on, that publication of it will not infringe upon the rights of any third party, and that I have not granted any rights in it to any third party.

In the event Bedford determines to publish any part of the Essay in one of its print books, I will receive one free copy of the work in which it appears.

Student's Signature _____

Name _____ Date _____

Permanent Address _____

Phone Number(s) _____

_____

Email Address(es) _____

_____

A Note to the Student:

When a writer creates something — a story, an essay, a poem — he or she automatically possesses all of the rights to that piece of writing, no trip to the U.S. Copyright Office needed. When a writer — a historian, a novelist, a sportswriter — publishes his or her work, he or she normally transfers some or all of those rights to the publisher, by formal agreement. The form above is one such formal agreement. By entering into this agreement, you are engaging in a modern publishing ritual — the transfer of rights from writer to publisher. If this is your first experience submitting something for publication, you should know that you are in good company: every student who has published an essay in one of our books entered into this agreement, and just about every published writer has entered into a similar one.

Thank you for submitting your essay.